MISHIMA
AESTHETIC
TERRORIST

An Intellectual Portrait

Andrew Rankin

University of Hawai'i Press

Honolulu

Printed in the United States of America

24   23   22   21   20   19   6   5   4   3   2   1

Library of Congress Cataloging-in-Publication Data

Names: Rankin, Andrew, author.

Title: Mishima, aesthetic terrorist : an intellectual portrait / Andrew
  Rankin.

Description: Honolulu : University of Hawai'i Press, [2018] | Includes
  bibliographical references and index.

Identifiers: LCCN 2018007919 | ISBN 9780824873745 (cloth ; alk. paper)

Subjects: LCSH: Mishima, Yukio, 1925–1970—Criticism and interpretation.

Classification: LCC PL833.I7 Z79 2018 | DDC 895.63/5—dc23

LC record available at https://lccn.loc.gov/2018007919

ISBN 978-0-8248-8308-9 (pbk.)

Cover art: "Ordeal by Roses," photo by Eikoh Hosoe. Used with permission.

University of Hawai'i Press books are printed on acid-free
paper and meet the guidelines for permanence and
durability of the Council on Library Resources.

MISHIMA
AESTHETIC
TERRORIST

Dedicated to my parents
David and Margaret Rankin

CONTENTS

AUTHOR'S NOTE

All extracts from Mishima's writings in this book are translated from *Mishima Yukio ketteiban zenshū*, the edition of his complete works published by Shinchōsha in forty-three volumes between 2000 and 2005. Each extract is identified with an in-text citation showing the volume number followed by the page number. References for quotations from all other authors are given in the endnotes. All the translations from Japanese are my own.

Introduction

On January 26, 1948, twelve people were killed in a bizarre robbery and mass poisoning incident at a branch of the Teikoku Bank in central Tokyo. A man posing as a government health worker tricked the bank's staff into drinking cyanide; as they lay dying, he made off with some cash. After several months of investigation the police still had no leads. Under intense pressure to solve the case, they arrested an artist, a minor but popular painter in the Japanese style. On the basis of what appeared to be extremely flimsy evidence, the artist was charged with robbery and twelve counts of murder. People in the art and literary communities were appalled. Many issued statements demanding the artist's immediate release. Newspaper pundits expressed skepticism that a man of high culture could be responsible for such a horrendous crime. There was, however, one brashly dissenting voice:

> It was obvious to me from the start that this extraordinary crime was part of a secret pact with the problem of beauty. This crime went so far beyond comprehensible norms that any talk of motive is surely redundant. The perpetrator's profound insensitivity toward human suffering was matched by his exquisite sensitivity toward his own actions, a sensitivity that suffused his unique powers of imagination. Clearly, an act that should have been carried out conceptually within the world of beauty had, for some reason, veered in the wrong direction and spilled outside. Considered in purely aesthetic terms, this crime was an ugly one. But this was not an ugliness of *essence*. It was the ugliness that is manifest when the good and the evil of mankind, all the creative possibilities that we call humanity, are condensed into a single event: a crime. Works of art are things of imperfect beauty. If ever a work of art is made perfect, it becomes a crime. (27:96)

This perverse analysis was written by a virtually unknown twenty-three-year-old novelist named Mishima Yukio. Both in content and in style it is wholly characteristic of his manner and simultaneously offers a manifesto and a self-portrait. Most of Mishima's core attitudes are on display here: a willful contrariness, a refusal to empathize, a narcissistic concentration on the self, a substitution of ethical categories with aesthetic ones, an equation of beauty and evil, and a conception of artistic creation as an antisocial activity. Mishima is an aesthete with bad intentions, and he wants us to know it. His own lifelong pact with the problem of beauty will follow almost exactly the formula he outlines here, leading him, ultimately, to condense all his creative possibilities, both good and evil, into a single, extraordinary, seemingly incomprehensible artistic-criminal event.

A year after writing the article containing the above passage, Mishima published *Confessions of a Mask*, the novel that launched his literary career. For the next two decades Mishima was a formidable presence in Japan's cultural scene. Immensely productive, he published work in almost every genre: novels, both literary and popular, plays in modern Western and traditional Japanese forms, literary criticism, literary translations, journalism, travel writing, autobiography, poetry, opera libretti, and ballet scripts. His work as an actor and filmmaker also won him attention. Mishima was unashamedly a "celebrity" intellectual, an indefatigable self-promoter, socialite, and public speaker, whose eccentric nonliterary antics frequently brought him ridicule. While expressing contempt and condescension toward Japan's increasingly consumerist culture industry, Mishima took every opportunity the industry offered him, participating enthusiastically in musicals, cabaret shows, photo shoots, boxing matches, samurai and gangster movies, and much else. People called Mishima a sensationalist, a contrarian, an irrationalist, an egomaniac, a fake, a buffoon, a nihilist, a genius, a fascist, a madman. Provocatively, he articulated his antagonism toward postwar Japanese society in the language of the wartime militarists and formed a civilian militia of one hundred volunteers dedicated to defending the emperor, whom they revered as the supreme symbol of Japan's enduring cultural unity. Yet Mishima's traditionalism, his veneration of the imperial throne, and his worship of cultural purity, strength, and manliness were continually offset by his cosmopolitanism and by his irreverent and campy exhibitionism. The ranting nationalist rebel was also a sultry homoerotic pinup. Each aspect of his persona seemed to be contradicted by another, so that the result was an awkward hybrid that often appeared to lapse into parody.

Mishima was therefore dangerous or irrelevant, reactionary or experimental, heroic or comical, depending on the point of view. His outrageous samurai-style suicide in the winter of 1970 set the seal on a frantic whirlwind of a career. Moreover, it was a seal that looked unbreakable. Throughout his career Mishima had pursued a fiercely eroticized vision of violent death, and after repeatedly writing his own death sentence (and acting it out) in art, he had finally carried it out in reality (or in an art that was real?), thereby accomplishing, so it seemed, a perfect unity of artist and work.

Nietzsche says, "One does well to separate the artist from his work, which should be taken more seriously than he is."[1] The dazzling, exhilarating, bewildering case of Mishima Yukio severely tests Nietzsche's dictum, for here we are confronted with an artist who *became* his work and whose masterpiece is his own death.

The scandal of Mishima's suicide had a long-term silencing effect on his Japanese contemporaries. This was understandable. A militant nationalist shouting *banzai* to the emperor and committing seppuku at an army base: this was not the image of itself that Japan wanted to present to the world. For nearly twenty years after his death Mishima's name was virtually taboo in Japanese academic and literary circles.

This left the field wide open for foreigners, who, equally understandably, were fascinated by Mishima. As a result, the most interesting statements about Mishima during those years came from abroad. In 1974 John Nathan, an American translator who had known Mishima personally, published an authoritative critical biography that no one has yet surpassed. This biography was followed in 1975 by a simpler biographical portrait by Henry Scott Stokes, a British journalist who had also met Mishima. The French novelist Marguerite Yourcenar published an admiring study of Mishima in 1983. Essays on Mishima by Henry Miller, Gore Vidal, Colin Wilson, and V. S. Naipaul were a lot less admiring. A film titled *Mishima: A Life in Four Chapters*, directed by Paul Schrader and produced by Francis Ford Coppola and George Lucas, was released in 1985. The film enjoyed international critical success, and the three books on Mishima mentioned above were translated into many languages.

The reception of these works in Japan, however, was less than warm. Some influential Japanese critics disliked what they saw as Nathan's vulgar Freudian reduction of Mishima to a pathological phenomenon, as if Mishima's work had no significance other than as a sublimation of his neuroses.[2] Mishima's widow, Yōko, who was ruling his estate with a guardedness that no one seems to have anticipated, took exception to Nathan's allegations about her late husband's secret sex life, and she successfully pressured Japanese booksellers to remove the book from their shelves. Schrader's film did not fare any better. Due to fears of violent protests by Japanese right-wing groups, the film was dropped from the 1985 Tokyo Film Festival, and even today it has still not officially been released in Japan. More generally, foreigners' leering fascination with Mishima's grisly suicide has been a source of irritation for many Japanese.

Tentative appraisals of Mishima's work by Japanese authors began to appear in the late 1980s. At first they came from nonacademics: poets, novelists, and former friends of Mishima. More substantial critical studies appeared after Yōko's death in 1994. Most of these authors denied that the silence of the previous twenty years was the result of sensitivity to Mishima's vociferous nationalism. Mishima had constructed his life and work so carefully and so defensively, they argued, that it was difficult to find an original perspective from which to approach him. There is some truth in this. Mishima's self-reflexive lucidity is indeed remarkable, and his mischievously deprecating commentaries on his own works have a knowingness and a sense of finitude that have intimidated many commentators. Saeki Shōichi, an English literature specialist who had worked with Mishima, opened his 1988 book on Mishima with these remarks:

> Why is it so difficult for us to write about Mishima? Because we cannot help feeling that Mishima is always one step ahead of us, that he has anticipated everything we may try to say about him. It is extraordinarily difficult to find something to say about Mishima that he has not noticed himself. And what is the point of a critical study of an author that cannot evade the author's own calculations?[3]

Virtually all Japanese commentators on Mishima have viewed him as problematic in some way. Apparently there is a *Mishima mondai*, a "Mishima problem" that needs to be solved. Okuno Takeo, a literary critic who had also known Mishima personally, wrote these lines in 1992:

> What was Mishima Yukio to us, and what will he be in the future? I still do not know. In my mind I cannot comfortably link together the man that I knew as a friend, the writer whose work I hungrily devoured every time he published something new, and that mind-boggling act of self-destruction. I find it impossible to fit them logically together to construct a total image of Mishima.[4]

Tanaka Miyoko, an editor and critic who has spent more than half a century studying Mishima's work, has recently written:

> We Japanese are still repeatedly confronted by the awkward question: What is/was Mishima Yukio? Like a mysterious ore that emits an intense radioactive beam, he keeps calling to us, as enticing and appealing as ever, yet also generating a twinge of spiritual pain.[5]

Depending on whose account we are reading, the "Mishima problem" can stand for any one of a bundle of shared anxieties about Japan's cultural identity, about the fate of the Japanese language in modern times, about the distinctive characteristics of Japanese art and literature, about modern Japan's spiritual well-being and creative vitality, and of course about the meaning of Mishima's final terroristic actions. During his lifetime Mishima assumed an array of attitudes that put him fiercely at odds with his contemporaries. Yet most Japanese commentators now regard him as paradigmatic of the Showa era (1925–1989) in which he lived, and which he both loved and hated.

Mishima's reputation in Japan has grown in the new century. The Mishima Yukio Literary Museum, newly built near the shore of Lake Yamanaka in order to house his manuscripts and letters, opened its doors to the public in 1999. The following year Mishima's publishers began releasing a new edition of his complete works; containing much new material, this edition comprises a total of forty-three hefty volumes. Today there is no question that Mishima is a popular writer in Japan. Even his minor novels have proved surprisingly durable, and a play by Mishima is performed at a theater somewhere in Japan almost every month of the year. His essays and critical writings have also made a comeback, a fact that is surely not unrelated to Japan's recrudescent nationalism. Mishima's criticisms of the blandness of modern Japanese society, of its declining artistic and literary standards, of unimaginative bureaucratic interference in cultural matters, of apathy and lack of vigor among Japanese youth, and other such complaints appear to strike an even stronger chord among the general public today than they did fifty years ago.

Even those who are not sympathetic to Mishima express admiration for his virtuosic mastery of the Japanese language. Hisaaki Yamanouchi says, "In its logical clarity and rhetorical richness his prose style is by far the most distinguished in modern Japanese literature."[6] The Mishima Yukio Literary Museum runs regular "recitation seminars" in which members of the public take turns reading aloud passages from Mishima's works. The purpose, according to the museum's website, is to enable people to "listen with their hearts to the true beauty of the Japanese language" as manifest in Mishima's prose. Anyone who is familiar with Mishima's studious absorption of Western literary styles will smile at the glow of patriotic pride emanating from that statement. Even so, the existence of these recitation seminars indicates the degree to which Mishima has come to be regarded as a beacon of literary excellence in Japan and a standard bearer for the Japanese language.

The new century has also seen a boom in Mishima scholarship. Today there is more *serious* interest in Mishima than ever before. Books on Mishima are appearing at the rate of roughly half a dozen each year, and many are highly ambitious critical ventures. Some Japanese intellectual heavyweights, most notably philosophers, have recently muscled their way into Mishima studies, and much of the best writing on Mishima now comes from scholars working outside the field of literature.

In contrast to all this, writing on Mishima by scholars in the West remains limited. While there is no shortage of lightweight popular treatments, which are predictably obsessed with Mishima's death, intelligent critiques of Mishima's work are surprisingly scant.[7] Nathan's biography has been hugely influential in establishing an image of Mishima as a frivolous figure whose work lacks intellectual depth. Scholars who write about Mishima in English seldom venture beyond the decades-old translations of his most famous novels, and the tone of their commentaries is often impatient or dismissive, as if Mishima is not worthy of serious critical engagement.

I have been working on Mishima for a long time. Initially I had the dismally unoriginal idea of writing yet another biography. Starting in the late 1990s I conducted interviews in Japan with many people who had known Mishima: literary colleagues, publishers and editors, actors and movie production staff members, political activists, former members of his army, former friends, enemies, and lovers. Already there were clear signs that Japanese attitudes toward Mishima were changing. On November 25, 2000, the thirtieth anniversary of Mishima's death, I attended his annual memorial service at the Kudan Kaikan Hall in Tokyo. An impressively large and varied crowd of people were in attendance: academics, novelists and literary critics, public officials, business executives, schoolteachers, some right-wing activists, and of course some former friends and colleagues of Mishima. Although I was only an anonymous student, I was led to the front of the hall and ushered onto the stage, along with half a dozen bigwigs, to lay a wreath before a giant portrait of Mishima sensei. I realized that, as the only white face in the crowd, I was being paraded as evidence of Mishima's international stature.

Meanwhile I continued to work my way through Mishima's letters and his lesser-known writings, and I read all the Japanese studies of his work. Eventually I recognized the futility of this project. I had become aware of the gap between the simple facts of an artist's life and the complex fictions of an artist's art, which no amount of purely biographical research can bridge. Moreover, it is this unbridgeable part that is often of the most interest. I put Mishima aside and spent several years working on other projects, returning to Mishima in 2009 for my doctorate at Cambridge, where I wrote the first draft of this book.

As I see things now, I think it is prudent to acknowledge from the outset that, strictly speaking, there is no Mishima Yukio. No such person ever existed.

Mishima was the creation of a Japanese writer, actor, and performance artist named Hiraoka Kimitake (1925–1970).

Hiraoka was born in central Tokyo and lived there his whole life. He was educated at the exclusive Gakushūin, known in English as the Peers School, and graduated from the University of Tokyo with a degree in law. After a brief period of employment at the Ministry of Finance, he became a full-time writer at the age of twenty-three. He married in his early thirties and had two children. He died by his own hand at the age of forty-five.

Biographers, swayed by the dramatization in *Confessions of a Mask*, have exaggerated the significance of the events of Hiraoka's formative years, which were not extraordinary by the standards of his day. A sickly child, until the age of twelve he was raised mainly by his grandmother, a neurotic and controlling woman. With his adoring mother he developed an intensely symbiotic relationship that lasted his whole life. At the age of nineteen, certain that he would soon be killed in the war, he wrote his last will and testament. He duly received his conscription notice but failed the army fitness test, a humiliation that almost certainly saved his life. During the final months of the war he became engaged to the sister of one of his school friends, but after a brief and awkward courtship the girl's family broke off the engagement.[8]

One fact about the history of Hiraoka's family is important enough to deserve mention. They were descended, via the neurotic grandmother, from samurai stock. This too was not as unusual as it might sound. Although the samurai class had been abolished in 1871, samurai pride lingered for generations and many middle-class families were still boasting of their samurai heritage by the time Japan entered its period of militarism and war. Boys who grew up in such families encountered a reactionary mindset: pretentiously aristocratic and superior, contemptuous of modern ways, full of nostalgia for an irretrievable past. The boys heard terrifying legends about their forefathers, warriors who were so fearless they could cut open their own stomachs.

Hiraoka's one truly exceptional feature was his prodigious fluency with language. This is already apparent in his earliest surviving compositions, little poems written when he was six years old:

Autumn has come.
Autumn has come.
As I stand alone in the garden
The leaves are rustling down,
Aiming at me.
(37:24)

We cannot blame a six-year-old for egocentrism. But we can say that in forty years his worldview did not change. These lines do not record an experience of reality so much as they express the stubbornness of a will to impose an aesthetic upon that experience. Recognizably it is an aesthetic governed by decadent principles. *Summer is over, the world is against me, and I am alone, and this is beautiful.* The word translated above as "aiming" is *megakete*, a slightly literary verb one would not normally expect to find in the vocabulary of a Japanese first-grader. The poem's emphatic ending already seems to indicate an awareness of dramatic form. There is even a hint of violence.

By his early teens this precocious child had written nearly one thousand poems, along with scores of short prose pieces in a multitude of literary styles. Grown-ups began to call him a genius, a label he did not dispute.

"Mishima Yukio" began as a pen name. He did not choose it for himself. It was given to him when he was sixteen by a group of scholars and critics who were helping him launch his writing career. This group was an offshoot of the literary movement known as Nihon Rōmanha, the Japan Romantic School, which by the 1940s was espousing a fanatical aesthetic patriotism similar to that of poets and critics in Nazi Germany. The group printed Mishima's poems and prose pieces in their magazine and sponsored his first book, a collection of stories titled *A Forest in Full Bloom* (*Hanazakari no mori*), which was published, almost miraculously, during the devastating Tokyo bombings of 1944.

After Japan's defeat, the writers of the Japan Romantic School were vilified as warmongers and fascists. At this juncture Mishima could have chosen to discard his wartime pen name. Instead he kept it, the first sign of a resistance against the postwar era that would never soften. Over the next twenty-five years he developed his pen name first into a literary persona and then into a full-blown alter ego. Mishima spilled off the page to become *Mishima*, a furious self-dramatization enacted in multiple media.

A specific psychological impulse drove this project: Hiraoka was tormented by the elusiveness of his own existence. He experienced this elusiveness in a most literal way, having only a flimsy cognizance of his own physical reality. His project of becoming Mishima was essentially a quest for a solid identity, and like all such quests it entailed a symbolic vengeance on everything that had hitherto obstructed or denied him. It is easy to see that Mishima is predicated on everything that Hiraoka was not. The sickly, delicate, bookish boy, smothered in female power and too weak to join the emperor's army, transforms himself into an athletic, dominant, hypermasculine warrior who now claims to be too *strong* for the emperor's army. This is, at the very least, a remarkable demonstration of self-overcoming.[9]

We do Mishima an injustice, however, if we limit ourselves to such psycho-biographical observations. Since opening to the Western world in the middle of the nineteenth century, Japan too has often been troubled by the elusiveness of its own existence. In Mishima's furious sensationalization of his identity crisis, in his search for authenticity and relatedness, in his restless vacillations between East and West, in his violence and his melodrama, and even in his emptiness, many Japanese have recognized reflections of national anxieties that remain unresolved. Hence the "spiritual pain" that Mishima continues to induce.

The book I have finally written about Mishima is not a biography but a critique of his artistic and intellectual themes. Its primary objective is to challenge the prevalent frivolous image of Mishima by demonstrating the intelligence and seriousness of his best work, without being blind to his indulgences. As much as possible, I lift Mishima from the confines of the specialized field of modern Japanese literature and discuss his work within a broad intellectual context. This has the double effect of illuminating the relevance and consistency of Mishima's thought while diminishing his apparent eccentricity and exoticism.

Undeniably, the "Japaneseness" of Mishima is interesting. It is interesting to Japanese readers, as all the scholarly and critical studies attest. It is interesting to non-Japanese readers, for whom Mishima often epitomizes a distinctively exotic Japanese phenomenon. And of course it is interesting to Mishima, who contrives to make a gigantic issue of the matter. We cannot talk sensibly about Mishima's work without addressing his cultural identity. But at the level of his fundamental intellectual and existential concerns Mishima is not a uniquely Japanese phenomenon. His work addresses a universal experience of modernity and its attendant anxieties that is congruent with that of twentieth-century Western thinkers. Indeed, part of Mishima's curse was his recognition that he himself was already irreversibly modernized and Westernized, and this is one of the features that gives his project a self-punitive and fatalistic dynamic. Mishima is concerned with such problems as the forfeiture of certainties and traditional meaning, and what he sees as modern culture's depletion of its erotic energies. He fears the decline of strong cultural identities in an age of increasing uniformity and globalization. He laments the diminishing importance of art and the demise of myth, tragedy, and the sacred.

The title of my book is adapted from Mishima himself. He coined the term *bi-teki terorizumu*, translatable as "aesthetic terrorism" or possibly even "beautiful terrorism," a few years before his death. He used this term primarily to describe the acts of political terrorism that have been a feature of the history of modern Japan: the various attacks, rebellions, and assassinations, and the suicides that almost invariably followed them. Mishima speaks of Japan's "genealogy of aesthetic terrorism" and strives to add his name to this genealogy. But "aesthetic terrorism" is a malleable term that can also cover a number of other tendencies and ideas that are integral to Mishima's project. It suggests the inevitable antisocial or amoral consequences of an extreme form of aestheticism that prioritizes beauty above all else. It denotes the aggressive shock tactics of modern art and the avant-garde. More precisely, it suggests the notion of an attack *on* aesthetics, accomplished by an aggressively sensual art that strives to erase the possibility of the disinterested pleasure of aesthetic appreciation; this was the sense in which Theodor Adorno famously objected to the "terrorist emphasis" of Wagner's operas.[10] "Aesthetic terrorism" also implies a general view of art as transgressive and oppositional, which is the only view that Mishima says he will accept. And, needless to say, the term aptly describes the carefully choreographed spectacle of violence that was Mishima's valedictory gesture.

I apply the term "aesthetic terrorism" retrospectively over the whole of Mishima's career. Each chapter of this book traces one of the constituent elements of this term as Mishima develops it in his work. Each of these elements takes the form of a proposition: art as sublimation, beauty as evil, life as art, narcissism as the death drive, culture as myth, eroticism as sacred. Each of the chapter titles is an extract from Mishima's writings.

Though I proceed broadly according to chronology and give contextual explanations where necessary, my interest is not in connecting Mishima to his times but in demonstrating the originality and consistency of his thinking and the ingenuity with which he creates himself as a character. I pay minimal attention to Mishima's biography (to the life of Hiraoka) and concentrate on the voice that speaks to us in the writings, essentially treating Mishima as a performance unfolding in the work.

I pay less attention to Mishima's fiction, and more to his nonfiction, than previous scholars have done. Mishima's essays and critical writings make up roughly one-quarter of his enormous oeuvre, and in my view they contain much of his most brilliant writing. Though he offers an opinion on virtually every subject imaginable, Mishima's main concern is always with art, culture, and eroticism, all broadly defined, and those are the subjects that dominate the discussions in this book.

Throughout the book I stress the pervasiveness of Mishima's aestheticism. Like Oscar Wilde, whose career and work he had studied carefully, Mishima treats art as the supreme reality and life as a mode of fiction. Mishima's way of thinking about the world is based largely on artistic models, which is why critiques that focus on his "nationalism" or his "politics" tend to miss the point of what he is trying to accomplish. Mishima presents himself as a radical conservative, a traditionalist struggling to preserve an ancient cultural essence that faces extinction in modernity. My thesis is that he never abandoned his decadent principles. Mishima says that Japan is in decline, and he bemoans the exhaustion of creative and erotic energies that he believes is symptomatic of this decline. A typically modernist pessimism about the future of culture, and not only Japan's, is a major premise of Mishima's outlook. But there is also a sense in which Mishima *wants* Japan to be in decline so that he can be its last defiant hero, a kamikaze of Japanese beauty. I read his entire project—in which I include his literary works in all genres, his essays and critical writings, his public lectures and media appearances, and his violent suicide—as a single, sustained decadent lyric that ironically flaunts its own contradictions and its futility. Mishima's work is suffused with a sense of ending—the end of art, the end of eroticism, the end of culture, the end of the world—and it conforms to a decadent aestheticism that holds that beautiful things radiate their most intense beauty on the cusp of their destruction.

In order to grasp Mishima's aspirations fully, though, it is necessary to think even further, beyond Japan and beyond modernity altogether. For while Mishima is, like all artists, like all of us, the product of a specific history, his myths and his archetypes are transhistorical. The aesthete who is killed by beauty. The lovers whose love is perfected in death. The ascetic priest. The warrior-poet. The religious martyr. The mad god.

There is one more point I want to make in this introduction. Facile readings of Mishima typically portray him as a man with an insatiable craving for death. Unquestionably, death was the romanticizing principle of Mishima's life and work. But it is careless to reduce him to a pathological death wish. A man who simply craves death need only get on with it and kill himself, or orchestrate his own killing. But Mishima does not rush toward death. On the contrary, he takes his time. Assiduously and manipulatively he constructs a narrative that will enable him to give a logical cohesiveness to his character, to link himself to myth and to tradition, to turn his eroticism into an ethical obligation, and to make his death serve as the terroristic culmination of his desire to impose his conception of beauty on the world, whether the world likes it or not. That is the project investigated in this book.

CHAPTER 1

A Zone of Unfeeling

One furthers one's ego always at the expense of others.

Nietzsche, The Will to Power

The first piece of writing bearing the name of "Mishima Yukio" appeared in the monthly journal *Bungei bunka,* translatable as *Literary Culture,* in the autumn of 1941, when its author was sixteen years old. By that time he had already written scores of short prose pieces and nearly one thousand poems, many of which he had published, under his real name of Hiraoka Kimitake, in various small-circulation magazines. A fact that seldom gets mentioned is that even after he began publishing as Mishima, he continued to publish under his real name for four more years. During this period he was selective about his choice of publications. He sent most of the Mishima works to *Literary Culture,* whose editors, all members of the Japan Romantic School, were mentoring him and supporting his career. He sent the Hiraoka works to publications with less overt ideological agendas, such as poetry magazines, book club magazines, and university literary magazines. The Mishima works are exercises in the sort of Romanticism that would have pleased his mentors. They are filled with lyrical expressions of longing and rapturous adulation of morbid types of beauty, declarations of the uniqueness of Japanese culture and the imperishability of the Japanese spirit, and so on. The Hiraoka works are more varied in style and form; they are more somber and more theoretical, but also more erotic and more decadent. Not satisfied with nostalgic praise of classical beauty, they also show a serious concern with the future of Japanese literature. Significantly, the final Hiraoka manuscripts, most of which remained unpublished, indicate that their author had been studying the writings of Hegel and Nietzsche, thinkers who expressed impatience with Romanticism.

Books on Mishima typically begin with some of the poems and stories he contributed to *Literary Culture,* or with *Confessions of a Mask,* his later fictionalized account of his childhood and adolescence. But I want to begin by looking at one of these unpublished Hiraoka manuscripts, since they offer us, I believe, a glimpse into the author's mind at a crucial moment of self-questioning and self-determination, before he had fully assumed the persona we recognize as Mishima.

A collection of literary and philosophical reflections titled "Poetic Theory" (*Shi ron*) is signed with Hiraoka's name and dated "May to June, 1945," that is to say, shortly after his abortive engagement and his failure to pass the military fitness test, and shortly before Japan's surrender. He wrote it at the naval base in Kanagawa to which he and his university classmates had just been transferred. That was how the twenty-year-old spent the last chaotic months of the war: alone in an office room at the naval base, feverishly recording his thoughts on literature. We know that he prepared two versions of this work, presumably a draft and a finished manuscript; the draft survives intact, whereas nearly all the pages of the second version, which appears to have been much longer, have been lost. Since *Literary Culture* had closed down in the previous year, "Poetic Theory" cannot have been intended for publication in that magazine. Given the timing and circumstances of its composition, it was probably not intended for publication at all.[1]

The subject of "Poetic Theory" is not poetry but the psychology and worldview of a type of artist referred to throughout as a "poet of aestheticism" (*yuibi-ha no shijin*). The word *yuibi*, usually translated as "aestheticism," literally means "beauty only," and an awareness of the ethical implications of assuming an extreme aesthetic attitude is clear in Hiraoka's opening assertions: "Poets of aestheticism, whom most people think of as delinquent vagabonds, are actually much more serious in their outlook than the supposedly serious people of the ordinary world, for the poets protect beauty instead of morals" (26:531). Beauty *instead of* morals. The poet of aestheticism is an amoral exclusionist whose sole concern is with the beautiful.

As if seeking to establish a logical justification for the above claim, Hiraoka devotes several paragraphs to an attack on conventional morality. His specific target is the virtue of compassion (*dōjō*). Compassion, he declares, epitomizes human weakness. It is the "fundamental sickness of the human race," nothing more than a "degenerate love" (532). With considerable technical assurance, Hiraoka forwards the argument that compassionate values are not founded on objective truths:

> Tears of compassion should be counted in the same type as tears of joy, rather than being linked to righteous indignation. Indignation is the coupling of a specific moral concept (a sense of justice or such like) with emotion, and the strength of the indignation is directly proportionate to the strength of the conviction of this coupling. But conviction can lend

necessity even to an accidental coupling. Thus, while indignation stands far above the moral concept that forms one element of the coupling, and far above the conviction of that coupling, it can nevertheless be made the object of a value judgment. Tears of compassion, on the other hand, are a coupling of straightforward emotions, just like tears of joy, and cannot be the object of any kind of value judgment. Yet society has long made the mistake of judging these "tears of compassion" from their results, or from the actions that they produce, thereby making them the object of value judgments. (532–533)

Worse still, a tendency to empathize with the suffering of others is liable to prevent the poet of aestheticism, whom Hiraoka wants to see as a superhuman figure, from achieving his full potential. If the poet merely "wallows in sensibility," he will eventually suffer fatigue of the senses and will be "devoured" by his own sensitive nature; to prevent this, he must meet the world with a "bright cruelty" (537). In these thoughts Hiraoka is closely following Nietzsche, who had denigrated compassion and altruism as symptoms of spiritual lethargy. Specifically, Hiraoka seems to have been studying *The Will to Power* (1885), where one of Nietzsche's core assumptions is that "life always lives at the expense of other life."[2] Hiraoka too is adamant that egotism and self-interest are essential to the formation of a great individual. The first step toward rising above the herd-like masses is to stop caring about them. Hiraoka is hostile to the "weak" emotion of compassion because he wants to make a Nietzschean move beyond morality, beyond good and evil, to a position of affirming that *everything* is good, everything, that is, that assists the genius, the poet whose concern is with nothing but beauty, in becoming all that he can be.

Interspersed among these opening statements are some self-dramatizing flourishes:

I am a demon in the human world. My nostrils seek out the stench of humans in their offices, in their dormitories, and in their clubs. That is my only gesture of affection toward these humans, yet it seems to make them rather uncomfortable. Evidently, they do not understand that for me to gobble them up and eat them would itself be a form of affection. (534)

Yet then we hear that the poet, for all his demonic propensities, is a fragile and unhappy figure. Though his self-awareness and intuitive powers far exceed those of ordinary mortals, he suffers from an existential malady Hiraoka calls "purity" (*junketsu*):

At the poet's core is a fierce and scorching purity. It is as though this is his punishment for having being born a poet, and his entire life, including even his old age, which for ordinary people is an opportunity for peaceful respite, will be shot through with the pain of wild passions. The poet's works are the result of his *attempt* to see how far he can *endure* this fierce purity, and it is an attempt that will continue for as long as he lives. However, in the troubled marriage between *enduring* (a matter of experience) and *attempting* (a matter of the will) there resides an essential tragedy. I am speaking here of a special mode of formation. (535–536)

This passage appears to offer a variant of the Romantic idea of the "beautiful soul," a mind that withdraws from the world in order to concentrate on itself, on its own thoughts and pleasures and desires, and thereby strives to attain an absolute or "pure" mode of self-consciousness. But it seems undeniable that the purity being spoken of here also has a sexual connotation. Purity, the above lines imply, is a congenital condition. The poet is doomed to spend his whole life struggling against his own "fierce" impulses. For the sake of his well-being he must strive to convert his "wild passions" into the dispassionate refinement of art. Success will depend on his ability to counteract the agony of this self-repression by bringing beauty into the world through his artistic creations.

The notion of artistic activity as the sublimation of sexual energies is familiar to us from Nietzsche and Freud. What is unusual about the artist defined in "Poetic Theory" is that he performs this process of sublimation knowingly. He observes and monitors himself as he channels his energies into art. He appears to have no Freudian unconscious: "The poet, paradoxically, always stands outside the poet" (538). Yet the poet is already resigned to the certainty that he will not be able to sustain this process of sublimation indefinitely and that it is bound to end badly for him.

Similar claims about the equivalence of suffering and poetry, or suffering and artistic creation in general, appear in some of the other unpublished Hiraoka manuscripts. An undated fragment, possibly written after "Poetic Theory," contains these lines:

If the appellation of genius depends on the works that one produces, then clearly I am no genius. And if genius means dying young, then obviously I am even more unqualified.

And yet there is genius here. It is I. A spirit that suffers day and night in ways ordinary people cannot understand. A child born for tragedy, a child of the gods. (26:633)

It is not just that the genius is doomed to suffer; his suffering is integral to his genius. Or perhaps he is a genius *of* suffering. Suffering conceived of in this way is like an aristocratic pride. Yet there is surely a hint of irony in this declaration of genius. The ironical concept of a self-proclaimed "child born for tragedy" (*umare-nagara higeki no ko*), a hero who actively seeks a tragic end for himself, and by doing so undermines the sincerity of his own drama, is already forming here.

In "Poetic Theory" Hiraoka illustrates the poet's self-conscious psychological process, the poet's "mechanism" as he calls it, with this startling image:

> Compared to ordinary people, the poet is inside out. His skin is on the inside, while his flesh and blood are on the outside. On the inside he embraces, on the outside he is alone. He is exposed to the external world with a stinging excess of sensitivity to pain, yet he transcends the level of sensations to create a mercilessly scathing zone of unfeeling [*tsūretsu muzan na fukan-tai*]. (536)

This image of an artist defiantly exposing his innards to the world is bound to shock our hindsight, since we know, of course, that Mishima will literalize this idea in his gruesome suicide. The suggestion here is of someone who forces himself to display his weaknesses in the hope that his exhibitionism will desensitize him and will thereby increase his power in relation to the external world. The poet's "mechanism" is self-defensive in that he shields himself from the world by refusing to invest in it emotionally: "The poet must learn the function of a frozen zone of unfeeling, like an impenetrable insulator all around him, when he confronts the external world" (537). The sexual subtext continues here, since the word *fukan* (unfeeling) can be also used to denote sexual frigidity. (Scribbled on an earlier page of the manuscript is this line: "It is not love that is complicated but the relations between man and woman.") And yet Hiraoka's language often seems to yield to a sadomasochistic delight in anticipating the pain and damage, both to himself and to others, that might ensue from the poet's unfeelingness and his refusal to empathize. Again and again we hear that the poet should cultivate cruelty and coldness, that he should confront the external world with a "ferocious and extreme iciness." All the while, he inflicts torments on himself. He resembles "a hungry snake trying to eat its own tail" (536); he is like "a crab tearing off its own shell" (538). Hiraoka insists, however, that he is not talking about the stereotype of the self-destructive artist. "This is not a destruction performed in order to end existence," he writes. "The poet slaughters himself in order that he may live. His is the self-destructive growth of existence itself" (537–538).

From these enigmatic remarks Hiraoka shifts to a consideration of the relationship between artists and history. He is keen to differentiate the history of art (poetry) from other types of history (the history of science, philosophy, etc.) by rejecting the notion of artists' historicity, their relation to a specific time and place. To do this he employs an eclectic vocabulary, mixing Buddhist terms such as *kuon* (the remote past) and *rinne* (the cycle of rebirth) with German words such as *Einmalig* (uniqueness; literally "once-only"), which he seems to have found in his reading of Hegel:

> The entire history of Japanese poetry can be expressed in a single line: "The flowers are in blossom" [*hana ga saite iru*]. No matter which poet speaks, the idea being proclaimed is the same. This is the poetic sentiment of all the great classical poetry collections and also of the modern lyric poets. In its relationship between the singular and the totality, between the particular and the universal, the history of poetry achieves a synthesis of the "specifically universal" in a manner similar to that of general history. However, the history of poetry must be viewed differently from general history, in that it lies beyond the laws of causality. A poet and his works cannot be explained easily, since they are absolute in their *Einmalig* yet they transcend the notion of the remote past and participate in the cycle of rebirth itself. [. . .] It is possible, and indeed appropriate, to base the history of poetry on Hegel's method; that is, as the development of a single theme according to a view of history as having a specific objective. And this theme can be summed up in the line: "The flowers are in blossom." (538–539)

Thus Hiraoka wants to construe artistic values as supra-historical, unaffected by historical contingencies. His argument connects to an ambition that no doubt exists in the minds of all serious artists: that their work will one day attain an aura of universality that reaches beyond the constraints of its immediate time and place. As Hiraoka then acknowledges, however, in modern times poets face a challenge, for the dominant language of modern literature is not poetry but prose: "In the present era the word 'flower' becomes a hindrance" (*hana to iu kotoba ga jama ni naru*). The challenge for modern poets is to find new ways of affirming the eternal poetic idea: "It ought to be possible to express the poetic idea of flowers in blossom by using a different word" (539).

With these thoughts "Poetic Theory" is moving closer to the ideology of the Japan Romantic School. The Romantics had deplored the spread of realism in modern Japanese literature, typified by novelists who fictionalized the often tawdry events of their own lives. For the Romantics, literature's duty was not to replicate life but to beautify it. Ancient Japanese poets had sung of the emperors, the gods, and the beauty of Japan. The Romantics believed that modern writers should do the same. Japan's cultural identity was inscribed in its classical poetry, which was nothing less than the repository of the spirit of the Japanese people. The Romantics revered the *Man'yōshū*, a collection of more than four thousand poems compiled in the eighth century, and the *Kokinshū* and other collections compiled by poets of the imperial court between the tenth and twelfth centuries. Since the oldest poems in the *Man'yōshū* are believed to date from the fifth century, the Romantics were inclined to think of themselves as guardians of a Japanese cultural essence that was unchanged since that time. "To protect the true literary arts of Japan is to live a dream that the Japanese people have cherished for 1,500 years" was the sort of statement they liked to make.[3] And they reminded their readers that their enemy, the young upstart nation of America, had no such heritage.

In "Poetic Theory" we hear that the modern poet of aestheticism, who faces the inconvenience of having to live among "non-ancients," must endeavor to become an "intermediary" (*chūkansha*) who can link modern readers to the spirit of Japan's ancient literary classics and thereby establish an "equilibrium" between present and past. Hiraoka makes it clear that he is not arguing for neoclassicism, and he even rebukes some unnamed modern poets who had attempted to imitate the poetic conventions of the *Man'yōshū* and the *Kokinshū* in their own work. Hiraoka's ideal poet does not simply mimic the past. He seeks new words, new forms, and new modes of representation, which may perhaps deviate from language altogether. Newness is a virtue:

> It is the newness of one who is born from a fundamental principle and yet who stands on the outermost edge of that principle to become its external existence. It is the newness of an absolute intermediary who creates a beautiful equilibrium. (539)

After a string of lofty claims about the "indestructibility" of the great works of Japanese classical literature, Hiraoka ends with an ominous declaration:

> A classic first comes into being as something unique, something that localizes an historical actuality at a single given point. But over time it transcends history, soars into the sky above subsequent generations like a new constellation of stars, and acquires an absoluteness to which nothing can be added and from which nothing can be taken away. It belongs in a wholly different category from the classic works of science and philosophy, which, once they have fulfilled their unique historical role, withdraw from the cycle of rebirth and acquire an historical materiality in the foundations of systematic knowledge. . . .
>
> In the process of becoming a classic, a work of literature passes through the absolute intermediary of its author(s) and changes from something

autonomous and internal to something that is purely external; thus the work sheds its contemporaneity and attains universality. It leaves behind its poets (authors) and becomes the property of all people, a work written by unknown authors and read by nameless readers. The classics are not the property of any single individual, but are equidistant from all readers. They are neither normative nor exemplary, neither loved nor despised. What the classics signify is an extreme longing for our homeland, for our "ferocious mother," for our "terrifying mother." (540–541)

Romanticism had cherished the myth of a mother-goddess who symbolizes the reproductive and destructive forces of nature. Japan's mythical mother is Amaterasu Ōmikami, the sun goddess from whom all the Japanese emperors are said to be descended. True poetry, Hiraoka now declares, is a homecoming, a return to mythic origins, to the savage forces that give birth to culture. There is a blatant contradiction here between the poet's desire for self-mastery, which we heard so much about in the first part of the essay, and this longing to subordinate himself to the "terrifying mother" (*ifu subeki haha*) of culture. Romanticism is, of course, full of such contradictions, and Hiraoka shows no eagerness to resolve them. On the contrary, throughout the essay his rhetoric escalates in proportion to the excitement he obtains from the tensions he has created within his self-description. A few pages earlier he had written, "The formation of the poet is itself a contradiction. The poet is a contradiction that transcends contradiction" (536).

So far, Hiraoka has promoted two main ideas: the importance of the poet's "unfeeling zone" and his craving for unity with the allegedly supra-historical "absoluteness" of the classics. In the final lines of the essay Hiraoka attempts to fuse these two ideas by claiming that it is precisely the poet's unfeelingness that qualifies him to fulfill the role of intermediary between modernity and antiquity:

It is in his unfeeling zone that the poet senses the vast depths between himself and the classics. The poet sings at the outermost edge of his own existence; hence he is closer to the classics than anyone, while at the same time he is furthest from the classics than anyone. For non-ancients, the unfeeling zone of the poet is the only bridge that can lead them to those depths, and it is a bridge that must be crossed. [. . .] Only by crossing it can we eliminate [*ridatsu*] (by death) the absolute intermediary that is the poet, and thereby enter the realm of the classics. (542)

The syntax is crumbling in these lines, and anyway the heavy rhetoric renders the meaning extremely opaque. The strange assertion that the poet's emotional frigidity brings him closer to the classics is not explained, and the only clear suggestion here is that of the poet as sacrificial martyr. The word *ridatsu*, another

Buddhist term, denotes liberation from the endlessly repeated cycle of life and death. Japanese Romantics exalted poets as tragic figures, superior even to military heroes, since a poet bonds with the whole of Japanese history. That seems to be what Hiraoka has in mind for himself here. The poet of aestheticism does not aspire to assert his individuality but to merge with an archetype defined in classical literature.

"Poetic Theory" records the anxious, egotistical reflections of a young artist writing at a traumatic moment in his life. It is therefore not the sort of text in which we would expect to find great clarity of expression or coherence of thought. And it is, let us remember, a draft and not a finished work. Nonetheless, beneath its rhetoric it presents a remarkably accurate description of the phenomenon we know its author will attempt to become. There is the disdainful attitude toward the state of affairs called reality, the coldheartedness and the praise of cruelty, the longing for an ethereal beauty, the aggressive egotism paired, paradoxically, with an ambition to transform himself into an archetype, and the almost religious faith in Japan's classical literature as the definitive foundation of Japanese cultural identity.

We should also take note of the fact that although "Poetic Theory" was written at a time when its author was closer to death, to the possibility of actually being killed, than at any other time in his life, it does not glorify death. The metaphor of the artist as a person turned inside out is shocking but not morbid. This work is written by someone who knows that he may die yet who wants to live, and who is determined, if granted the opportunity, to live in a most extraordinary way.

In support of that assertion I want to quote the content of a postcard he sent two months later to one of his former school friends, a junior boy from the Peers School Literature Club. The postcard is dated August 16, 1945, the day after Japan's surrender. Hiraoka, now on the verge of permanently assuming the name of Mishima Yukio, had apparently received a despairing message from the boy. This was his reply:

> Please do not lose hope. You must stay alive, and you must live for what is most pure, most noble, and most beautiful. The mission of military men has come to an end. Now the true mission of literary men begins. Ours is the language of the emperors and the gods, and our literature and the poetic spirit that sustains it are not the monopoly of any individual person. Please live purely and vigorously. Weak though I am, I too will stay alive, and I will fight. (38:313)

CHAPTER 2

Problems of Beauty

> There are corpses buried beneath the cherry trees!
> There must be. How else could the blossoms be so beautiful?
> *Kajii Motojirō, "Beneath the Cherry Trees"*

"Poetic Theory" is concerned chiefly with the psychology of the artist and offers no statement about beauty itself. In this sense it is atypical. In the writings of all other stages of his career Mishima is tirelessly preoccupied with the category of experiences that he calls *bi* (beauty), with objects and people he considers *utsuku-shii* (beautiful), and with modes of action he considers *bi-teki* (beauty-oriented or aesthetic). Even in his earliest poems and jottings, written before he began publishing his work, we find him investigating the multitude of intuitions, emotions, and sentiments that fill the category of beauty as he wants to understand it. The following five aphorisms are dated May 24, 1939:

> All distant things are beautiful,
> For they exist in the realm of our imagination.
>
> Beauty does not always accompany goodness;
> Sometimes the beauty of evil surpasses that of good.
>
> One must not approach too near to beauty;
> It should be kept inside a glass shrine.
>
> The beauty of the weak as perceived by the strong
> Will always surpass the beauty of the strong as perceived by the weak.
>
> Throw away the light, and watch the moment when darkness meets it:
> That is Beauty!
> (37:337–338)

The prioritizing of imagination over reality is no surprise in a teenage dreamer. But note that imagination here goes hand-in-hand with distance. This beauty is experienced most intensely in reveries or dreams, where it is beyond reach or lost in time. No desire is being expressed here for a sensory experience of beauty in the present moment. These lines exalt an *unreal* beauty. It is a beauty that, if made real, would be too dangerous to approach; to touch it would be to touch death. We also perceive an assertion of the essential amorality of beauty, along with hints of beauty as tragic suffering. Lastly, and most characteristically, comes a vision of beauty as a spectacular and destructive union of mutually negating forces.

A short prose piece with the title "On Having Seen a Sunset" (Yūyake o mita koto), written one year after the above aphorisms, contains the following passage, which attempts to conceptualize more clearly the allure of "unreal" beauty:

> In my view, there is no beautiful thing that does not contain death. The ecstasy we feel when we see a thing of beauty, the joy we feel, together with a chilly kind of sadness that deserves to be called tragic [*hisō*]—all this is so similar to a sense of confronting death that the two experiences are quite inseparable. And when we see such a thing we realize that those ancient people who situated the most beautiful thing of all—heaven— in the world of death had created a truly exquisite idea. Heaven is our beautiful ideal, yet we die without ever having seen it. The people who first imagined heaven treated it not as something to be visualized, but as a metaphysical problem, something too profound to be kept secret, yet always beyond the reach of mankind. (43:130–131)

This image of tragic beauty situated in an otherworldly realm brings to mind the aesthetics of the Noh theater, where beauty often lies half hidden in shadows, dreams, and ghostly visions. Sometimes in Noh there is an intimation of a beauty too fragile to survive in the real world, or, conversely, a toxic beauty that would be too dangerous for this world to withstand. Beauty of this kind must be constrained within strictly prescribed forms or confined to the realms of the imaginary and the unreal. In his mature writings on Noh, Mishima is always keen to emphasize this point about constraint:

> The long line of Noh dramatists and actors beginning with Zeami Motokiyo [1363–1443] were, I suspect, thoroughly familiar with the terrifying quality inherent in beauty. That, indeed, is why they took care to seek beauty only in the ruined, shutting up beauty within the confines of dreams, of reminiscence, and of death. It was their rule that even the most perilously seductive beauty should be nothing but an apparition from the

dead, that it should be already over, with no power to threaten us in actuality and no existence in reality outside the bones lying in the grave. (36:601)

In his twenties Mishima made modern-language adaptations of eight plays from the classical Noh repertoire. The plays he selected all share a common theme: the eternal return of obsessive desire.[1] Perhaps the most poignant is Mishima's adaptation of the play known as *Komachi at Sotoba*, which dates from the middle of the fourteenth century.

Every Japanese person knows the legend of Komachi, a famous noblewoman of ancient Japan who was celebrated for her beauty. Komachi tells one of her suitors that she will give herself to him only after he has visited her a hundred times. The man obediently visits her night after night, but on his hundredth visit, he dies. Komachi's extraordinary beauty, it seems, is beyond the reach of any mortal man. In the Noh play, events unfold long after Komachi has passed away from old age, and they are confined in an unreal world: the ghost of Komachi appears in the dream of a sleeping monk and tells him her story.

Mishima, in his modern-language adaptation, arranges the scenario as a nighttime encounter in a park between an elderly homeless woman and a young man who turns out to be an aspiring poet. When we first see Komachi she is sitting alone on a park bench, counting cigarette stubs she has collected from the ground. The young man, who is noisily drunk, wanders into the park and strikes up a conversation with her. To his astonishment, she guesses instantly that he is a poet. She tells him she is ninety-nine years old: "All the men who called me beautiful are dead. So, the way I see it now, any man who calls me beautiful is certain to die." The young poet laughs at her. "If that's the case," he sneers, "then I'm in no danger" (21:531).

Suddenly a waltz begins to play. Couples dressed in old-fashioned clothes appear and start dancing. Komachi and the poet have been transported back in time eighty years to what we understand is a fashionable dance hall of the Meiji era (1868–1912). The two of them begin to dance. Soon the poet is delirious with joy. In his mind Komachi is now a beautiful young woman and he is her lover. Komachi realizes that the poet is losing grip of his senses and warns him not to tell her that she is beautiful: "If you say it, you will forfeit your life!" She implores him to look at the web of wrinkles on her face. But the poet is blinded by his fantasy. Unable to restrain himself, he whispers to her, "Komachi, you are beautiful—more beautiful than anything in this world" (541).

The moment the poet utters those words, his hands and feet turn cold. After promising to meet Komachi again in the same place one hundred years from now, he dies. Komachi's last words to him: "It is already one hundred years!" (542).

Komachi has done her utmost to keep her beauty confined safely within the world of dreams and memories, but she has failed. In the silence that follows, we understand that the transcendent beauty we have just glimpsed was not Komachi's death-inducing beauty, nor the illusion of her beauty's eternalness that the poet thought he was embracing. It was the fate of the poet himself, the eternally beautiful idea of a young poet dying for the sake of beauty.

And yet, in a way that is typical of Mishima, the play lightly mocks the sentimentalism of its own idea. In the final moments a policeman arrives on the scene. He discovers the poet's dead body and tuts in annoyance. After questioning a few people in the park, the policeman has the body unceremoniously dragged away. Now Komachi is again sitting on the bench and counting cigarette stubs, exactly as she was at the start of the play. Everything continues as before. The beautiful death of a romantic young poet has not had the slightest effect on the world.

Did it even happen?

Ecstasy of Being Enfolded

Other feelings Mishima wants to include within the category of beauty are too aggressive to find adequate expression within the stately and ritualized world of Noh. Mishima complicates beauty by investing it with his own sexual volatility. He is very strongly drawn to the sadomasochistic potential of beauty conceived as an overwhelming force, a force to be violently resisted or deliriously embraced. Mishima's attitude toward beauty is therefore paradoxical. He loves beauty because it is the value through which he asserts his will to power, but at the same time he resents beauty because it forces him to subordinate himself to it. He wants to confine beauty safely within prescribed forms, as in Noh, yet also he dreams of drowning in an unstoppable tidal wave of beauty. At other times Mishima pursues beauty as a limit-experience, a point where extreme pleasure coincides with extreme displeasure, where ecstasy coincides with agony, or where a distinction between the two becomes untenable.

Mishima finds manifestations of the kind of beauty he seeks in exquisite objects, people, and creatures that have been subjected to spectacular acts of violence. A lover hacked to death. A religious martyr pierced with arrows. A temple set on fire. A peacock torn to pieces. A kitten strangled and dissected. A samurai cutting open his own stomach. Constant at the center of Mishima's work is the belief, akin to a religious faith, that for a beautiful thing to be made perfectly and eternally beautiful, it must be destroyed. This act of destruction resembles a ritual sacrifice that releases the essence of the thing or creature that is destroyed and renders it transcendent. In his highest flights of rapture Mishima even dreams of a beauty so deadly that it would destroy itself, and he wants to throw himself into such beauty, to become beautiful with it, to merge with it at the moment when it burns itself out and vanishes from the world.

The literary critic Tasaka Kō says, with some exasperation, "For Mishima it often seems as if the beautiful [*utsukushii*] and the terrifying [*osoroshii*] are synonymous."[2] Tasaka thinks this is perverse, and he goes hunting for explanations in Mishima's supposedly abnormal upbringing. But the matter is less perplexing if we reformulate it in the language of modern aesthetics, by saying that Mishima refuses to separate the beautiful (conceived as a pleasurable awareness of harmonious form) and the sublime (an awed or terrified awareness of formless power) into different categories, and uses the word *utsukushii* (or *bi*) as inclusive of both.

Western thinkers first introduced the aesthetic category of the sublime in the eighteenth century to denote the feeling of awed pleasure aroused by spectacular natural phenomena: great mountain peaks and high clifftops, giant icebergs, raging seas, thunderstorms, and the like. Japanese scholars of the late nineteenth century dutifully concocted an equivalent Japanese term: *sūkō*. One historian of aesthetics tells us that the two kanji that form this word suggest lofty mountains, an intention to soar upward, and "the spiritual energy that creates all things."[3] The word *sūkō* did not win broad acceptance until the 1930s, when the writers of the Japan Romantic School appropriated it into their lexicon. In their first manifesto they declared their passionate resolve to "defend that which is most beautiful and to honor that which is most sublime."[4] Mishima, in contrast, seldom uses the word *sūkō*, and that is one reason why his pronouncements on beauty can be so difficult to fathom or to sympathize with. Occasionally he makes his meaning clearer by differentiating between beauty that depends for its effects on formal qualities, and another kind of beauty, which he calls "true beauty" (*shin no bi*) and which is characterized by volatility, danger, and boundlessness, all characteristics we associate with the sublime.

Elisions of the beautiful and the sublime into a single category are most familiar to us from late Romanticism. We think of Rilke's famous lines:

For Beauty's nothing
but beginning of Terror we're still just able to bear,
and why we adore it so is because it serenely
disdains to destroy us.[5]

Or the passage from the Madonna-Sodom episode of Dostoyevsky's *The Brothers Karamazov*, which Mishima quotes as an epigraph to *Confessions of a Mask*:

Beauty is a terrifying and a horrible thing! It's terrifying because it can't be defined, and it can't be defined because God has set nothing but riddles. Here the two banks of the river meet, and here all contradictions exist together. . . . The Devil only knows what's at stake here, that's the truth of it! Things that seem ignominy to the mind, to the heart are nothing but beauty. Beauty in Sodom—can that be true? You may be certain that it is precisely there that beauty resides for the vast majority of people.[6]

By the early twentieth century, Japanese writers too were challenging assumptions about the intrinsic goodness of beauty by promoting the beauty of the perverse, the dangerous, and the wicked. For centuries Japanese poets had exalted the beauty of nature. Modernists attacked this tradition by stressing the naturalness of disease, ugliness, and pain. The poems of Hagiwara Sakutarō (1886–1942) are littered with unpleasant insects, animal carcasses, and putrid filth. Mishima was fond of quoting a prose poem by Kajii Motojirō (1901–1932) that depicts cherry trees bursting into blossom from a pile of rotting corpses.[7] The aim of these decadent distortions and inversions was not to desecrate beauty but to reconsecrate it by liberating it from the staleness of convention and cliché. Many of Mishima's own works explore similar scenarios of beauty being revitalized by contact with its opposite. But Mishima still yearns for something darker and more sinister, for aesthetic gestures that erupt into violence and destruction. He routinely places beauty far beyond the pleasure principle, as when he declares, "True beauty is something that attacks, overpowers, robs, and ultimately destroys" (36:600).

Mishima offers a sumptuous evocation of his ideal of "true beauty" in the very first work he published under his pen name, a lyrical prose piece titled "A Forest in Full Bloom" (Hanazakari no mori). This was the work that first established Mishima's name in Japan's literary circles and convinced people to call him a prodigy. In one of its episodes a young woman has just moved from Kyoto to a remote coastal town, where for the first time in her life she encounters the sea. Mishima's precocious linguistic brilliance is on full display:

The sea was glistening like a ribbon of satin in the distance, yet the
    unending rumble of the waves assailed her where she stood.
Covering her eyes, she raced toward the beach. The sea wind assaulted
    her ears as the sound of the waves grew louder. When at last she felt
    the warm dry sand beneath her feet, a shudder hurtled through her
    body.
Then she uncovered her eyes.
The seascape stretched magnanimously before her, as though it was
    the most natural thing in the world that it should be there. The sky

was serenely clear. The golden clouds were as static as if painted on a scroll. The cape, still covered here and there with verdant patches, was cupping the bay tightly like an elegant shell.

Now, at last, the fertile sea carved its mark in the young woman's heart. Yet just as a violent wound affords no pain at the instant of its infliction, she felt none of the fear she had anticipated. From this first encounter, the gods of the sea lived within her.

She was enraptured by an inexplicable ecstasy, such as a murder victim feels the moment before the killer strikes. A moment of distinct premonition, yet one which sheds no light on the present. A beautiful and isolated present. A disconnected moment as pure as anything in this world.

She became completely passive. Once she had been active, and soon she would be again. But for now she collapsed into passivity, or rather, into the pure abstraction of mind that accompanies such a collapse, accepting all and becoming nothing, as if being clasped to her mother's breast.

All of a sudden she was ejected from this indescribable plenitude, this ecstasy of being enfolded. An unbearable heaviness and a sense of dread descended over her. The sea continued to rage within her and seemed ready to overflow. She fled back to the house and closed the shutters. (15:501–502)

There is something unsettling about a sixteen-year-old who writes likes this. The experience he is describing could perhaps be characterized as that of a violently erotic sublime. The woman's encounter with the vast formlessness of the sea induces her to postulate an infinity that is beyond the capacity of her imagination. She feels herself reduced to nothing, and consequently she is overcome with terror. But at the same time, she experiences an illumination of consciousness that detaches her from her terror, lifts her above it, and grants her a moment of blissful reflection on her capacity to recognize this incapacity, to imagine that the world is larger than she can imagine it to be. This is the familiar paradox of "negative pleasure" afforded by experiences of the sublime.

Yet this alone is not enough for Mishima. He cannot resist adding images of violent physical penetration: a wound carved in flesh, a fatal stabbing. The subliminal eroticism of stabbing is a constant idea in his work, and, as we shall see later, he routinely uses female characters to disguise his male-centered fantasies. Here the young woman's orgasmic swoon is also an orgasmic union with the colossal force that threatens to destroy her. What she experiences in her momentary "ecstasy of being enfolded" (*tsutsumareru koto no kōkotsu*) is an intimation of the shattering of her own autonomy, but it is also a spiritual exaltation that comes from transcending her sense of her own individual self.

Such is the moment of "true beauty" to which Mishima and his characters ceaselessly aspire: a liberation from self-consciousness and individuality, a feeling of oneness with the totality of existence, a pleasurable apprehension of a hostile and deadly force—what we might call an appreciation of terror.

Sweet Violence

Mishima's fascination with the triad of beauty, eroticism, and violent death is not as idiosyncratic as many commentators have suggested. To a large degree it is of its time, connectable to the violent history of Japan in the first half of the twentieth century: the aesthetics and propaganda of Japanese militarism and emperor-centered fascism, the fake-traditional martial code of bushido promoted before and during the war, the beauty of the kamikaze squadrons and the banzai suicide charges, and all the apocalyptic madness of the war itself. The blood-soaked sexual fantasies described in *Confessions of a Mask* stand alongside declarations of "a sensuous craving for the destiny of soldiers, the tragic nature of their profession, and the manner of their deaths" (1:185).

Japanese boys of Mishima's generation had no choice but to think about how they were going to die. Most took it for granted that they would not live long past the age of twenty. Japan's military promoted an ideology of glorified death, instructing soldiers never to surrender but instead to "shatter like crystal" on the battlefield. School textbooks, popular songs, theaters, and films exalted the virtue of "falling like cherry petals" for the emperor. The writers of the Japan Romantic School assured their young male readers that death in battle was equivalent to poetry and that soldiers who fought suicidally to the end would attain a "divine spirit" (*kamigokoro*).[8] Barely concealed beneath all this frenetic glorification of death was a resignation to certain defeat, embodied in the ubiquitous propaganda image of cherry blossoms. The fall of the petals is not only beautiful, it is inevitable.

For boys who absorbed this ideology yet who, like Mishima, did not actually go to war and who lived on after Japan's defeat, the war years remained in their memory as an exhilarating encounter with danger and doom, an experience they could never recapture during the subsequent years of peace.

Here is the political theorist Hashikawa Bunzō (1922–1983), Mishima's contemporary and one of his most astute readers, reminiscing two decades after the end of the war:

For those of us, like Mishima and myself, whose boyhood and youth coincided with the war, it is impossible to remember that time without a certain guilty feeling of pure pleasure. It is the memory of a pagan orgy, of the intoxication of consecrated crime. The schema of that era comprised an astonishing amount of freedom, a miraculous self-indulgence and innocence, and an acosmic [sic] harmony of beauty and logic. The whole world seemed imbued with a unity of transparent indolence and sweet violence.

To us boys, those days felt like the days of an endless summer, a vacation that was going to last forever. The gods had come down to earth to fight as tribal gods, and the deep inner anguish of humanity could not exist under the skillful political shamanism of that time. If I may borrow a term that Max Weber used to describe his experience of the First World War, what guaranteed such intoxication was our *Totengemeinschaft*, our "community unto death." We knew that we were going to die young. Therefore everything was permitted.

Needless to say, this orgy was a repulsive irony produced by the phenomenon of total war. Amid the stubborn perversity of those years, there was nothing unpatriotic about living in a dormitory at a naval factory, as Mishima did, engrossed in solitary aesthetic pursuits, indifferent to the progress of the war. As far as we were concerned, if a silver grenade smashed a boy's skull into pieces and spattered his blood over a summer garden, even that had a self-evident beauty about it.[9]

This passage displays a kind of savage honesty, both in its confession of pleasure and in its acknowledgment of perversity. As described here, the intoxication generated by the *Totengemeinschaft* (a term Hashikawa renders into Japanese as *shi no kyōdōtai*, a "community of death") has a profoundly disturbing effect on the sentiment of beauty, such that even the most decadent beauty can lose its aura of decadence and become normal or "self-evident." Hashikawa's religious terminology ("pagan orgy," "tribal gods," "consecration," "shamanism") and his oxymoronic conjunctions ("consecrated crime," "sweet violence") well evoke the rapturous collisions of contraries that generate the sublime experience that Mishima and his characters crave. And Mishima's aesthetification of bloodshed and destruction surely loses some of its peculiarity if Hashikawa can find beauty in a smashed skull. This passage also helps us to understand how Mishima's contemporaries were inclined to interpret his work and his persona: as the expression of a trauma that was not his alone, but which was embedded in the minds of young Japanese men of his generation who had experienced the intoxication of the community unto death and yet, randomly and unexpectedly, had outlived it.

Mishima's teenage writings endlessly manifest the sort of decadent indulgence recalled by Hashikawa. Many of them could be characterized as stylistic exercises in the beautification of evil. In an unfinished story titled "The Mansion" (Yakata), dated November 1939, an aristocrat with a lust for cruelty hires a team of artists to paint a picture of hell on the walls of his mansion:

> Oh, what words can describe the terrifying images they painted there? It would be no exaggeration to say that they exhausted the limits of human atrocity in their depictions of the vilest, cruelest, ugliest, most fearsome, most shameful scenes imaginable. Perhaps this is what is meant by the beauty of evil. It was as if those paintings were made by men who had seen hell with their own eyes. So cruel, so ugly is this hell, that its beauty sucks the helpless spectator into its vortex and drowns him in a sea of blood. (15:175–176)

A poem titled "Evil Things" (Magagoto) is dated January 15, 1940:

Night after night
I stand at my window,
waiting for signs of the mysterious.
A sandstorm surging through the streets
like a rainbow after dark.
The pink pyroxene of an evening sky,
floating through trees that are dead and dry as sea sponge.
A sunset mixed from a thick tincture of iodine.

When I see the colors of evil things
a curtain of satin closes over my heart.
The Dark Ones appear
and battle furiously through the night,
until blood drips from the stars
and pandemonium rings out in my room.

I am waiting for evil.
To me, good news is bad.
Black are the faces of the mangled and the dead.
Crimson is my blood, and cold as ice . . .
(37:400–401)

The following undated fragment, which has the title "Extermination of the Americans" (Beijin ōsatsu), was presumably written toward the end of the war:

> Americans, leave this earth! That is your duty. Leave no trace of yourselves. It is your only honorable course. Die, Americans! Become extinct. Do not

hesitate. Let your swords be drenched in your own blood. Die, every one of you. Never walk this earth again. Die, Americans! You disgust me. I cannot stand the sight of you. Die, you blind herds who show no fear before the Sun! Since you look to the Sun with hatred rather than with respect, I shall stamp on your faces . . .

Your foul stench is revolting. Get away from me, don't come near me. One whiff of your breath and even the flowers in the garden draw their daggers. Your breath rots fish in the clearest streams. You are mothers of flies. Be gone, loathsome ones. Dogs of dogs! Swine of swine! Wretched filth-eating spawn of Babylon! You will be mowed into the ground, and poisonous flowers will sprout from your corpses. You will be stamped on and trampled on and crushed like crabs. Do not dare to spill your blue brains on this soil! (36:547)

Perhaps the most remarkable of Mishima's wartime texts is the journal he kept of his visits to the theaters: Bunraku, Kabuki, and Noh. His descriptions of the performances are meticulous to a professional level, recording idiosyncrasies in the actors' mannerisms and movements, the actors' precise delivery of specific lines, deviations from convention, failures of timing, textual alterations, and so on. But what most strikes the reader is the journal's utter indifference to realities beyond art. Virtually the only time Mishima acknowledges the existence of a world outside the theaters is when the government orders the theaters closed down in order to focus people's attention on the increasingly desperate war effort. In his journal Mishima fumes with outrage. How dare these ignorant government bureaucrats disrupt his theater schedule! When some of the smaller theaters tentatively reopen during the US bombings, the young critic is back to work, attending every performance he can. He does so with a grim diligence, walking to the theaters through the wreckage and rubble of downtown Tokyo. He attended a performance of the Noh play *Viewing the Autumn Leaves* staged, almost incredibly, in February 1945. Despite all his complaints, however, his journal makes it clear that these performances were among the most intense artistic experiences of his life. Like performances of Beethoven and Wagner in war-torn Nazi Germany, the proximity of death and the sense of imminent apocalypse created in audiences extraordinary feelings of luxury and guilt, as if it were immoral to be enjoying such beautiful art in such an ugly time. Under such circumstances, perhaps, art becomes evil.

If Mishima was at his happiest during the years of war, as he would later claim, it was because the war enabled a sense of harmony between the cruelty of the world around him and the cruel sensibilities that were innate within him. The prospect that he was soon going to be killed, that Japan was going to be defeated and destroyed, and that the whole world was coming to an end accorded perfectly with his own decadent aesthetic, according to which things give off their most intense beauty at the moment they perish and fade.

Hashikawa remembered the war fondly, though with an inescapable feeling of criminal guilt. For Mishima, however, it was the years of peace that struck him as criminal. He spent the rest of his life hankering for the time when the world had been infused with a sense of radical danger, of awe and dread, and when all things had seemed united by the "self-evident beauty" of impending apocalypse. He published the following lines in August 1965, on the twentieth anniversary of Japan's defeat:

> Only after the war ended did I come to understand that the war had been an erotic time. It was a time when all the little pieces of vulgar eroticism that proliferate today were gathered together and purified in one giant Eros. If I had died in the war, I would have been able to die within an Eros that was totally unconscious and self-sufficient. This was something I did not realize at the time, and so today I find it very difficult to block this thought from my mind. Those who preach peace may not like to acknowledge it, but the fact is that war is more than just misery. (33:490–491)

He made the following remarks during a later interview:

> Will there ever again come a time when it is not strange to write the words "Long Live His Majesty the Emperor" in one's last will and testament? Whether it comes again or not, the fact is that I once lived in such a time, and I remember a sort of ferocious happiness. Just what was that experience? What was that happiness? At the very least, I have never been as free as I was during the war. (39:681)

Dark Thoughts

The sentiments articulated in the above quotations are central to *The Temple of the Golden Pavilion* (1956), the novel in which Mishima presents his fundamental myth of beauty and destruction.

Mizoguchi, the young monk whose maniacal obsession with the beautiful temple ultimately compels him to burn it down, is, not surprisingly, a contradictory character. In psychological terms he seems to fit the profile of a sociopath. Introverted, narcissistic, socially awkward, and sexually impotent, he seethes with resentment at the world. Yet he is also reflective, analytical, logically meticulous, and endowed with a keen aesthetic sensibility. The novel is presented as his own written account of his life up to the moment he burned the temple. That it is a *written* account needs emphasizing. We are not listening to the thoughts in Mizoguchi's mind; we are reading his autobiography. After burning down the temple he has taken the trouble to turn his crime, and himself, into a work of literature, though we never learn when he wrote it, or for whom, or why.

On a simple level, the various stages of Mizoguchi's relationship with the temple resemble those of a disastrous love affair. When we first see him he is yearning for the temple from a distance. He longs to possess its beauty and share its secrets. Then a crisis brings him and the temple closer together. Now he dreams of dying with the temple, and he attains his highest degree of happiness when it looks as if his wish will soon be fulfilled. But events thwart his apocalyptic dream, and when the temple seems to spurn him Mizoguchi turns vengeful. Now the temple's beauty is unbearable to him. Malicious thoughts grow in his mind. He begins to plot against the temple, against its redundant excess of beauty, and against the world that has denied him his desire. He wants to destroy the temple, to erase its beauty from the face of the earth. If *he* cannot have it, then *no one* shall have it. And so he kills the thing he loves.

However, the density of Mizoguchi's philosophical reflections, and the tortuous shifts in his consciousness as he progresses toward what he believes is a state of enlightenment, preclude such a simple reading. I say that Mizoguchi's reflections are philosophical because his malaise has a metaphysical nature, and although he obsessively pursues an idea he calls "beauty," the text he has written is not only, or even primarily, about aesthetics. It explores issues such as the phenomenology of imagination, the nature of art, of the sublime, of freedom, of evil, and the quest for the absolute. In what follows I shall focus on the aspects of the novel that help to shed light on Mishima's own project of aesthetic terrorism.

Mizoguchi informs us, "It would be no exaggeration to say that the first truly difficult problem I confronted in life was that of beauty" (6:27). For Mizoguchi the problem of beauty, initially at least, is not one of definition but of estrangement. As a young boy he hears from his father, a country priest, that the Temple of the Golden Pavilion in Kyoto is the most beautiful thing in the world. Mizoguchi is enthralled by this notion. But he is also disturbed at the alleged presence of such beauty in the world, antecedent to and separate from him: "If beauty really did exist there, it meant that my own existence was estranged from beauty" (28).

This seemingly childish logic is founded on a subtle imaginative process. His father's words have presented Mizoguchi with a concept, and, utilizing this concept, Mizoguchi creates an image in his mind. But the image he creates is nonetheless independent of causality. A primal image of the most beautiful thing in the world surges into his consciousness, and he equates that image with the Temple of the Golden Pavilion. It is something so beautiful that any attempt to represent it using human skill would almost certainly be inadequate. But Mizoguchi does not immediately think in this way. He assumes that the wondrous beauty he has imagined is an intrinsic quality of the actual temple in Kyoto, and that this beauty will be apparent to him the moment he sees the building.

That, of course, is how we commonly articulate our feelings about beauty. We speak of the pleasure we derive from a beautiful object as if it were a quality that the object itself possesses, rather than an emotion or feeling generated within us through our response to the object.

When he visits the temple for the first time, Mizoguchi discovers the falseness of his assumption. Arriving in Kyoto, he expects to see the most beautiful thing in the world. What he finds is a bland old wooden building standing next to a pond. Mizoguchi is despondent. How is it possible that the real temple is inferior to the temple in his mind? As he puts it, "How can beauty be so unbeautiful?" (31).

After the death of his father, Mizoguchi moves to Kyoto and becomes an apprentice monk at the Golden Temple. Now he must face the object of his obsession every day. In his reveries he addresses the temple directly:

> At last I have come to live beside you, Golden Temple! . . . Some time, it needn't be right now, please be kind to me and reveal your secret to me. I feel that I am so close to being able to see your beauty, and yet I cannot see it. Please make the real Golden Temple look more beautiful to me than the image of it in my mind. And if it is true that you are more beautiful than anything in this world, please tell me why you are so beautiful, why it is necessary for you to be so beautiful. (41–42)

These lines have the feel of a prayer about them, and the argument could be made that Mizoguchi's yearning for a transcendent absolute, which he strongly intuits yet cannot define and to which he gives the name "beauty," is proximate to a religious attitude. The new idea appearing here is necessity. Mizoguchi rejects the contingency of things—that they might not have been as they are, that they might not have existed at all—and demands something that will enable him to experience the world as if it exists *necessarily*.

War breaks out, prompting Mizoguchi to reflect that the fifteenth-century temple was built in an era of social turmoil when wars were frequent and when it was not unusual for temples to be destroyed or burned in fire. Could this be the temple's secret, that it is not a celebration of beauty but a crystallization of anxiety? Are fear and danger somehow embodied in its structure?

Thinking in this way, Mizoguchi is excited to hear a rumor that American bombers will soon come to Kyoto. Now there is a real possibility that the temple will be destroyed in an air raid, and he along with it. This sense of shared danger enables him to superimpose the image of the temple in his mind onto the actual temple, which for the first time appears no less beautiful to him than his mental image of it. Thereafter he enjoys a delirious sense of unity with the temple, as if drowning in its tragic beauty.

Mizoguchi's thoughts and feelings up to this point are not, I think, implausible. It is a common enough experience for us to inspect an object or artwork that people of earlier centuries revered as religiously sublime or magically beautiful, or perhaps feared as magically dangerous, and find to our disappointment that to our modern critical consciousness, the object has lost its sublime or magical aura and is merely aesthetically pleasing. It is also true that a beautiful thing can seem more precious to us, more beautiful, when we fear that we are about to part with it or lose it forever. And surely most people have sensed, at one time or another, a lack of meaning in the contingency of their lives. As for Mizoguchi's delirious dream of total annihilation, this is none other than the community of death recalled by Hashikawa. On a radical level, this delirium connects to an idea with which many of us can probably feel some sympathy; namely, that life is only lived authentically in the face of extreme danger, at a point that is almost beyond life. Brooding on the prospect of imminent destruction, Mizoguchi attains an absolute perspective that enables him to bypass self-reflection and thus overcome his contingency. All of Mishima's characters who contemplate their own deaths like this obtain the same alimentary effect: liberation from self-consciousness. It is not that Mizoguchi craves death. What he craves is a feeling of being *alive*, and it is only when convinced of the chaotic excess that makes death an imminent possibility that he can obtain this feeling.

But Mizoguchi's dream of destruction proves to be overly optimistic. The American bombers spare the city of Kyoto. (They did so, let us note, largely for aesthetic reasons: in an irony unknown to Mizoguchi, Kyoto was saved from destruction by the beauty of its temples.) The Temple of the Golden Pavilion survives the war, thereby contradicting Mizoguchi's apocalyptic vision. It turns out that he is not going to die violently in the heart of the most beautiful thing in the world. He is going to live. And the temple, it seems, is going to live forever. Thus Mizoguchi once again finds himself in a world of contingency. Dismayed and frustrated, he sinks back into angst.

The wartime temple had functioned symbolically as an embodiment of Mizoguchi's tragic longing, manifesting in sensuous form the evanescence of all things. But the postwar temple has lost this aura. It is as beautiful as ever, but its beauty lacks the metaphysical dimension that previously supported it. Now the temple is needlessly, inexplicably, meaninglessly beautiful. It has been reduced, he feels, to the status of "cultural heritage." It is a relic of the past, something that tourists come to take snapshots of. Mizoguchi is maddened by what he feels is this hypertrophy of historical awareness within which the temple is becoming entrenched. He wants the temple to burn, as temples have burned in the past, as he hopes they will burn in the future, for it is, he believes, the supra-historical essence of their tragic beauty to burn.

These thoughts force Mizoguchi to rethink his theory of beauty. He comes to understand that the experience he has been calling "beauty" is not derived from sense-perception but originates as a primal element of his own psyche. Beauty, he now realizes, does not arise directly *from* the temple but indirectly *through* it. His ideal beauty is a kind of faith, whereas the temple itself is merely an object made from wooden planks and iron bolts:

> If you inspected the beauty of the details—the beauty of the pillars, the railings, the shutters, the ornamented windows, the pyramid-shaped roof, the various sections of the design, the temple's shadow on the pond, the tiny islands, the pine trees, even the mooring-place for the boat—beauty did not reach its culmination in these details; rather, each detail contained an intimation of another beauty to come. The beauty of the details was itself filled with unease. While dreaming of perfection it knew no completion and was urged on to the next beauty, to an unknown beauty. One intimation led to another, and it was these intimations of a beauty *that does not exist here* that constituted the fundamental idea of the temple. Such intimations were signs of nothingness. Nothingness was the very structure of this beauty. (267)

Over the beauty of the actual temple, Mizoguchi is determined to privilege "a beauty that does not exist here" (*koko ni wa sonzai shinai bi*). Ivan Morris' English translation of the novel inexplicably omits the preposition "here" and thereby alters the meaning of this crucial phrase, even though Mishima has emphasized it with italics. It is not that Mizoguchi accepts that his beautiful ideal is nonexistent, a fantasy of his own invention. On the contrary, he clings fanatically to his belief in a transcendent, ineffable absolute that he calls beauty, and which, he now understands, cannot be adequately represented within the realm of worldly phenomena. In destroying the Golden Temple, Mizoguchi knows that he will "reduce the amount of beauty that humans have created in this world" (206). But he is sure that his act of destruction will open people's eyes to a superior beauty that no object made by humans can replicate. It is precisely this impossibility, the insufficiency of human abilities to represent this sublime idea, that he will expose to the world.

The claim could be made that this is also what happened in reality. As is well-known, Mishima based his novel on the actual burning of the Temple of the Golden Pavilion (to be precise, the burning of the pavilion) by a deranged young monk on July 2, 1950. But we should pay attention to the time lag between the burning of the temple and the composition of the novel. Mishima did not begin writing the novel until late in 1955. That was the year in which the newly rebuilt temple had been opened to the public. Photographs taken before 1950 show that the temple that burned down was not very golden. Five and a half centuries of rain and wind had eroded most of its gold leaf. The reconstructed temple, on the other hand, glittered with new gold leaf, as the original temple had once done. The point is not that by burning down the temple the monk had unwittingly prompted the restoration of its beauty. Rather, by destroying a rebuildable wooden structure known as the Golden Temple he had unwittingly demonstrated that the Golden Temple is not the wooden structure. The Golden Temple is really an *idea* of a Golden Temple. Temples may burn, but the beautiful idea is eternal. And perhaps there are even times when it is necessary for a temple to burn in order to remind us of this truth.

The problem of beauty for Mizoguchi is thus not a matter of aesthetics but of anti-aesthetics. He refuses to accept an experience of beauty that is founded on the disinterested pleasure of aesthetic enjoyment, on the calm and detached contemplation of beautiful things. In its place, he craves a beauty that cannot be confined with prescribed forms or experienced without fear and trembling, a beauty that is fraught with danger and tainted by the stench of death. The ultimate purpose of his act of aesthetic terrorism is to destroy aesthetics.

Now that we have followed the novel almost to its conclusion, let us take another look at Mishima's five early aphorisms on beauty:

All distant things are beautiful,
For they exist in the realm of our imagination.

Beauty does not always accompany goodness;
Sometimes the beauty of evil surpasses that of good.

One must not approach too near to beauty;
It should be kept inside a glass shrine.

The beauty of the weak as perceived by the strong
Will always surpass the beauty of the strong as perceived by the weak.

Throw away the light, and watch the moment when darkness meets it:
That is Beauty!

Is the argument of *The Temple of the Golden Pavilion* not already discernible in these lines, which were written more than ten years before the actual burning of the temple? For Mizoguchi, the temple is most beautiful when it is distant from him, when it exists only in the realm of his imagination, as it does at the beginning and the end of the novel. This is the principle of unreal beauty, central to Japanese Romanticism. We noted the religious nature of Mizoguchi's longing, as he struggles to fathom the disjunction between the temple as empirical reality and the transcendental temple in his mind. The idea that goodness cannot fully contain the problematic feeling of beauty gradually comes to dominate Mizoguchi's thinking. Via a typical nihilistic reversal, his insecurities and thwarted desires are transformed into a lust for euphoric violence and a will to commit evil. His hostility toward the postwar world, in which transcendence is no longer possible, engenders in him a particular kind of vengefulness; it is the vengefulness of the weak that Nietzsche calls *ressentiment*. In the final scene Mizoguchi sets fire to the temple at night, happy in the confidence that he is returning its beauty to the realm of the unreal. Then, from a hillside overlooking the burning temple, he watches the sublime moment when darkness meets the light. That moment is true beauty.

Lastly, in order to prepare ourselves for the subsequent development of Mishima's career, we must take note that the first readers of *The Temple of the Golden Pavilion* were likely to discern in it a specific allegorical meaning. Like Mizoguchi, all the first readers of the novel were war survivors. During the war they too had harbored in their minds a beautiful idea: the *tennō*, the Japanese emperor. Not the emperor as an objective reality, but the emperor as a sublime, transcendent, quasi-religious ideal.

In the desperate final weeks of the war, the emperor's most fervent supporters hoped that he would die, whether by bombing or by suicide. But the emperor did not die. And after the war the Americans spared his life, just as they had spared the Golden Temple. In Japan's calendar scheme, each era is named after the reigning emperor. Hence the death of the Showa emperor in 1945 would have meant the end of the Showa era, and a new era would have begun afresh. But the emperor survived, and so the Showa era continued, dragged on, as Mishima will later say.

To the first readers of Mishima's novel, then, the Golden Temple could function as a metaphor for the emperor, though no reviewer dared to say so in print when the novel was first published.

The first person to acknowledge this point was a young critic named Noguchi Takehiko, who in 1968 published an enormously impressive study of Mishima's major works, which still exerts influence over scholars today. In his reading Noguchi stressed the importance of recognizing what he called the "dark thoughts" of Japan's war generation, which, he says, underlie the novel's discussions of beauty and destruction. Though Noguchi chooses his words carefully, we can sense the figure of the Showa emperor implicated behind them: "The burning of the temple, which was not martyred in Japan's defeat and instead ignominiously continued to live, is a sort of religious drama for wreaking vengeance on the 'postwar,' which is really a synonym for a world that ought to have died and yet did not die."[10]

Once we accept this reading, the allegorical symbolism of the temple becomes so clear that there are many pages of the novel where we can replace the words "Golden Temple" with the word "emperor" without any loss of meaning. I have done so in the following passage, which appears in an episode where Mizoguchi and one of his university classmates are walking in the temple grounds, one year before the end of the war:

> [For young men like us] this was to be our final summer, our final summer vacation, our final day. . . . Our youthfulness was standing on a dizzying edge. And the emperor was standing on the same edge, facing us, talking to us. Our expectation of air raids had brought us and the emperor this close together. [. . .] The possibility that the emperor might be destroyed by a bomb meant that his destiny had come very near to our own. Or perhaps the emperor would perish before we did. This prospect made us feel that the emperor was living the same life as we were. (51)

The dizzying intoxication of this community of death came to an end on August 15, 1945. And what Noguchi wants us to understand is that the memory of this intoxication lingered, engendering confused and difficult feelings among many Japanese: nostalgia for that lost intoxication, a frustrated sense of destiny unfulfilled, a profound guilt at having survived the war, and even an unutterable resentment that the emperor too had not perished. Mizoguchi's mind is a storm of such dark thoughts, and that is why it is wrong to dismiss him as a psychopath or a madman. For readers of Mishima's generation who understood the novel like this, Mishima had found a way of giving expression to these frustrations and resentments while ingeniously disguising them as talk about aesthetics.

In the years since Noguchi published his study, other commentators have taken up his idea of the temple as a metaphor for the Showa emperor.[11] But I think we can pursue the idea one step further.

As I noted at the beginning of this section, the novel is presented as Mizoguchi's own written account of the arson; he has turned a crime into a work of literature. So too, of course, has Mishima, and not only in the sense of literary adaptation. In its covert attack on the "ugly" emperor who survived the war, *The Temple of the Golden Pavilion* is an audacious transgression committed in a work of literature. In the early half of his career Mishima is content to do things covertly in this way, and we shall be looking at other examples. But the later Mishima will not be satisfied with metaphors and innuendo. It is not just that Mishima will become like Mizoguchi; he will also become like the Temple of the Golden Pavilion. In his monstrous egotism Mishima will try to usurp the temple as he has depicted it in his novel, to assume all of its symbolic functions, to turn himself into a sublime object, and by implication to usurp the Showa emperor. Then the terroristic destruction of Mishima Yukio, beautiful, unique, glittering, iconic symbol of centuries of Japanese cultural tradition, will have the function of a spectacular religious ritual for wreaking vengeance on a world that ought to have died and yet did not die.

CHAPTER 3

Originality in the Arrangement of Fate

To treat life in the spirit of art is to treat it as a thing in which
means and end are identified.

Oscar Wilde

At one point Mizoguchi muses, "When people think only about beauty, they unwittingly confront the darkest thoughts in the world" (6:55). As we have seen, the poet who devotes himself to "beauty only" is a foundational paradigm of Mishima's thought. But is it really a meaningful idea? After all, what sort of person thinks *only* about beauty? In this chapter we will look more carefully at the implications of Mishima's extreme aestheticism.

One way of describing the experience of beauty is to say that when we experience an object as beautiful we perceive it as something other than it really is. Everyone knows the experience of stepping closer to a beautiful painting in order to inspect its beauty in greater detail, only to find that there is nothing there but some brushstrokes of paint on a canvas. Where has the beauty gone? We feel as if we have been tricked by an illusion. In order to experience the painting aesthetically we must, for a moment at least, cease to acknowledge its objective reality (the canvas, the paint, the brushstrokes). To perceive an object as beautiful we must first take a derealizing attitude toward it, as Mizoguchi gradually learns to do with the Golden Temple. In the state of aesthetic perception, reality is suspended and the tangible, "thingly" character of the object fades from our view. The beautiful image we perceive is dependent on the object, but it exists only in our imaginations. Jean-Paul Sartre, who during the 1940s and 1950s published some highly original studies of beauty and the imagination, emphasized this unreality of the aesthetic state and summarized the implications in sensational language: "Beauty is a value that can only ever be applied to the imaginary and that carries the nihilation of the world in its essential structure."[1]

For most of us, our experiences of beauty are fleeting ones. We pause to admire a beautiful object or landscape or work of art, we enjoy its pleasing impact on our senses, and then we move on. To attempt to perpetuate this state of derealization indefinitely would be to assume the attitude of aestheticism, and to the extent that this attitude prioritizes beautiful appearances over objective reality, aestheticism has potentially immoral tendencies. To think *only* of beauty, if such a fanatical aestheticism were achievable, would be to disregard content, ethics, truth, even death. Such an aesthete would be an evildoer.[2]

Mishima proclaimed his aestheticism in his first collection of essays, *Kari to emono*, published in 1951. The title literally means *Hunting and Prey*, but it is perhaps more smoothly rendered into English as *The Hunter and the Hunted*. Anyone who is familiar only with the later Mishima, the born-again samurai reactionary who rails against the corrupting influences of Western culture, will be struck by this book's heavy concentration on Western art and literature. In particular, the book showcases Mishima's familiarity with the fin-de-siècle of nineteenth-century Europe: the writers, artists, and dandies of English Aestheticism and the French Symbolist movement. Throughout his life Mishima maintained close intellectual friendships with Japanese scholars and translators who were working on European fin-de-siècle literature; he proofread their translations and enthusiastically reviewed their publications. Meanwhile, to the Japanese public Mishima presented himself as a connoisseur of beauty in the lighthearted manner of a dandy.

Yet Mishima could not resist flaunting the cruelty and immorality of his aestheticism. In an autobiographical sketch he imagines himself saying (but does not quite commit himself to saying), "I wouldn't care if they dropped the atomic bombs all over again. All that matters to me is whether it would make the shape of the world a little more beautiful" (32:301). His one-act play *Primary Colors* (*Sangenshoku*, 1950) preaches a haughty elitism founded on aesthetics. Its message is that for beautiful people there are no rules. "In my opinion," says one of the handsome young characters, "morals and rules and all things in the world revolve around *us*. If we think we are beautiful, well then, that becomes our morality, and the things we do become rules for everyone else" (22:389). Yet Mishima's mercilessly aesthetic evaluation of life inevitably inclines him toward a bleak nihilism. Elsewhere he writes, "One of my incurable notions is that old age is always ugly and youth is always beautiful. The wisdom of the elderly is an eternal illusion, while the deeds of young men are eternally pure. So, the longer you live the worse it gets. To live is to decay" (34:110). And on another occasion he says bluntly, "Beautiful people ought to die young" (27:113).

Mishima has no compunction about reducing morals to aesthetic judgments: "A sense of morality is like a natural work of art created by a community of people over a period of many years" (28:261). And Mishima's sadism often gives his aestheticism a brutal inflection. In a letter to the novelist Dan Kazuo (1912–1976) he wrote, "I never look at a beautiful boy without wanting to douse him in petrol and set him on fire" (38:690).

Choosing Oneself

The most brilliant piece in *The Hunter and the Hunted* is Mishima's meditation on Oscar Wilde. I call this piece a meditation because to say that it is "about" Oscar Wilde would be to misrepresent its intentions. Mishima tends to read historical figures as if they are fictional characters, and he reads historical events as if they are theatrical works. Mishima's method of evaluation is always uncompromisingly personal in the aestheticist manner. His principal aim, as he explains in a separate piece, is "to determine my own attitude [to the work]" (*jibun no taido-kettei*; 28:579). The basic question he always asks is "What effect does this work have on me?" Mishima almost never writes about writers or works of literature that he does not admire; consequently there are few negative pieces among his literary essays. (His most persistent complaint is of the poor quality of Japanese translations of foreign works; on this matter he is merciless.) On occasion Mishima queries the purpose of the genre of criticism itself: "I am rather suspicious of the need for an intermediate zone between intuitive appreciation and self-criticism (or autobiography, confession, etc.). Criticism that lacks style [*buntai*] is not qualified to critique style, while criticism that has style . . . becomes a work of art in its own right" (27:431). In this spirit, Mishima intends his most ambitious essays to stand as works of literature in their own right, and it is a matter of much less concern to him whether his remarks faithfully correspond to people or ideas that once existed in reality. Truth is never his primary objective. To point out errors or implausibilities in his readings, therefore, is often to miss the point of what he is trying to accomplish. Even when Mishima is reflecting on the works of other writers and artists, his first topic of interest is always himself. Mishima is reading in order to write, and he is writing primarily in order to develop and realize himself as a character, rather than to offer scholarly or critical comment on the works of others.

His essay on Wilde, mischievously titled "A Theory of Oscar Wilde" (Osukā Wairudo ron), is exemplary of Mishima's method. Mishima wrote this essay while working on his novel *Forbidden Colors*, which chronicles the spiritual corruption of a beautiful young man by a cynical older man, a formula obviously derived from Wilde's novel *The Picture of Dorian Gray* (1891). In his reflections on Wilde, Mishima develops the idea of self-mastery that he had first articulated in "Poetic Theory." There the central vision was of an artist consciously redirecting his raw impulses into productive artistic work. Now Mishima begins to expand his conception of "artistic work" by envisioning an artist who treats his own life as a work of art, specifically as a work of literature, and who sets out to become the hero of his own life, in the sense of a "hero" of a novel. Mishima's essay also has the feel of a stylistic impersonation, being studded with pithy aphorisms very much in the manner of Wilde.

We might expect Mishima, writing on Wilde, to discuss dandyism, satire, the theater, the artist as celebrity, and the like. Instead his themes are fate, crime, and suffering. Connected to these within this context is the issue of homosexuality, to which Mishima alludes quite boldly in his opening lines:

> For a long time I was obsessed with Wilde. To be honest, it was probably the saga of his troubles with Lord Alfred Douglas that fascinated me more than anything else. I refuse to acknowledge an attachment to any writer or literary work that is not founded on lust. At times, this lust is merely searching for an object; at other times it is a consolation that only those of the same type can know [dōrui nomi ga shiru isha]; and sometimes it resembles a deep hatred. Remarkably, Wilde was all of these to me. (27:284)

The word dōrui, "the same type," obviously has a strong connotative meaning here. In his nonfictional writings this is about as close as Mishima ever gets to coming out about his sexuality. A thrilled sense of transgression is discernible in most of his subsequent comments in the essay:

> The first work of Wilde's I read was Salome. I was still a boy at the time, and this was the first book I had ever chosen and bought for myself. [Aubrey] Beardsley's illustrations naturally influenced my choice. But then, what difference was there between choosing Beardsley and choosing Salome? Was it not the atmosphere of an era that I had chosen? The more I tasted the fruit that my innocent boyish hand had plucked in the darkness, the more I became convinced that my instinct had been correct. Ultimately, I feel, we all choose ourselves like this, long before our lives unfold. (284)

As is well-known, Wilde's scandalous fall from grace proved disastrous for him. After his release from prison, where he had served two years for gross indecency, he exiled himself to France and died in poverty and obscurity. Mishima sees Wilde as the lead character in a drama he authored himself. In a simple sense this is uncontroversial, given that it was Wilde who instigated the legal proceedings that eventually led to his own downfall. But Mishima perceives masochistic yearnings in Wilde from the outset, as if his downfall was really a self-inflicted punishment. In support of this view Mishima quotes a striking remark by the Austrian essayist Hugo von Hofmannsthal (1874–1929): "Though Wilde's fingers plucked orchids to pieces and his feet lay among cushions of ancient Chinese silk, deep within they were filled with a fatalistic longing for a bath that ten convicts had used before him" (284). Mishima comments, "If we think of criticism as essentially being the ability to choose oneself, then Wilde, who proclaimed that criticism is the true act of creation, was undoubtedly a person who created his own fate" (285).[3]

What does it mean to speak of "choosing oneself" (*jiko wo sentaku*) or "creating one's own fate" (*unmei wo sōzō*)? In "Poetic Theory" Mishima talks about "realization" (*keisei*) rather than "self-realization" because he dislikes the idea that there is a core self waiting to be realized. From his remarks about Wilde it becomes clear that Mishima's way of thinking about the self derives from literary models. A character in a novel is not the realization of a pre-existing self, but is simply the totality of the actions performed by that character. Could Mizoguchi have decided not to burn the Golden Temple? The question is irrelevant and in any case unanswerable, since this action is indispensable to the character named Mizoguchi. The most memorable literary characters are those whose words, traits, and actions all feel indispensable in this way. We admire such characters for their unity, for the smooth and comprehensive integration of their traits. Mishima applies this method to Wilde, essentially defining "Oscar Wilde" as no more than the totality of actions performed by Oscar Wilde, just as if he were a literary character.

This idea of life as a work of art had been articulated most clearly by Nietzsche, Wilde's contemporary, who early in his career espoused a sort of philosophical aestheticism. Nietzsche had written:

> *One thing is needful.*—To "give style" to one's character—a great and rare art! It is practiced by those who survey all the strengths and weaknesses of their nature and then fit them into an artistic plan until every one of them appears as art and reason and even weaknesses delight the eye. . . . In the end, when the work is finished, it becomes evident how the constraint of a single taste governed and formed everything large and small. Whether this taste was good or bad is less important than one might suppose, if only it was a single taste![4]

Note the insistence that this artistic plan must be all-inclusive. The ideal is to construct a character that does not have any extraneous or inessential features, in exactly the same manner as a novelist aims to construct a literary character. As Nietzsche urges, it is not a matter of *discarding* personal weaknesses but of *subordinating* them. What matters is the formal consistency, the cohesive unity of the whole.

A similarly extreme aestheticism, one that insists on applying artistic values to life, had featured in the writings of the Japan Romantic School. During the years of militarism and war the Romantics were understandably keen to show that there was more to literature than the appreciation of beautiful words. Poetry was certainly not to be thought of as something confined to the pages of books and literary journals. "Japanese poetic expression is not limited to writing," declared Yasuda Yojūrō, the leading figure of the Romantic School, in 1943. "It can, of course, take other forms."[5] Any beautiful expression of the spirit of the Japanese people could be counted as a poem. The Romantics found examples of such "poems" in the lives of those reactionary samurai who, in the early years of Japan's modernization, had fought suicidally against the encroachment of Western ideas and practices. For the Romantics, these men were not political activists but aesthetes who worshipped a beauty they believed to be distinctively Japanese, and their violent protests and acts of terrorism were tantamount to artistic gestures. Yasuda called them "ultimate poems" (*shi no kyokuchi*).

Such are the daunting standards by which Mishima proposes to judge Oscar Wilde. In Mishima's reading, Wilde is both author and protagonist of the work of literature that constitutes his life and which comprises not only his plays and stories but also his criticism, his recorded conversations, and even his speeches during his court trials, while the people surrounding Wilde are merely subsidiary characters in this work. Mishima detects in this project the sort of cold unfeelingness he likes to associate with aestheticism: "Instead of allowing his life to consume his soul and his pain, like other people do, Wilde gave that job to his literary works" (27:291). But Mishima thinks that Wilde underestimated the cruelty of human nature. "I cannot rate Wilde highly as a tragic actor," he writes. "His faith in the will to tragedy was encumbered by naïve assumptions regarding the Bohemian lifestyle of the Romantic poet" (290).

In regard to *De Profundis*, the long and self-pitying letter that Wilde wrote to Alfred Douglas from prison, Mishima has this to say:

> Few works illustrate so vividly how a man of art is defeated by a man of life. In comparison with Douglas, Wilde, who attempted a balancing act between life and art, led such a narrow life! Gide tells us that Douglas' personality was more clearly defined than Wilde's. But personality impedes the kind of "power of imagination" that Wilde held dear, and provides a constant logical reference for life and art. Douglas acted according to a logic of his own, whereas Wilde lived without logic. . . . There is a

scene where Douglas abandons the sick Wilde (who had stayed up all night taking care of Douglas) and goes off to have fun in London. Here, I feel, Douglas himself becomes another of Wilde's dazzling creations. (27:388–389)

Mishima politely takes issue with virtually every feature of Wilde's persona. Wilde is not original enough, not aggressive enough, not subversive enough, not shocking enough, not perverse enough. Mishima delivers his criticisms in a hectic tour de force of name-dropping that challenges readers to keep pace with its erudite author:

Sarah Bernhardt writes in her memoirs of how, on her first visit to London, a "turbulent young man" who looked like "a German student" flung an armful of lilies on the ground at her feet; it was the young Wilde. But the scruffily dressed disciples of Victor Hugo had indulged in these sorts of eccentricities with greater daring. Yes, Wilde engaged in homosexuality; but Verlaine and Rimbaud had lived together openly in London in 1872. By the time Wilde was enjoying himself in Algeria, Rimbaud was living among savages. Wilde served time in prison; but the Marquis de Sade had been incarcerated from the age of thirty-eight to fifty-one. (In *De Profundis* Wilde wryly places himself between Gilles de Rais and Sade.) Wilde won celebrity, though not as much as Victor Hugo. Wilde experienced poverty; but Villiers had written with watered-down ink and used floorboards for a writing desk. Wilde's proud demeanor seems to mock the mediocrity of nineteenth-century English society. But there were people in England who were wallowing much deeper in decadence than Wilde. Goncourt's diary tells us of an establishment in London where customers paid for the privilege of sticking needles into young girls, and of a certain aristocrat who attempted to have his books bound with the dried skin of an African female. (293)

Mishima scrutinizes some of Wilde's celebrated paradoxes and finds them to be flawed. The standard equivalent Japanese word *gyakusetsu*, literally a "reverse argument," does not fully capture the meaning of "paradox." Mishima tends to favor the transliteration *paradokkusu*, which he uses liberally though not always precisely. Strictly defined, a paradox is a set of propositions (with Mishima there are never more than two) that individually appear to be true yet when considered together are clearly inconsistent. A successful paradox makes us aware of a fundamental problem in our reasoning and thereby allows us to glimpse a truth that is perhaps beyond the grasp of our language. "At the heart of a genuine paradox," wrote the literary critic Kobayashi Hideo, "there must always be fiercely direct observation, and intelligence keen enough to perceive a reality that is impenetrable to reason."[6] A paradox that accomplishes this is no frivolous gesture, but is a creative action in its own right. It presents a view of the world that strikes us as rationally unacceptable or intolerable, a view of the world that we instinctively resist and reject, yet it ultimately forces us to accept this view as true. This is why Mishima is so drawn to paradoxical statement: a genuine paradox generates knowledge that undermines our stability and our confidence, conveying a truth that is almost *painful*.

Here are some of Mishima's paradoxes, taken from his piece on Wilde and from other, mostly early, writings:

He who possesses the fiercest subjectivity also possesses the fiercest objectivity. (26:534)

Genius is the slaughterer of adolescence. (631)

I am a realist who is trying to produce a realistic depiction of a Romantic spirit that could never exist in reality. (1:611)

God created the Devil for hygienic purposes. (27:288)

Society is like a jealous woman: she loves a man most at the very moment she vents her fury upon him. (291)

Casanova, that genius of life, how fated he was to meet women! Each one appeared in his life like a messenger knocking on his door at night. Casanova was simply being obedient. (294)

My definition of a writer: a person who devotes his whole life to words in the full knowledge that those words will never be understood. (298)

Calling someone a fascist turns him into one. (28:358)

It is only the souls of poets that make history. (29:133)

No matter how sweet and sentimental little boys or girls may seem, they all possess a deep-rooted cruelty. Kindness only develops with the hypocrisy of adulthood. (30:331)

A writer who enjoys talking about his earlier work is like a madman who delights in his own feces. (34:25)

Most of these are, I think, successful to some degree in delivering a kind of outrageous truth. But paradoxes do not always achieve this effect. Sometimes a paradox is merely shocking or contrarian and accomplishes nothing more than a brief evasion of truth. Umberto Eco has wittily demonstrated that many of Wilde's famous paradoxes make equal sense even when their meanings are reversed.[7] Mishima too recognizes the evasiveness that characterizes the pose of the dandified aesthete as epitomized by Wilde. Rather than condemning such evasiveness for its indifference to truth, however, Mishima explains it as another element in the aesthete's project of self-punishment, which he now attempts to equate with something resembling saintly martyrdom:

> A paradox is never a complete evasion. It only evades a given situation. The paradoxical man pursues himself with paradoxes until he forfeits the right to be evasive. That is why he is often the most sincere person of all. It is now that he comes closest to touching God, humanity's final evasion. One might say that paradox is a shortcut to the divine. (27:285)

Prior to his downfall Wilde had famously claimed that he had put his genius into his life and only his talent into his work. Mishima balks at this distinction:

> Many commentators got caught on Wilde's paradoxes. Among them was André Gide, who wrote of Wilde: "A great writer, no, but a great *viveur*." This echoes Wilde's own painfully self-defensive paradox: "I have put my genius into my life—I have put only my talent into my works." But surely genius and talent are inseparable? Gide knew this, of course. These two drugs that Wilde explains as an error of usage, Gide categorized as an error of essence. Gide really did see only talent in Wilde's works. But I believe that the tragedy of Wilde lies in the sincerity of this paradox within a paradox. It is the tragedy of trying to split a complex chemical compound into its constitutive elements, only to find that, the instant you do so, it becomes none of them. (285–286)

Mishima's extended metaphors sometimes have an obfuscating tendency, and the above statements are perhaps only vaguely meaningful. Mishima seems to be accusing Wilde of betraying the decadent principle of collapsing all distinctions. *Everything* you do, Mishima insists, again taking literature as his model for understanding life, is essential to the person you are.

Needless to say, this is not a call for sincerity. A person who sets out to become the hero of his or her own life narrative must to some extent become an actor, and acting is an artificial mode of behavior. "Acting is the ultimate deception, the peak of artificiality," writes Mishima. "It is the realm where the script that is the human language finds its most loyal companions" (298). As that last remark indicates, Mishima follows Wilde in believing that the first duty in life is to be as artificial as possible. Indeed, Mishima consistently asserts that "artifice" (*jinkō*) is more truthful than naturalness. At the age of twenty-one, in a letter to the novelist Kawabata Yasunari, he had written, "Is artifice not the most pure and honest of human desires? Is it not founded on something stronger in human nature than the desire to reproduce reality?" (38:246).

Wilde had famously preached the truth of masks, and Mishima readily adopted this idea. "Poetic Theory" contains these lines:

> Modern people are most uncomfortable when they are commanded to lay bare their true emotions. It is a cruel command that is impossible to obey. Modern people have all sorts of faces available to them. But "true emotion" has become just another one of those masks. Indeed, it is actually *easier* to believe that it is a mask. Hence laying bare one's true emotions is really no more difficult than choosing a mask. (26:532)

The same idea was clearly guiding Mishima's ambitions in his "sexual autobiography," the paradoxically titled *Confessions of a Mask*, which he published one year before his piece on Wilde. In one of the numerous prefaces he provided for that book Mishima informed his readers, "My aim has been to write a completely fictional confession" (*kanzen na kokuhaku no fikkushon*; 1:674). This paradoxical statement challenges the assumption that there is such a thing as a true literary confession. Is not every supposedly truthful autobiography or memoir riddled with deliberate falsehoods? Anyone who expounds on a self-image called "I" is always, to some degree, engaging in a process of creation. And confession is one of the most duplicitous of all creative processes, since it is really a process of creating a confessor. "In my autobiography," Mishima writes, "I have no intention of swearing allegiance to the idol of truth. I shall let my lies roam free and feed wherever they please. My lies will thus become sated, and they will stop nibbling away at the truth" (676). This statement builds on the paradox of the first one, reminding us not only that the lies we tell about ourselves are one of the elements that constitute our real selves, but that our lies can often reveal more about our real selves than our truths. Our truths are generally uninformative and invariably dull. It is in our artificiality—our posturing, our false confessions, our dramatic fabrications and exaggerations—that our real and interesting selves reside.

There is an obvious ethical problem, however, in the idea of living life as a work of art. "To treat life in the spirit of art," Wilde had said, "is to treat it as a thing in which means and end are identified."[8] But if the only goal is to organize your life into an artistically coherent unity, then this is a purely formal matter, independent of any question of ethical content. If all that matters is stylish presentation, any content will do just as well as any other. A serial killer, say, could organize his career such that means and end are identified, and then declare himself an artist of life. So could a professional criminal or a terrorist. In the case of literary characters this is not problematic. We can admire fictional villains, as long as they are depicted well. But a person as a *living* work of art is a principle with latent immoral implications, since a work of art need not obey moral laws.

In his essay on Wilde, Mishima highlights the moral problem in an unusual way by depicting Wilde as bored by his own amoralism: "I suspect that Wilde was well aware of how easy it is to commit a crime" (27:288). But that, says Mishima, made the idea of transgression empty and meaningless. Wilde needed to seek out pleasure in order to have an awareness of the thrill of transgression: "He felt that crime ought to be pleasurable. The quest that this proposition demanded of him was no more than a quest to evade the proposition, giving it a paradoxical structure from the outset" (288). This led ultimately to a masochistic craving for pain and punishment: "For pleasure to be criminal, it must be a hardship. And for pleasure to be a hardship, it must be painful." The suggestion here, surely, is that of the repressed homosexual aesthete as guilt-laden self-punisher. His aestheticism is an evasion or displacement of his guilt. He takes refuge in a world of beauty and treats life in the spirit of art, but the work of art he creates is a tragedy that culminates in his own condemnation and destruction. "Could it be true," asks Mishima, "that Wilde's pain was in fact the pain of stabbing others in order to stab himself?" (290).

As if anticipating a criticism that will frequently be made of his own writing, Mishima observes that Wilde seldom depicts suffering in his fictions. Due to this failure or unwillingness to express suffering in his art, Mishima suggests, Wilde was forced to transfer his ability to express suffering to his life:

> Wilde was haunted by the realization that his own life could never satisfy him. This, surely, is one of the functions of suffering, one of the reasons why suffering exists at all. And so he manufactured suffering from nothing, as when mirrors are arranged face to face so as to produce infinite reflections. The perception of Wilde as a "genius of life" is due principally to this psychological "manufacturing" ability. (290–291)

Mishima believes that Wilde intentionally made himself a figure of derision and orchestrated his own downfall:

To begin with, Wilde succumbed to the poison of vulgar success (if I may call it that). It was partly vanity, and partly his natural sincerity (to him these were the same thing) that made him long for the distinction of being despised. Society is like a jealous woman: she loves a man most at the very moment she vents her fury upon him. A circus acrobat grows bored of impressing the crowds; he wants to shock them instead. And so he walks the tightrope, at great danger to himself. English society had its own unique form of death, the "scandal," which was bound to appeal to the tightrope walker. People had stopped being offended by the "beauty of ugliness" that Baudelaire saw in the suffering of Catholicism; in fact they were enjoying it. And so, in order to be despised, Wilde had to make himself sick. He smiled the ascetic's smile of secret pleasure, and gradually immersed himself in that vice, that spiritual leprosy. (291–292)

The social function of artists' suffering is one of the questions Mishima raises in his novel *Kyoko's House* (*Kyōko no ie*, 1959), where Natsuo, the young painter, ruminates on the relationship between artists and society. Why, Natsuo wonders, do people not only assume that creative artists will be unstable, emotionally tortured misfits, but actually seem to demand that they be so? Even if we acknowledge that artists are people who are likely to inflict unusual kinds of psychological suffering on themselves (one of the assumptions of "Poetic Theory"), this does not explain the fascination their suffering seems to exert over other people. Natsuo develops a theory of artists as symbolic sufferers. He reasons that society has always needed a few individuals to serve as its "anguish specialists" (*kunō no senmonka*) and that artists are simply the latest inheritors of that role: "In ancient times, fearsome holy people had fulfilled that function, but at some point in history the holy people were replaced by artists" (7:372).[9] In Natsuo's view, artists suffer so that ordinary people don't have to. He explains this state of affairs by pointing to what he calls the "bourgeois desire" to ensure that suffering is something that only happens to other people. Moreover, the therapeutic power of artists' suffering derives from the perception that their suffering is meaningless: "The abstract nature of artists' suffering, the fact that it is socially worthless, has the effect of soothing people's fear of real suffering in their own lives." From the comfort and safety of their boring lives, the middle classes view artists as sick people who are suffering from a disease that they (the middle classes) will never catch: "Suffering that cannot become a general rule, suffering that has no connection to general human existence, this is what the bourgeois loves in the artist" (373).

Natsuo, who speaks to us from the 1950s, is thinking of novelists, poets, and painters, who at that time still had a reputation as self-destructive hell-raisers.

Today his argument perhaps applies better to the media performers we call "celebrities," whose unhealthy vices and vulgar excesses are put on public display so that we can all feel better about the fact that our own lives are dull by comparison.

Mishima sees Wilde's project as an attempt to become a scapegoat of this type, a heroic "anguish specialist" who suffers on behalf of the timid masses. In this context, Mishima's remarks toward the end of the essay indicate that he had drawn some important lessons from Wilde's extraordinary portrait of Christ in *De Profundis*. Christ, according to Wilde, was no altruist. Christ did not live for other people; he lived in order to perfect himself. He was an incorrigible egotist ("No one comes to the Father except through me") and a dispenser of paradox ("Love thine enemy") whose values are really aesthetic ones: he preached love simply because it is more beautiful than hatred. Christ does not actually teach us anything, says Wilde; he hypnotizes us with the sheer charm and power of his personality. He is "just like a work of art himself" and his life is "the most wonderful of poems." By reading Christ in this way, Wilde empties him of moral meaning and presents him instead as the first Romantic artist of history, a supreme individualist who created himself out of his own imagination and who used the world as his stage.[10]

Mishima likes this interpretation, but he places greater emphasis than Wilde on the sublime tragic effect of Christ's death scene. The Passion of Christ, the drama of his suffering and martyrdom, was the means whereby Christ realized his conception of beauty:

> Life can never be wholly original. Fate, on the other hand, can. Christ's originality lay not in his life but in his Fate on the Cross. It is only originality in the arrangement of Fate that makes life appear original. (27:293)

According to this view, the quest for formal perfection in art *and in life* is the attempt to show the subject as identical with its own inevitability, again in the same manner as a well-crafted literary character. The past is an inevitable part of oneself because it is, of course, unalterable. The effect that Mishima calls "originality in the arrangement of fate" (*unmei to iu mono no hairetsu no dokusōsei*) is to be accomplished by unifying one's past with one's present in an aesthetically satisfying conclusion. This is the last and indispensable step in the lifelong process of "creating oneself."

Whatever events or characters he is considering, real-life or fictional, Mishima always looks first for "logical consistency" (*ronri-teki ikkansei*) and "orderliness" (*chitsujo*), by which he means the architectural or structural order that is established by coherent form. Thus in another piece he writes, "When I am interested in particular incidents or frames of mind, it is only because they possess a logical consistency that closely resembles the orderliness of works of art, and the reason I love fictional characters who are 'obsessed' by things is that, to me, obsession is synonymous with logical consistency" (20:533). In a separate note on Wilde's *Salome*, for example, Mishima says that Salome knowingly chooses her fate: "She desires her own fate and forces it into realization [*unmei o muriyari jitsugen shite shimau*]" (39:350). Fate, as the inevitable outcome of one's life, should not, of course, need to be "forced into realization."[11] Mishima expresses it this way because he sees fate not as an externally imposed determinism but as a kind of internal formal coherency. We might think to translate *unmei* here as "destiny." But Mishima probably has in mind Nietzsche's formula for greatness in a human being: *amor fati*, love of one's fate. Necessity is again the governing principle. To love one's fate is to love that which is necessary. Central to Mishima's thinking is the aestheticist idea that a work of art need only be consistent with itself. This consistency is what he calls "logic." And whereas "fate" suggests a passive attitude to life, logic is something that one can actively demand and pursue.

In these purely formal terms, what Wilde's life-drama lacks, obviously enough, is a beautiful death. Mishima blames Wilde for this "failure," essentially accusing him of giving up on art altogether:

After Wilde left prison he became mediocre. He fell silent, after writing one essay on socialism. He was already dreaming of a world where people would have no more need for art. (27:298)

Contemplating the difficulty of creating oneself with the formal exactitude of a literary character, the Nietzsche scholar Alexander Nehamas says, "To make a perfectly unified character out of all that one has done . . . may involve us in a vicious effort: we may have to be writing our autobiography as we are living our life, and we would also have to be writing about writing that autobiography."[12] This is exactly what Mishima sets out to do, with his endless self-commentaries, auto-fictional pieces, and his "analyses" of his own works. Many scholars uncritically quote Mishima's commentaries as if they can illuminate his self-dramatizing fiction, failing to recognize that these commentaries themselves are extensions of the fiction. No matter what topic Mishima pretends to be writing about, his prose always functions performatively in this way, his objective being to create an organically unified character called Mishima. More precisely, we should say that the objective of the totality of Hiraoka's project is to create the biography of the character named Mishima, the actual "life" of Hiraoka being of no consequence.

His piece on Wilde is no exception. Needless to say, Mishima's theory of Wilde is really a Wildean theory of Mishima.

Wilde's miserable downfall had demonstrated the limitations of aestheticism, both as a form of cultural critique and as a mode of life. Mishima resolves to avoid the same failure. He is acutely aware that creative people who can make beautiful things often make a disastrous mess of their own lives. And though Mishima accepts the idea of art as sublimation, he does not accept the idea of art as therapy. In his letter to Dan Kazuo he had written:

> I hate the impatience of sick people who say they want to get better. That is not how you overcome decadence. If you want to get better, go and be a communist or follow Christ. Literature's duty is to let sick people develop an ability to acquire a wild sort of healthiness that ordinary people can never experience. (38:690)

The biographies of Japanese writers and artists in the early decades of the twentieth century contain an abundance of misery: psychological disorders, destructive relationships, alcohol and drug abuse, chronic illness, premature deaths, and suicides. Mishima frequently sneers at artists of this ilk and is scathing of what he calls their spiritual weakness, their lack of discipline, and so on. But his principal objection remains an aesthetic one: though they may have created beautiful works, they have allowed their lives to become ugly. Mishima is determined that the same will not happen to him, and that is why the only laws he recognizes are artistic ones. Some notes that he made for an unwritten novel contain this Wildean maxim: "A genius must not lead a wretched life, no matter how prematurely he dies" (43:436).[13]

Seeing the Literature in Paintings

Mishima's writing on the visual arts constitutes a small but enduringly popular part of his oeuvre. In setting out to build a reputation for himself as an art critic, or at least as a literary person with strong opinions about art, Mishima was following a career path first established by the European aesthetes, many of whom had written prolifically about the visual arts. The readiness of aesthetes to venture into art criticism was consistent with their confidence in the potential for transposition between different art media. The project of aestheticism was innately interdisciplinary in its attempt to translate visual images, and also music, into words, as if painting with language. The French novelist, artist, and filmmaker Jean Cocteau (1889–1963) was among those who continued this project in the twentieth century, and Mishima followed suit with his various crossovers between prose, theater, film, and photo shoots.

His friend Shibusawa Tatsuhiko tells us something interesting about Mishima's way of thinking about the visual arts. "Talking to Mishima about Dali," writes Shibusawa, "I said that dreams are just a kind of visual decadence that unsettles things and causes them to dissolve. But Mishima refused to acknowledge the idea of visual decadence. Even when he talked about decadent art, in the end he was really only seeing literature in the paintings."[14] Shibusawa means that last statement negatively, as if to suggest that Mishima lacked a vital apperceiving faculty. But it would be hard to think of a better characterization of aestheticist art criticism than as an attempt to "see the literature in paintings." Oscar Wilde himself had coined the term "art literature" and he praised any critic who tried to make "a prose-poem out of paint."[15] Mishima works along similar lines in his essays and articles on art, providing literary equivalents for the imaginative effects that paintings and sculptures have produced in him. Hence his commentaries are subjective, tendentious, and unscholarly, yet always sensual and artful in their own right.

As an example of Mishima's method, here is a passage from his meditation on Jean-Antoine Watteau's *Embarkation for Cythera* (1720), which he wrote two years after his essay on Wilde:

> The essence of the Rococo spirit, I believe, was to escape the inevitable evils of mankind by eradicating fierce passions and submitting oneself to the pure rules of pleasure; there is something almost musical about such a scheme. Paintings of the later Classical and Romantic movements reveal the inevitable, and hence each work has an inevitable conclusiveness about it. We are shown the end of tragedy, the end of happiness, or some sort of theatrical apodosis. But the Rococo paintings of Watteau always establish a moment ruled by chance, where everything wavers indeterminately, where the concerns of life are focused on frivolous matters, and where the dominant theme is nothing but the playfulness of love.
>
> A music that never ends, a love that never wanes—two similar things. The first exists only in music, and can only be fulfilled by music, while the second exists only in a particular moment of pathos, and can be fulfilled only within the imaginary endless chain of that moment. These are the pleasures of Watteau's Rococo scenes, and there were also, one feels, the rules of pleasure itself. (28:282)

These beautiful lines accomplish a kind of transmutation, as Mishima takes Watteau as a starting point for a new creation of his own. He begins in scholarly manner, but quickly shifts into creative reverie. His tone becomes lyrical, and his definition of the Rococo style is almost a prose poem in itself. Mishima clearly sees Watteau as a refraction of himself, concluding that Watteau exemplifies the artist whose spirit is obsessed with "bright external surfaces" as a means of evading the "inner crisis" of fierce emotions. In the world of Rococo, Mishima muses, "there are no true feelings other than those transmitted via art" (285).

Mishima only writes about art that he admires, and the range of his interests is predictably narrow: Greek sculpture, art and sculpture of the Italian Renaissance, the decadent art of nineteenth-century Europe. He generally has little interest in landscapes or genre paintings; the human form is what interests him. In his commentaries he tries to make readers aware of the suggestive depths of intense facial expressions, flexed muscles, and contorted limbs. His aim is not simply to re-present the artwork to the reader as a form of voluptuous sensual experience. Mishima sees the human form as an embodiment of an eternal Idea. As he puts it, "To reach the ultimate Idea one must first pass through the gate of physical beauty" (35:70). Having described the sensual reaction the work in question induces in him, Mishima tries to identify the feature of the work that leads away from its specificity to some indissoluble universal idea, usually to a kind of quasi-metaphysical yearning that is, he says, the source of the work's seductive power. Here he is reflecting on the bust of Antinous at the Vatican:

> The fact that the Greeks made statues of such youths, whose lives were cut short at the peak of their fullness and vitality, hints at the tragic principle latent in the Greek notion of the monumental. Antinous was the last flower of Greece who did not submit to Christian baptism, the last remnant of Greekness prophesying the day when Rome would sink into decadence. Standing again today before this beautiful statue of Antinous, I cannot help but recall the "pessimism of strength" and the "suffering of superabundance" that Nietzsche saw in the pessimism of the Greeks that comes from an excess of life. These are the words that Silenus speaks to King Midas in the Greek folktale related by Nietzsche in the third section of *The Birth of Tragedy*: "The best of all things is something entirely outside your grasp: not to be born, not to *be*, to be *nothing*. But the second-best thing for you—is to die soon." Antinous' melancholy is not his alone, but represents the pessimism of long-lost ancient Greece. (27:637)

In *The Birth of Tragedy* the "wisdom of Silenus" is offered as the finest possible insight into the nature of the real. The Greeks, says Nietzsche, had no naïve illusions about life. They recognized the absurdity and meaningless, the purposeless repetitiveness of human existence. But having been granted this terrible insight,

Nietzsche argues, the Greeks embraced life all the more passionately. They did not succumb to the nihilism of Silenus. Instead they found redemption in the healing powers of Art: "She alone can turn these thoughts of repulsion at the horror and absurdity of existence into ideas compatible with life."[16] Mishima's sympathy with the fin-de-siècle artists lies partly, he tells us elsewhere, in their ambition of achieving "a tragic affirmation of the real world, as in Greek tragedy" (27:464).

Of course it is not for philosophical reasons that Mishima's eye always lingers on images of beautiful boys. As in the above example, it pleases him to find hints of "tragic fate" and "transcendent suffering" in their expressions and in their postures (34:323). Of Michelangelo's *Dying Slave* he writes:

> The boy's deep spiritual suffering . . . is not expressed in the form of physical anguish, but in a feeling of the gentle and anxious lethargy of life as it wavers before death. The expression on the boy's face is peaceful and filled with resolve. He seems almost unaware of his physical pain, so that the unease and suffering in his body give rise to a sort of musical inflexion. The powerful anguish inside him becomes a languid and elegant uncertainty. The sculpture seems to say that a boy's suffering is most beautiful when it is hidden from view. (323–324)

In a series of essays on beautiful youths for an art magazine, Mishima elaborates on his admiration for the Greeks and their cults of beauty. Mishima envies their belief in "the spirituality of the human body" (34:321). The decline of this belief is one aspect of modernity that bores him. It is a problem that, he says, concerns both art and literature. The culprit, as always for Mishima, is consciousness: art has been "poisoned by self-reflexivity." A belief in physical (bodily) spirituality is required in order to appreciate the ancient statues of the human form, which have no "allegorical interiority" (319). Over centuries, however, the minds of artists have suffered a "distortion due to self-awareness." The idea of the universality of beauty surpassing a realistic representation of the human form has come to be regarded with suspicion: "A young man gazing hopefully to the heavens looks ridiculous to us now" (320). When we see statues of youths today, Mishima says, we tend to think of the individual model: "We do not believe enough in the spiritual nature of the body to infer universality and general validity from them" (321). The lack of young male characters in modern literary fiction shows a transition in the understanding of youth: "Literature is born from the assumption that the interest of youth is on the *inside*" (318).

Similarly, Mishima complains of the "absence of the body" in modern-day art. What this signifies, he says, is not a decline in physical vitality but a decline in "the universality of representations of the body" (320). This is the familiar argument that our modern tendency to adopt a critical stance toward artworks has become so strong that it renders us incapable of identifying with them. Instead we strive to represent the work to ourselves within a critical framework provided by aesthetic judgment.

If the work of art no longer satisfies the spiritual needs that it did in earlier times, the status of artists is degraded. On more than one occasion in his critical writings, Mishima reminds us that Plato had thought highly enough of the powers of artists (poets) that he banned them from his ideal city. The Greeks saw the imagination as a fundamentally deceptive force, capable of permanently warping a person's character and morals. In one of his essays Mishima approvingly quotes these lines from Edgar Wind's influential book *Art and Anarchy* (1963):

> [Plato believed that] before an artist can be condemned he must receive the highest possible honor, something like the Order of Merit. Plato understood what few seem to understand today, *that the really dangerous artist is the great one: "a rare and holy and delectable being"* (Mishima's italics).[17]

In Plato's day the experience of art had very little to do with what we moderns think of aesthetic enjoyment. There was a prevailing fear of the potentially dangerous effects of the inspired imagination, which Plato characterized as "divine terror." Mishima laments the historical decline of this fear of the imagination, our loss of the "divine terror." As Mishima sees it, this decline eventually precipitated a rift between the various artistic genres that signaled the start of modernity: "From the Impressionists onwards, art parted ways with literature and became pure art" (27:632). The close companionship between art and literature was lost, as artists "stopped depicting marathons and started painting apples and crazed suns" (31:498).

Inevitably, perhaps, since he is writing on Western artworks for Japanese readers, Mishima occasionally makes observations that may seem simplistic or clichéd to Western readers more familiar with the works in question. Yet his main agenda of restoring the sensual to art was innovative for its time, even when set against Western conventions. Admiring Guido Reni's *Saint Sebastian*, Mishima notes what he calls the painting's "pornographic" character and asks impatiently, "When will art historians speak frankly to us about the beauty of this decadent pagan art?" (28:123). This reluctance to see the eroticism at the surface infuriates him. Elsewhere Mishima complains about "the sickness of the modern consciousness" (27:188). If tragedy and modernity are contradictory, he says, it is because our critical consciousness makes the object of our reflection seem comical: "The only weapon of the modern mind is cynicism." Critical interpretation undermines strong emotion and leads us into "nebulous uncertainty." The only solution, says Mishima, is to "bring back great emotions and passions" (189).

I wrote above that Mishima's approach was innovative. It is possible, for instance, to find common ground between Mishima and the American critic Susan Sontag (1933–2004), who in the early 1960s was making a name for herself by challenging modern modes of art interpretation. In her celebrated essay "Against Interpretation" Sontag observed that we have lost "the innocence before all theory when art knew no need to justify itself, when one did not ask of a work of art what it *said* because one knew (or thought one knew) what it *did*."[18] To interpret art, Sontag argues, is to impoverish it by reducing it to its content. (Sontag is not talking only about the visual arts.) In the same spirit as Mishima she notes a contempt for appearances that typifies modern interpretive methods, and appeals for greater attention to form than to content. Her conclusion: "In place of a hermeneutics we need an erotics of art."[19]

That exactly is the theme of Mishima's lament. What worries him is atrophy of sensibilities, which he regards as a specifically modern malady. The problem, he holds, is that we are in danger of becoming *immune* to art. He sneers at the Kantian conception of the beautiful as disinterested pleasure. For Mishima, art is a mode of expressing psychic and erotic energies that cannot be apperceived disinterestedly. If one removed the sensual from art, Mishima insists, nothing would remain.

Like Sontag, Mishima wants an erotics of art. He calls for an impressive (as opposed to expressive) criticism that engages honestly with the sensuality that works of art connote. Furthermore, he dreams of creating a work of art that would purify the experience of beauty by somehow eliminating the opportunity for critical reflection by those who encounter it, and thus recuperate the "divine terror."

The Artist as Criminal

As I noted earlier, Mishima's aestheticism diverges from Wilde's in its conception of nature. Mishima had a strong intuition of nature's cruelty and indifference and of the reality of evil as a force in the world. For Mishima, and for many of his characters, aggressive antagonism of the self toward the world is a primal psychic fact. This antagonism, Mishima repeatedly asserts, is the true origin of human endeavor: "At the root of the desire to create is a force entirely opposed to that desire" (27:85).

Similar assumptions about the aggressive core of human subjectivity have often featured in theories of artistic creation. Hegel located the origin of art in the boy who throws a stone into a pond to enjoy the ripples this creates. The initial impulse here is a destructive one. The boy throws the stone because it pleases him to disrupt the pond's calm, and he enjoys the ripples because he knows they are the product of his little act of vandalism. He throws the stone *at the world*, to dominate and possess it, and for a moment it answers to him.

"Whatever you do in art there is always an impulse toward destruction," Mishima declares (29:185). But often Mishima wants to take this idea further, specifically equating art with antisocial activities and with crime.

To some extent Mishima's thinking here was a convention of his day. In the early half of the twentieth century, disdain for poets and writers of fiction was common among the Japanese middle classes. Mishima's father had done everything in his power to prevent his son from becoming a professional writer, and although Mishima defied his father, as sons invariably do, he inherited much of his father's prejudice. In addition, the war exacerbated hostility to literary fiction. During the years of militarism it was not uncommon in Japan to hear *bungaku* (literature) derided as *bunjaku* (weakness). In his mid-twenties Mishima wrote:

> There has always been a part of me that thinks of literature as a vulgar activity, something that no young man should really be doing. A genuine young man should fight with all his heart against contradiction and wrongdoing, and either kill himself or get himself killed. (28:476)

A strong belief that literary fiction was an unhealthy deviation from normality remained with Mishima his whole life, and his career as a novelist represented a transgression for which he would one day have to atone.

These thoughts lead us to one of Mishima's favorite formulas: the artist as criminal. That there is no essential incongruity between art and crime was another of the principles of fin-de-siècle decadence. Wilde had written, "One can fancy an intense personality being created out of sin."[20] Though such statements were daring in Wilde's day, the incongruity of art and crime is now no longer controversial. It became a commonplace in the twentieth century, epitomized by the commandants of Nazi concentration camps, who could end a day of mass murder with a Beethoven string quartet and a glass of claret.

But Mishima is not satisfied with an acknowledgment of incongruity. He rejects the possibility that aesthetic sensibility and maleficence could coexist in a person without being somehow connected to each other. Mishima wants to see artistic creativity and criminality as manifestations of the *same* underlying drive.

For that argument to work, it is clear that only special types of crime will do. Mishima treats them obsessively in his fictions. He favors gratuitous crimes, irrational crimes, inexplicable crimes, motiveless crimes. In a short story titled "The Circus" (Sākasu, 1946) a sadistic circus owner orchestrates the double murder of two of his acrobats during their performance, simply to please the crowd. In the stage play *The Black Lizard* (*Kuroi tokage*, 1961) the heroine decorates her home with the flayed skins of beautiful murder victims. In *The Sailor Who Fell from Grace with the Sea* (*Gogo no eikō*, 1965) a group of teenage boys murder a sailor and dissect his corpse, having judged that he lacks heroic potential. In "The Peacocks" (Kujaku, 1965) a bored aesthete dreams of committing what he is sure will be the most beautiful crime ever committed: the slaughter of a flock of peacocks; eventually he discovers that his dream self has been slaughtering the birds in reality. *Runaway Horses* (*Honba*, 1969) tells the story of an aspiring young terrorist who cannot fathom the source of his own rage toward the world; all he knows for sure is that he yearns to commit "a little act of pure evil" (13:734). Many more examples could be given.

The energy of Mishima's aesthetically minded criminals always flows unilaterally. Victims are passive and compliant. In some cases they are even complicit. Ideally they are mute. Or violence is directed against wordless creatures and objects: a kitten, a sword, a temple, a peacock. Narrative pressures often oblige Mishima to provide motivations for his protagonists; these tend to be the weakest parts of the work. Mishima does not really want to have to explain crime, because a crime that can be explained is not wholly evil. Even though Mishima tracks the processes in his criminals' minds from the crime's conception to its execution, he is usually unconcerned with motivations. Crimes committed for material profit are unsuitable because they cannot be said to express pure evil. Mishima's compulsion toward evil is fueled by a vertiginous desire. He craves transgression for its own sake, beyond any consequences he can obtain from it. His criminals commit their crimes in order to have committed them, or in order to be *seen* to have committed them. "Evil for evil's sake" would be the slogan of Mishima's criminal aestheticism.

Again it is Mizoguchi who most obviously embodies this notion of the artist as criminal. Recalling his school days, he tells us how he liked to dream alternately of being a brutal tyrant and a great artist: "On the one hand I enjoyed imagining how I would execute all the teachers and classmates who tormented me every day, while on the other hand I imagined myself as a sovereign of the inner world, a great artist endowed with the purest lucidity" (6:11). Implicit in those thoughts, and in many of Mishima's own claims about art and crime, is an assumption that every act of creative genius has its counterpart in an act of destructive evil.

In his essays and articles Mishima asserts the various affinities, as he sees them, between the artistic mind and the criminal mind:

Rather than analyzing the current situation around them, writers and poets often make sense of things by taking a symbolic structural view. This somewhat resembles the experience of dreaming. Criminals do likewise, since in their minds they often have a symbolic structural view similar to that of writers, or they are troubled by similar obsessions. The criminal differs from the writer in that one day he suddenly actualizes his symbolic structural view of things *in reality*, without the use of any medium. He himself never even knows the meaning of it. (31:590)

It pleases Mishima to think that the novelist, more than any other type of artist, is closest in spirit to the criminal:

Nothing stimulates the novelist's imagination, challenges him, and excites his creative impulse more than a crime that conventional morality has deemed indefensible. It helps him to feel proud of his isolation from the judgment of society, brings him into close affinity with the pride of an unrepentant criminal, and thereby makes the novelist wonder if he is on the verge of discovering a hitherto unknown value standard. (34:745)

The affinity between novelists and criminals derives, Mishima says, from the simple fact that both specialize in researching "probabilities" (*gaizensei*) that are beyond the reach of the law. "Society wears a mask of humanism," writes Mishima, "but the novelist knows that behind that mask lurks a lurid curiosity, and indeed fondness, for evil. No one who ventures beyond that point is unconnected to the loneliness of the criminal" (745).

Mishima does not deny the influence of social or economic factors on criminal behavior; he simply finds them uninteresting. Mishima is looking for something deeper in the consciousness of the criminal, a propensity for evil that does not stem from external pressures but is rooted in human nature. "What is this privileged flash of light we perceive in crimes?" he asks. "What is the secret that criminals never confess in their statements to police and prosecutors?" (746). Religious traditions have posited the existence of a radical evil grounded in the human subject. Christianity has the idea of original sin, while Buddhism explains evil in terms of *karma*, the spiritual cycle of cause and effect. Mishima too has a strong intuition of evil, not as something produced by the selfishness of individuals, but as a reality in the world. Hence his characters do not *commit* evil so much as they *actualize* it.

Mishima makes an attempt to theorize the psychology of real-life crime in his analysis of the phenomenon that the Japanese call *tōrima*, the "passing devil."

This term refers to a person, often deranged, who randomly attacks a stranger or strangers on the street, typically by cutting or stabbing them with a knife. The problem of random slashings first began making headlines in Japan during the 1950s, and some commentators had suggested that it was symptomatic of a kind of existential angst or stress peculiar to the postwar years. It hardly comes as a surprise to find Mishima taking a keen interest.

For his analysis, Mishima considers a (fictitious) example where a man armed with a knife cruises the streets at night on a bicycle. The man spots a young woman; he approaches her, cuts her once, and then flees into the darkness without waiting to see what happens to her. Another apparently meaningless and gratuitous crime. Mishima writes,

> On the face of it, this is no more than a series of actions. Yet, other than the necessary preparations and escape, we can see that these actions have all been naturally extended from the symbol of a criminal at the moment of stabbing. But this symbol was not generated directly from internal impulses. There was one foundational idea that the criminal warmed and nurtured, while carefully contemplating the possibility of turning it into reality. And the moment he carries it out in reality, that first idea lives once more. (590)

In Mishima's idealized example, it is significant that the slasher does not linger to observe the reaction of his victim. Since the slasher has no interest in seeing her suffer, it is clearly not cruelty that motivates him; therefore we cannot call him a sadist. "Rather than the sensory experience of grasping reality and stabbing it," writes Mishima, "it would probably be more accurate to say that he has chosen an experience of a reality shaped like a first idea, positioned on the border between dream and reality" (590). The most striking feature of this formula is its emotional sterility. There is no sense of voluptuous self-release, no sadistic excitation, no rapture. Between the faceless victim and the equally faceless man who cuts her (Mishima's word is *sakka*, a mere "grazing") no communication of any sort occurs. Mishima explains, "At the moment one commits this type of crime one does not expect great intoxication, but rather something sweetly beautiful lurks in his successful re-experiencing of that first concept" (590). This is a criminal who, rather than submerging himself ecstatically in the moment of his crime, turns away and hurries off to ruminate on it in solitude, an onanist of transgression:

> The absolute solitude [*zettai kodoku*] of the man who carries out this act, his urge toward union, and his urge to commit murder—these three things

paradoxically exist together. For an instant he simultaneously accomplishes unified consciousness and murder. Then he flees . . . (591–592)

A lot depends here on the meaning of *kodoku*. Normally this word means "loneliness," but in Mishima's work it often seems to imply something different. In *The Temple of the Golden Pavilion* we hear a lot from Mizoguchi about his *kodoku*, and the connotation is usually that of estrangement rather than loneliness; perhaps "solitariness" would be the best translation. Mizoguchi is never lonely, because his own mind is fascinating to him. Although he does not crave the company of other people, he recognizes that his solitariness is unhealthy. He talks about it as if it were a medical condition: "Once again my solitariness had begun" (*mata watashi no kodoku ga hajimatta*; 6:139). In his unending solitariness he knows that he is alienated from meaning. Yet he has no intention of giving up his solitariness. He aspires, in fact, to a kind of cosmic solitude. An excess of consciousness, an overly strong self-awareness and sense of his individuality, robs his life of its symbolism. This is the broader and more urgent implication of *kodoku* in Mishima's writings. It denotes an antagonism toward the world that is, Mishima suggests, intrinsic to human subjectivity, since the subject necessarily exists in opposition to the world, to all that is not himself.[21]

Mishima's random slasher, languishing in his state of *kodoku*, is similarly alienated from meaning. He exists in a sort of existential vacuum. What he craves is not union so much as a symbolic act of union, which need only last for a split second. What he slashes is not another human being, Mishima tells us, but merely a concept of a human being. The slasher demonstrates that union is possible in the act of rejecting it, and by his act of evil he makes his isolation absolute; he "guarantees" his solitariness, as Mishima puts it.

Perhaps this is one way of understanding the people, nearly always men, who commit random mass shootings, and who, we invariably hear later, were "solitary," "reclusive," "socially awkward," and so on. It is not that a lonely outsider suddenly breaks from his solitude to communicate his presence to the world through an outrageous act of violence. Rather, his intention from the start is to declare his refusal to communicate and thus to make his solitude absolute. Paradoxically, however, he makes this declaration of absolute solitude via a monstrous act of communication that no one can ignore. Thus he rejects the world at the very moment he proves that union is possible. And although Mishima is scrutinizing a phenomenon he assumes is specific to contemporary Japan, in his analysis of an alienation that seeks to express itself through an outburst of indiscriminate violence, we can easily discern the outline of a psychopathology that is more familiar to us today under the name of terrorism.

The Fine Art of Murder

Needless to say, the crime that exerts the most powerful hold on Mishima's imagination is murder. He obsesses about murder in endless variations, about the prospect of killing, of being killed, and of killing oneself. He was virtually incapable of writing a story that did not culminate with a killing of some sort. *The Temple of the Golden Pavilion* is not an anomaly, since arson is equivalent to the murder of a building. For Mishima, murder is the supreme crime because it permanently changes the world and causes it to be haunted by an absence. But a killing is often also a union: of murderer and victim, of the executioner and the condemned, of two lovers in a suicide pact. As the philosopher Kiyoshi Mahito says, "In Mishima's works, the act of killing connects the killer directly to the world, to space, or to Being, and enables a kind of bonding. In this sense, killing is experienced as a metaphysical act with an existential significance."[22]

One of Mishima's wartime prose works bears the extravagant title "Extracts from the Posthumous Philosophical Diary of a Medieval Serial Killer" (Chūsei ni okeru ichi-satsujin jōshūsha no nokoseru tetsugaku-teki nikki no bassui, 1943). This miniature text, which fills barely six pages, consists of a sequence of diary entries in which the killer records his killing spree:

> Today's victim: Ashikaga Yoshitori, Twenty-Fifth Shogun of the Ashikaga Shogunate. He was in bed at the time, puffing on his opium pipe while casting an eye over a selection of gaudily clad girls lined up before him. Lazily he reached for his bedside bell and rang it. Little did he know he was summoning the man who would cut his throat. Moments later, the shogun's blood was turning the tatami mats the color of cinnabar. (16:145)

The diary offers no story, no background, no reason why the victims must die. Each entry describes an aesthetic metamorphosis in which a brutal murder is transformed into a string of beautiful images:

> Today I killed Reiko, a nobleman's wife. How beautiful she looked as her eyes filled with soft tears and the tension receded from her frame. She seemed almost glad to be murdered. At first I felt a resistance to my sword. But then her fine gold and silver brocade caved in, and her spirit faded away. I can still picture her pretty little chin, white as porcelain, rising out of the darkness like a moonflower. An expression of the most sublime beauty, perched on the tip of an assassin's blade. (146)

Despite its simple format the text is rife with ambiguities. The narrative inexplicably skips back and forth between first person and third person and between present and past tenses. The diary entries are undated. Consequently we have no guarantee that their order is chronological. Out of necessity I have inserted some extra pronouns into my translation. But Mishima's Japanese here has a strategic vagueness. In the first entry it is not inconceivable that the shogun is his own killer. The tone of the diary is also strangely calm. Amid the relentless slaughter there is no sense of frenzy or joy in destruction. The only break in the killer's subdued manner is a flash of impatience when he is obliged to dirty his hands by dealing with the lower classes:

> Today was a most productive day spent slaughtering beggars, one hundred and twenty-six of them in all. Worthless maggots! They chewed on death as if they enjoyed the taste. (147)

The corpses pile up until finally the killer meets someone he does not kill: a pirate chief. The two board the pirate's ship and begin a sort of philosophical dialogue. The pirate boasts to him:

> For us pirates there are no laws, no boundaries. Nothing is impossible for us, and therefore nothing is possible. For us there are no laws, no boundaries.
> We pirates cross the ocean and return whenever we wish. We visit islands colored with blossoming flowers and find hidden there flames of gold. Yet for us there is no progress as such. The universe was ours from the day we were born. You speak of "creating" and "discovering." But to us, these things have always existed. . . . For us there is no other. (150)

Seeing that the killer is awed by this declaration of omnipotence, the pirate urges him to leap over the side of the ship:

> Killer, become the sea! When a sea breeze blows through the pines, something flutters in every pirate's heart, and we pray to the gods of war. We pray for what already exists, what is already determined. Such are the prayers of those like us, those who have no other.
> Killer, become the sea! The sea is in the infinite finite. . . . Killer! What are you thinking? You must become a pirate. No, you *were* a pirate, and now you must return to your destiny. Or do you say that you cannot return? (150)

The killer can offer no answer. Tears stream down his cheeks as he curses "the distance between himself and others."

On a simple and obvious level, "Diary of a Serial Killer" treats killing as a metaphor for artistic creation: the killer is a specialist in the fine art of murder. But there is more to this work than metaphor. After all, the title announces it as a "philosophical" diary. We must ask what this means.

The diary describes an unhappy existential predicament. The killer perceives the world as being filled with separate objects and persons, but he suspects this is an illusion. Beneath these individual experiences, he feels, is a vast, unchanging unity. The pirate, who has "no other" (*muta*), represents the possibility of experiencing this unity, of obtaining a rapturous sense of oneness with the world. The killer, for his part, feels eternally shut out from the possibility of such an experience. This sense of isolation and estrangement is the origin of his desire to destroy and of his desire to create. Many of his victims seem to be types of people he would like to become; they possess attributes that he covets, that he would like to incorporate into himself. We sense the pull of identification, the killer's yearning to break free from his monad and merge rapturously with another person. There is also a suggestion of regaining a lost experience, possibly of returning to a primal state: "Killing is a way of moving closer to a forgotten life" (146).

The killer believes that violence is the only means whereby he can impose his aesthetic on the world: "In my dreams, killing is the sole beauty in a world of chaos" (146). But *only* in his dreams. In reality he is frustrated. The instant he drives his sword into his victim and readies himself for merger and rapture, his mind begins a process that to him seems beyond his control. Rather than dissolving into an ecstatic embrace with his victim, he distances himself from the moment and experiences it aesthetically. He watches the victim die, and he watches himself watching. His problem is that he cannot forget himself. His monad remains intact: "The distance between himself and others—that is what traps him, and he cannot break free." The solution to his problem is already tragically clear to him: "The killer knows that only by being killed himself can he be made complete" (146). That line reminds us with a jolt that this is a *posthumous* diary. The killer survives by killing, while moving ever closer toward his own death.

"Aestheticism does not derive from an unconditional love of the beautiful," wrote Sartre. "It is born of resentment. Those whom society has placed in the background, the adolescent, the woman, the homosexual, subtly attempt to reject a world which rejects them and to perpetrate symbolically the murder of mankind."[23] The paradox of Mishima's serial killer is that while he strives to reject all symbolism by committing real-life murders, he then aestheticizes the murders themselves by rendering them into works of art. The suggestion is that he does so involuntarily, that he cannot stop himself from being an artist. If we followed Sartre's formula, the logical solution to the killer's predicament would be for him to reject the world of art that enslaves him and to perpetrate *unsymbolically* the murder of himself.

That seems to be the idea expressed in the vision of redemptive self-punishment with which the killer's diary ends. Like so much in Mishima's early writings, this passage is strikingly prophetic:

> They say that killers die from being misunderstood. But birds still sing and flowers still bloom in that dense forest of misunderstanding. His mission is already a form of weakness. Consciousness too is already a weakness. In his quest to become a thing of peerless elegance, the day may yet come when this killer offers a cryptic prayer to the very weaknesses that he himself despises. (155)

Decadent Agony

Mishima considers an extreme form of aestheticism in his reading of the French novelist Joris-Karl Huysmans (1848–1907). Huysmans' name crops up in *Confessions of a Mask*, while in *Forbidden Colors* we are informed that Shunsuke, the aging novelist who is the central character, has published translations of three novels by Huysmans. Renowned in his day both for his fiction and his art criticism, Huysmans cultivated a fascinatingly perverse prose style characterized by ornate descriptions and an eccentric vocabulary, which we can be sure Mishima had studied carefully.

In 1962 Mishima's friend Shibusawa Tatsuhiko published the first Japanese version of Huysmans' 1884 novel *À rebours*, sometimes translated into English as *Against Nature*. Shibusawa rendered the inscrutable French title into Japanese as *Sakashima*, which means "in the wrong direction." Mishima obligingly wrote an enthusiastic review, though in a discussion printed later in a literary magazine he was quite critical of the novel.

À rebours is typically characterized as a breviary of decadence. It is the account of an aristocratic dandy named Des Esseintes, who, repelled by the vulgarities of modern life, retires to a suburban retreat to live a solitary and aestheticized existence. In a letter to a colleague Huysmans summarized the novel as follows: "The last representative of an illustrious race, appalled by the invasion of American manners and the growth of an aristocracy of wealth, takes refuge in absolute solitude. He is well-read, cultured, and refined. In his comfortable retreat he substitutes the pleasures of artifice for the banalities of Nature."[24] Each chapter of the book describes, in florid and exhaustive detail, one of Des Esseintes' eclectic obsessions: decadent paintings, early Latin texts, plainsong, rare books, perfumes, gemstones, tropical plants, and so on. Des Esseintes values art and artificiality above all else, believing that "artifice was the distinguishing characteristic of the human genius. . . . Nature has had her day."[25] But Nature retaliates by punishing him with headaches, insomnia, cramps, and syphilis. Unable to swallow food, Des Esseintes must take his nutrients "in the wrong direction": by enema. In this way, reality comically thwarts his aesthetic ambitions. At the end of the novel he returns despondently to Paris. His escapist enterprise has been a dismal failure.

"This is a book that must be read by anyone who wants to hold forth on the subject of decadence," writes Mishima in his review. "The dignity and comicality of decadence are all depicted here, and the luxurious wealth and cultural sophistication that are the necessary conditions for decadence are all displayed to marvellous effect" (32:115). Mishima admires what he calls the "eternal child-like purity" of Des Esseintes, whose increasingly extravagant indulgencies he declares to be "idle poems" (*mui no shi*) that have the sum effect of "bonding decadence with a child's view of the world."

Mishima later offers this first-person characterization of the psychology of the decadent aesthete:

> Living life in this way, I myself am the representative of beautiful things, and since no one is more sensitive to beauty than I am, there is no one who is sacrificing himself to serve beauty more than I. (40:187)

In discussing the passivity inherent in the decadent attitude, Mishima frequently employs the unusual verb *tayutau*, which has the meanings of wavering, drifting, or vacillating. Contrasting decadence with nihilism, he explains, "Nihilism has both positive and negative motions, whereas decadence is a state that has drifted into stasis [*tayutatte teishi shita jōtai*]" (40:188). This passivity, says Mishima, is not conducive to the creative process: "Decadence makes it easier to turn one's life into art . . . but makes it more difficult actually to create works of art" (191).

It is partly his fear of sinking into such decadent passivity that drives Mishima to his pseudo-visionary schemes and fuels his desire for machismo, action, athleticism, and revolt. Mishima was ready to sacrifice himself to serve beauty. But he had a horror of sensing in himself the docility and lethargy of the decadent aesthete. While his disdain for nature is equal to that of Des Esseintes, Mishima would rather be an agent provocateur than an impotent hermit. "There is nothing of the aggressor in Des Esseintes," complains Mishima, "he is merely unwell" (40:189). Des Esseintes is reclusive, anemic, fragile, and perpetually sick. Mishima inoculates himself against each of these ailments by his gregarious socializing, his strict fitness regime, his philosophy of action, and his cult of "the sun and the steel," and then relentlessly promotes these new aspects of his persona in his work. While Des Esseintes retreats into solitude to indulge his exotic tastes in private as if his pleasures were sins, Mishima makes of himself a public affair. He demands an audience for his extravagances and witnesses for his transgressions. Here we recall the startling image at the heart of "Poetic Theory," the aesthete who is turned inside out, with all his weaknesses on display, yet who internally remains sealed in solipsism.

Like Des Esseintes, Mishima will accumulate a collection of exotic obsessions: samurai ethics, Buddhist mysticism, yakuza machismo, the seppuku ceremony, swordsmanship and martial arts, fin-de-siècle dandyism and aestheticism, Kabuki theatrics, ultranationalist ideology, emperor worship, and much else. Japanese commentators have devoted many pages to analyzing the meaning of each of these things within the context of Mishima's work. But, as the literary critic Seikai Ken has said, the question we should ask is not "What is the meaning of these things?" but rather "What is the will that desires them?"[26]

A scholar of nineteenth-century French literature defines the decadent hero as follows:

> He is a metaphysical hero living à rebours, against the grain, a cerebral hero who is an aesthete, cosmopolitan, pervert, or all three at once. His roles are inextricably entwined. He is an ambiguous figure who personifies yet hates his society, one which he wishes to destroy yet cannot live without. This is the decadent agony. He is a megalopolitan primitive sentenced to life in the prison of the modern world. He abhors but feeds upon its artificiality.[27]

In this precise sense we can say that Mishima is a decadent hero. He is metaphysical because of his world-weariness, because of his belief that he has lived too long, which leads him to reflect morosely on his peculiar place in time and space. He is cerebral because he rejects reality and lives apart from it in an alternate world he has created for himself. He is an aesthete for his worship of beautiful things and his obsessive cultivation of his senses. He is cosmopolitan for his attachment to the city and city life, a consequence of his disdain for nature and his love of artifice. And he is a pervert for his contempt for the ordinary and his insistence on deviating from whatever society judges to be normal, as manifest in his narcissistic efforts to transform himself into an object, his denial of feeling and compassion, his love of crimes and evil, and his hedonistic indulgence in eroticism.

We might also recall Nietzsche's remarks about intellectuals and moralists who think that they can extricate themselves from decadence by waging war against it: "Extrication lies beyond their strength: what they choose as a means, as salvation, is itself but another expression of decadence; they change its expression, but they do not get rid of decadence itself."[28] Mishima, thinking along similar lines, is well aware of his predicament:

> In my early teens I could not bear to hear the shouts of the boys training in the kendo hall. It was as if their physiology was being turned inside out and released from their bodies. . . . It was like the stench of something raw. To my mind, that sort of thing was about as far as one could get from decadence. Since the physiology of young men was manifest in those shouts, I assumed that something healthy, something normal was being released. Years later I starting doing kendo myself, and now the shouting does not bother me at all. Actually, it gives me indescribable pleasure to let out that animalistic shout. But now I wonder if perhaps *this* is decadence. Anyone watching me will probably think: How wonderful that he's doing kendo and shouting so healthily! . . . But I don't know whether I was healthier when I used to hate this sort of thing, or healthier now that I am shouting along with the others. These two states of mind seem to be interrelated. (40:186)

The problem is that aestheticism itself is intrinsically decadent, since the emphasis on beauty leaves little room for nature. To prioritize beauty and art is already to go against nature. The message of *À rebours*, as Mishima well understands, is that such a project is ultimately doomed: "Art for art's sake" is no more than a temporary evasion. It is surely significant that Mishima perceives religious undertones in Des Esseintes' enterprise, characterizing him as a "priest" of the cult of beauty (40:187). Both Baudelaire and Wilde ultimately turned to Christ, each in his own way. Beardsley converted to Catholicism one year before his death and asked the executors of his will to destroy his most decadent works. Huysmans' conversion was the most extreme: just nine years after writing *À rebours* he entered a monastery. We know that Mishima too will eventually find God, and like Wilde with Christ he will fashion his God largely in his own image. But his early essays on aestheticism and the fin-de-siècle in *The Hunter and the Hunted* show us that Mishima had seen into the heart of the matter years earlier. "For the aesthete," he writes, "beauty can be no more than a relative salvation. What comes in the end is the absolute salvation of God" (27:63).

CHAPTER 4

The Leap of Narcissus

"I wish I could love," cried Dorian Gray with a deep note of
pathos in his voice. "But I seem to have lost the passion and
forgotten the desire. I am too much concentrated on myself."

Oscar Wilde, The Picture of Dorian Gray

By his early thirties Mishima was devoting a substantial portion of his writing to
chronicling his hectic social schedule, his kendo practice and his gym training,
his forays into the movie industry, his photo shoots, his trips overseas, and the
many other activities that constituted what he liked to called his "non-literary life"
(31:179). In the West today we are accustomed to seeing people turn their lives
into public theater. In Japan it is much less common, and in Mishima's day it was
almost unheard of. As his contemporaries struggled to make sense of Mishima,
the concept many of them initially reached for was narcissism. Mishima's inordinate interest in himself, his theatrical self-presentation, his love of surfaces and
visual effects, his lush and ostentatious prose style, his near-religious obsession
with beauty as an absolute value, all these things seemed to be manifestations of
a profoundly narcissistic mind.

Once again, however, narcissism is one of those aspects of Mishima about
which it is challenging to find something to say that he is not already saying
himself. Indeed, his interest in his own narcissism is so keen that one is tempted
to call it a narcissistic interest. As we have seen, his teenage writings contain outlandish declarations of his own genius and uniqueness. In numerous articles and
essays later in his career Mishima speaks more clinically, though quite unabash-
edly, about the nature of his narcissistic impulses, while his fictions are full of
characters who obsess about their beauty in ways that are liable to strike us as
unhealthy. Among Mishima's most memorable narcissists are Minami Yūichi,
the serial womanizer of *Forbidden Colors*, and Funaki Osamu, the self-enam-
ored young actor who appears in *Kyoko's House*. Neither of these two men has
any genuinely appealing qualities, yet both exert a strange fascination nonetheless. The same goes for the beauty-obsessed neurotics who appear in the stories

"The Goddess" (Megami, 1954) and "The Peacocks." Vanity and the transience of physical beauty are prominent topics in the play *The Terrace of the Leper King* (*Raiō no terasu*, 1969). In addition to these fictional treatments, Mishima discusses the psychology of narcissism in his critical and discursive writings, most notably in his studies of actors and acting, his essays on art and literature, and in his final auto-fictional pieces. In 1966 he published an extended essay titled "On Narcissism" (Narushishizumu ron), which has some affinities with Freud's seminal 1914 study of narcissism. Although Mishima, characteristically, does not even mention Freud's name, it seems clear that he intends some of the points he makes in this essay as counterstatements to Freud.

Mishima's ideas about narcissism derive from an idiosyncratic reading of the Narcissus myth, from his study of writings on narcissism by various European authors, and from self-observation. To understand him properly, we must first familiarize ourselves with the foundational myth. There are multiple classical sources for the tale of Narcissus, and their storylines differ markedly. The most famous is the one in Ovid's *Metamorphoses*, and it is this version that Mishima takes as his starting point.

From birth, Narcissus is a dual being. Of mixed parentage and apparently the result of a rape, he is not quite divine and not quite human. He is endowed with "a beauty that broke hearts." By the time he is sixteen years old, countless nymphs, both male and female, have become infatuated with him, but he has rejected them all. The nymphs pray for his punishment: "Let him, like us, love and know it is hopeless." The gods grant this vengeful prayer. While resting by a pool of water, Narcissus sees his reflection and falls instantly in love. At first he does not recognize that the reflection is himself. He plunges his arms into the pool and urges his reflection to come up onto the land. Finally he understands: "I am in love with myself." His very next thought is of death: "My beauty is in full bloom—But I am a cut flower. Let death come quickly." He curls up by the side of the pool and weeps in sorrow until he stops breathing. When people come to bury him, all they find is a single white flower growing at the spot where he died.[1]

The myth of Narcissus contains material for much more than a straightforward allegory about destructive self-love. Psychoanalysts have constructed theories around Narcissus' solitariness, his indifference to others, and his vulnerability to illusion. Mishima had studied literary treatments of the Narcissus myth by European authors who had explored the decadent implications of auto-eroticism. And of course the myth urges us to consider the nature of love itself. Mishima concentrates on three main ideas: the meaning and symbolism of the mirror image, the duality of mind and body, and the link between narcissism and the death drive. Let us look at each of these in turn.

Mirrors

Mirrors feature prominently in all Mishima's discussions of narcissism. He speaks of Narcissus' reflection as a "mirror image" (*kyōzō*) and in various essays ponders the changes in consciousness that occur during self-observation in a mirror. In *Kyoko's House* Mishima uses the kanji for "mirror" in the name of the eponymous Kyoko, whose patient listening skills enable her four neurotic friends to feel that they are being "reflected" in her mind. Often in Mishima's stories, young and beautiful characters gaze dreamily into mirrors. Aging characters stare in horror and despair.

The following statements appear in a memoir Mishima dictated in his early thirties:

> The narcissism at the boundary between boyhood and adolescence will use anything for its own purposes. It will even use the destruction of the world. The bigger the mirror, the better. At the age of twenty I could imagine myself as anything. A genius fated to die young. The last young man of Japan's aesthetic traditions. The last ruler of a depraved and decadent empire. Beauty's kamikaze squadron [*bi no tokkōtai*]. (32:278)

The bigger the mirror, the better. The narcissistic confession being communicated in the above lines is that Mishima could not imagine himself *as anything other than* a decadent hero.

We might think there is nothing unusual about Mishima's preoccupation with mirrors and mirror images, since the mirror seems an indispensable prop for any narcissist. But in the myth, of course, there is no mirror: Narcissus gazes at himself in a pool of water. Nonetheless Mishima insistently prioritizes the idea of a mirror:

> Narcissus' love begins from his discovery that the reflection he sees in the water is both himself and a pure existence separated from his self-consciousness. Without this rift between the mirror image and the mind, between the mirror image and consciousness, the exterior and the interior would become one. (34:143)

While it may be valid to speak of a "mirror image" reflected in water, Narcissus' watery pool cannot be substituted with a mirror without weakening the symbolism. A mirror is a static object. It is unnatural, geometrical, restrictive. Unlike water, it does not offer any depth for dreaming.[2] The material finitude of the mirror limits the mirror gazer's sense of self within its frame, as it does in Mishima's reading. Narcissus' beauty continues into the water. But the mirror gazer finds that his beauty comes to an end before the mirror; the materiality of the mirror keeps him out. This, I think, is what leads Mishima to make such a categorical division between "exterior" and "interior."

In a short piece titled "Love in a Mirror" (Kagami no naka no koi), Mishima employs a mirror scenario to argue, in a playful manner, for the superiority of surface over depth. Two young lovers are gazing at themselves in a mirror. "Which is real," Mishima asks, "the love in the mirror or the love outside the mirror?" The mirror gives only the lovers' form, showing everything they are willing to put on display and concealing everything they wish to conceal: "There are no emotions in the mirror image." That is a good thing, says Mishima, since emotions can ruin love as well as foster it: "Only as a form [katachi] does love last forever" (34:104). This is the aesthete's mantra that only beauty of form, not beauty of content, can attain an objectivity that transcends time. Mishima ends by imagining the young lovers being liberated from the potential complications and ugliness of emotions, as they find eternal happiness in the purely superficial world of the mirror.[3]

Mishima's obsession with the mirror sets him apart from other modern writers who have addressed Narcissus in poems and essays. André Gide situates Narcissus beside a gushing river, as a symbol of time's relentless flow. Paul Valéry's pool-gazing Narcissus suffers delusions in which he thinks he hears "the voice of the waters."[4] In Oscar Wilde's witty inversion of the myth, the watery pool falls in love with its own reflection, which it sees in Narcissus' eyeballs. In Mishima's version, the water has no life force like this, and his Narcissus always faces "a silent water mirror" (34:149). Why is the symbolism of the mirror so important to Mishima? One answer, I think, is to be found in the equivalence, as Mishima sees it, between mirror gazing and the apperception of art.

Ovid's Narcissus is essentially a Romantic, a lovesick dreamer. On encountering the beautiful face apparently floating in the water, he is desperate to embrace this "stranger who could make him happy."[5] In contrast, Mishima's mirror-gazing narcissist has coldly superficial eyes. The shallowness of the mirror image, its restrictive finitude, is for him a desirable effect. Mishima's Narcissus inspects himself in the mirror and sees "pure outer surface and nothing more" (143). He looks at himself as if he is inspecting a sculpture, or any art object. The static materiality of the mirror legitimizes and facilitates this object-like apperception of himself.

It was in a similar sense that Schopenhauer famously employed a mirror metaphor to explain how we contemplate works of art. One of the effects of art, says Schopenhauer, is to reduce our self-centeredness. Art diverts our attention away from our own needs and selfish interests, and by doing so art frees us from our subjectivity. That is why we can speak of "losing ourselves" in art. While contemplating a work of art, we forget our individuality and exist "only as pure subject, as clear mirror of the object, so that it is as though the object alone existed without anyone to perceive it."[6]

Mishima applies Schopenhauer's theoretical formula to the narcissistic gaze, in which the "work of art" the subject perceives is his own image. For a brief moment the subject's whole consciousness is preoccupied with this single object of perception. As Mishima explains it, the narcissistic mirror gazer succeeds in eradicating "the rift between mirror image and mind" to a point where "exterior and interior become one" (34:143). Perceiver and perception become indistinguishable, and it is as if the object alone—the mirror image—exists.

There is a second reason why the mirror better suits Mishima's idea of narcissism. The mirror gazer has a knowingness not given to the mythical Narcissus, whose tragedy is that he does not recognize his own reflection. It could be argued that, strictly speaking, Narcissus is not a narcissist at all: he loves himself in error and dies of a broken heart once he realizes that his reflection will never return his love. Narcissus' despair begins from the moment when "he learns to know himself," exactly as the oracle had predicted. His fear is that the mirror will show him what he does not want to see: signs of decay. For the narcissistic person who wishes to admire himself beyond a brief moment, to admire himself *indefinitely*, the mirror is a gateway to a cosmos of self-doubt. The narcissist needs the mirror in order to admire his image. But at the same time, he recognizes that the mirror is potentially fatal to his self-admiration.

Mishima had perceived this cruel psychology of the mirror. In one of his early poems, an unidentified woman rushes across a green lawn. She is wearing a wedding dress and is in great emotional distress. We are given no explanation; the poem depicts only this mysterious flash of panic. Then we read:

The surfaces of all the saffron flowers,
All the forests, all the lakes,
Every fountain and every cypress tree,
Were wrapped in invisible mirrors.
(37:424)

It is tempting to interpret this paradoxical image of infinite "invisible mirrors" (*me ni mienu kagami*) as symbolizing a kind of visual claustrophobia, a fear of being spied on from all sides by unseen eyes. Freud had wondered if delusions of being watched might contribute to the neurosis of narcissists. But what induces the woman's panic here, surely, is the *unavailability* of her own mirror image. An

invisible mirror is obviously useless, and an infinity of useless mirrors symbolizes the trauma of being constantly unable to see oneself. The woman is trapped
in a landscape devoid of reflecting surfaces, unable to confirm her own existence
through any visual means. A world that returned no reflection, the poem seems
to say, would be a narcissist's hell.

In his reading of the Narcissus myth, Mishima stresses that Narcissus attains
awareness of his own beauty purely from self-observation, by gazing at his "mirror image" in the water, and not from any external standard or evaluation, such
as compliments from other people. Narcissus does not care how other people see
him; indeed, he barely recognizes their existence. Mishima explains:

> The true form of pure narcissism has no need of praise from other peo-
> ple. Herein lies a very subtle and very difficult problem of beauty. Yes,
> Narcissus is beautiful. When other people see him they think he is beauti-
> ful. If Narcissus were not objectively beautiful to other people, the myth
> itself would not be beautiful. On the other hand, Narcissus is absolutely
> exclusionary [zettai ni haita-teki], and if he did not have such enormous
> confidence in the objectivity of his self-consciousness that the praise of
> others is irrelevant to him, the myth would similarly lose its meaning.
> Narcissus must know himself, he must be a master of self-criticism, and
> he must be so beautiful that no amount of harsh self-criticism can trouble
> him. (34:147–148)

According to Mishima, then, Narcissus does not need other people because
he gazes at his reflection in the objective knowledge that he is beautiful. The
"absolute objectivity of self-consciousness" (jiishiki no zettai-teki kyakkansei) is
a difficult notion (148). An ugly narcissist would certainly be a ridiculous figure.
But he would be ridiculous for his lack of objectivity, not for his ugliness. In
Mishima's scheme, objectively beautiful Narcissus attains "absolute objectivity"
at the moment he becomes conscious of his own objective beauty: "If we consider Narcissus' reflection in the water to be the pure wordless mirror of narcissism, other people are just secondary (though powerful) talking mirrors" (149). If
Narcissus' awareness of his beauty were dependent on the opinions of others, his
narcissism would not be "pure," as Mishima calls it:

> Once you have other people, rather than pure self-reflection, as your mir-
> ror, narcissism lapses into relativism, and you will not be able to avoid fall-
> ing into the hell of relativity. The essential form of all types of narcissism
> other than pure narcissism is anxiety. (149)

Freud had asserted that narcissistic tendencies are more commonly found in women. Mishima considers a number of different mirror-gazing scenarios—a woman doing her makeup, a bodybuilder admiring his muscles, a soldier checking his uniform—and concludes that pure narcissism, as he has defined it, is strictly a male phenomenon.

To reach this conclusion, Mishima first stresses the distinction between narcissism and vanity. Women's obsession with their appearance, he argues, is a manifestation of anxiety. This anxiety arises from a craving for the approval of others; it is vain, but not narcissistic in the pure sense. As Mishima keeps reminding us, Narcissus does not believe himself to be beautiful because other people tell him so; he *knows* himself to be beautiful from self-observation. Mishima says that women lack what he calls the "self-cultivation of self-consciousness" (*jiishiki no jiko-seichiku*) needed to achieve this level of objectivity. Even if a woman spends hours doing her makeup in front of a mirror, Mishima argues, her viewpoint remains purely subjective: "Women are not really looking at themselves" (139).

This gendered distinction is important to Mishima because, like Freud, he wants to link narcissism to the death drive. The myth ends, of course, with a death: the leap of Narcissus is fatal. Mishima insists that this death is not a metaphor but is to be taken literally. It is essential to the myth's meaning and signifies a psychological drive toward death that is, he argues, distinctively male. In a basic biological sense, men are expendable: "If women who gaze intently into their mirrors all leaped in and died, the human race would become extinct. . . . Narcissus can only be male" (139). And a few pages later Mishima writes, "I believe that narcissism is men's most fundamental impulse [*otoko no mottomo hongen-teki na shōdō*]" (146).

Following from this, it comes as no surprise that Mishima finds the epitome of male narcissism in the military world. The military, Mishima declares, is a "pure masculine world" where unfeelingness is the norm and "surfaces must be immaculate at all times." In such a world the mirror is an essential item. In the military, says Mishima, "man's external appearance is strictly regulated, and this exterior then regulates his internal self-consciousness, restraining his self-consciousness, so that the energy of a simplified and uniformalized self-consciousness is made to serve the superego" (144).

Mishima contrasts this "pure narcissism" of the military with the case of a bodybuilder admiring himself in a mirror. What the bodybuilder sees in the mirror is similarly "a pure other" (*junsui na tasha*), an "external surface that he has created by the force of his own will and energy" (146). Mishima insists, however, that a crucial element of narcissism is missing:

What is oddly lacking here is that mysterious operation that takes place during self-cultivation: when self-consciousness eats away at itself, the mirror devours the mirror, and thus generates a drive that compels the man to take the leap of Narcissus, in other words, to destroy himself. Bodybuilders lovingly cultivate their muscles and fill themselves with vitamins, calories, and so on. But male narcissism requires an active quality [*kōdōsei*] that urges men toward death. This kind of active narcissism attempts to smash the mirror by leaping into it. (146)

Mishima points to the universal male preoccupation with violent and dangerous activities as a clear manifestation of the narcissistic death drive. When men try to become beautiful, he says, they always move closer to death. Even war is only secondarily explicable as territorialism, nationalism, or tribal conflict; primarily it is a ritual of male narcissism: "Those Japanese boys who joined naval college just because they wanted the uniform and short sword of the naval officer, and then perished in battle, they all died the death of Narcissus" (145).

Anguished Muscles

Narcissism, as it is commonly understood, denotes an inordinate regard for oneself. There is a Japanese word *jikoai*, which translates literally as "self-love," though Mishima prefers the loanword from English, *narushishizumu*. Love of oneself is not a bad thing. After all, our survival instincts are rooted in self-regard. And we take it for granted that geniuses and high achievers will be selfishly engrossed in themselves. The attributes we associate with narcissism are the unhealthy or unappealing side effects of a self-love that has become excessive or unrealistic. We think of narcissists as narrow-minded and spiritually shallow. Loving another person is obviously contrary to the narcissistic impulse since it demands a degree of indifference to oneself. Narcissism seems shallow in its prioritizing of appearance over substance. We are likely to say of narcissists that they have lost touch with their origins or their surroundings, or that they have confused themselves with the fictional role they perform. In its most extreme forms, narcissism can lead to a dangerous dislocation from reality and a decline into paranoia or psychosis.

As we saw earlier, Mishima's aestheticism leads him to the view that the goal of life is to be successfully artificial, that is, to make a success of the artificiality that is an unavoidable feature of human life. Such an attitude facilitates the narcissistic split of the subject into self and image, and the subsequent prioritization of the image. In Ovid's tale Narcissus wonders, "Why can't I get apart from my body? This is a new kind of lover's prayer: to wish himself apart from the one he loves."[7]

This splitting phenomenon is most obvious in actors, who are split beings by profession. Even the most charismatic and accomplished actors often look shy and uncomfortable during media interviews and public appearances, when they are obliged to be themselves. It is in the roles they play, their artificial other selves, that they have invested their narcissistic energies.

Throughout his life Mishima was enviously fascinated by actors and the art of acting. He wrote the following lines at the age of thirty:

> The soul of an actor filled with self-consciousness is like Narcissus loving his own reflection in the water. To Narcissus, his own body is nothing but an object of love. If a successful acting performance can be compared to this, then an actor is a Narcissus who has leaped into the water, a spirit that has leaped into the world of "expression," a subject that has plunged into an object. The relationship between actor and role resembles that of Narcissus' mind and Narcissus' body reflected in the water. This is what I regard as a healthy manner of expression. (28:584)

Mishima is enthralled by this possibility of turning oneself into an art object, of displacing one's identity from self to image, and then using this artificial self-image to exercise a kind of devilish power over other people. In a later essay on the art of Kabuki he offers these remarks:

> The basic question for determining the talent and worth of an individual actor is probably this: How do beauty, narcissism, and evil come together and relate to each other in him? Beauty is the power of existence [sonzai no chikara]; it is a guarantee of objectivity. Evil is a seductive power, one that exhausts the limits of artifice and of human-made wisdom; it seduces people, possesses them, and whisks them away to a higher sphere. And narcissism, in the actor, is a power that forcibly merges beauty and evil. (31:259)

It is understandable, then, that one of the most memorable (and disturbing) narcissists in Mishima's work is an aspiring young actor. In the character of Funaki Osamu, one of the protagonists of *Kyoko's House*, Mishima meticulously tracks the development of an extreme pathological narcissism, from the mirror-dependency stage right up to the fatal leap.

Osamu is handsome, languid, and bored. He has no interest in the world around him, but is entirely concentrated on himself. This solipsism induces a sort of mental torpor. Osamu feels suspended in time like a statue, since his eyes see almost nothing that is extraneous to himself:

At the start of each day, Osamu saw vaguely through to the day's end. He knew the day would pass by with no changes of any kind, and his eyes were just about able to see to the end of it. He could see no further than that, and he did not try. What need was there for him to look? The future was veiled in gloom, and an arrogant darkness was blocking out his field of vision like a great black beast. (7:71)

Osamu knows that he is handsome, and he has the haughty sense of superiority that such knowledge typically brings. In his daydreams he imagines himself performing triumphantly on the theater stage, the greatest actor of his generation. Yet at the same time Osamu suffers from a strange form of anxiety. His problem is that he lacks a deep and continuing sense of being alive. He experiences this lack in the most literal way, having only a fragile sense of his physical, bodily existence. He feels trapped in an unstable existential state, which he describes as "quivering like a liquid," and he fears that he might cease to exist at any moment (55).

Osamu is forever checking his reflection in mirrors. He even keeps a small hand mirror beside his bed so that he can check his face the instant he wakes up, and also before and after sex. It is not vanity that makes him do this. Osamu is a mirror junky: without access to his own reflection he quickly becomes nervous and agitated. Mirrors, and all things that return his reflection, are reassuring to him, because they unfailingly confirm his existence. Yet while mirrors can relieve Osamu's doubts about his existence, at the same time they destabilize his sense of autonomy. He is frustrated by the fact that he and his mirror image are not one and the same. He would prefer the world in the mirror to be the real world. Gazing at his reflection he muses, "That is where I really exist" (57). He dreams of somehow becoming one with the beautiful young man who is gazing back at him from the mirror. This, of course, is the dynamic of Narcissus.

Osamu has sex almost as often as he looks in the mirror. He sleeps with a seemingly endless string of casual lovers. But he does so only for the satisfaction of watching them react to his beauty. He makes no emotional investment in them. He is not interested in them as human beings; to him they are merely human mirrors. When his lovers look at him, he sees himself reflected in their eyes. When they touch him or kiss him, it is the awareness of his own body, not theirs, that preoccupies him.

His dependence on the gaze of his lovers causes problems for Osamu during sex. As he watches one of his lovers losing herself in pleasure, it annoys him that she has stopped paying attention to him:

Once again his existence had become ambiguous. It had just melted away. The guarantee was gone. He felt alone, as if he had been left out of the sex.

The same woman who moments ago had been admiring his body, making him so clearly aware of his own existence, had now shut her eyes and plunged into the depths of her own ecstasy. She was no longer connected to his existence, and had drifted so far away that she would probably not even answer him if he called. (204)

Even worse, when Osamu tries to recall his sex sessions the morning after, he discovers with horror that he is absent from his own memory:

The sharp creases in the freshly starched bedsheet, the dripping beads of sweat, the over-sprung mattress wobbling like a little boat on water—he knew that all those things had been real. And the enormous sense of relief at the moment the pleasure subsided: that had definitely been real too. The only thing he was not sure about was whether he himself had existed. (32)

In this way, any person or object in which he cannot discern part of himself, anything that fails to return his reflection, triggers in Osamu a profound self-doubt. He begins to wonder if he would obtain a greater sense of being alive by increasing the size of his body. "Flesh is itself a kind of existence, a weight," he tells himself. "So, if I increase the amount of flesh on my body, will my sense of existence also increase? Will it become denser?" (55).

With these thoughts in his mind, Osamu decides to start lifting weights. At the gym he comes under the influence of a bodybuilder named Takei, who, with the implausible eloquence that is typical of Mishima's characters, lectures him on the profundity of surfaces:

What, really, is the value of human psychology or human emotions? Who says that psychology and emotions are the only things that can have deep and subtle meanings? The most subtle part of the human body is the muscle! [. . .] Anger, tears, love, and laughter are no richer in nuance than muscles. . . . Look at the sadness of muscles that are sad. They are more sorrowful than the emotion of sadness. Look at the grief of anguished muscles. They are more sincere than a grieving soul. No, emotions are not important. Ideas that cannot be perceived visually are not important! (77)

Osamu is encouraged by this line of reasoning. While lifting weights he feels he is reaching out to existence for the first time in his life. After his training sessions he relishes the pain tearing through his muscles, as though something is coming to life inside him. If he carries on training like this, he tells himself, one day his whole being will become muscle:

Then I will be a person who is made entirely of external surfaces, a person who has expanded completely into his own surfaces. A man without a soul, a man made of nothing but muscles. That is when I will really exist, and there will be no shadow or trace of the ambiguous person who is sitting here now, thinking these thoughts. (96)

The pleasure Osamu obtains from his muscle pain ominously indicates the direction his behavior is about to take. Months later, after he has bulked up and achieved the impressive physique he wanted, one of his lovers surprises him by suddenly taking a razor and cutting the skin over his rib cage. When he asks her why she has cut him, he gets the reply: "Because your skin is just too beautiful" (350). As he watches himself bleed, Osamu thinks he understands more clearly than ever the metaphysical significance of pain:

When he saw the blood trickling down his side, he felt a confidence in his existence that was greater than anything he had experienced before. Here was his young flesh, and another person's attention was fixated on his flesh so keenly that she could not stop herself from wanting to cut it. A desperate love had been directed at him, there was a moment of searing pain, and the blood pouring from the wound was unmistakably his own. Here, at last, the drama of his existence had been established, an existence that was guaranteed by pain and blood. It was as if a panoramic view of his whole being had opened up before his eyes. "So," he said to himself, "this is how it feels to exist on the edge of the world." (351–352)

As a psychology of one type of deliberate self-harm, this is persuasive. One undeniable effect of pain is that it eliminates existential doubt: I suffer, therefore I am. Osamu is jubilant at this discovery, and thereafter makes skin cutting a regular part of his life. Soon his body is covered with scars. Enjoying the exquisite pain of a salty bead of sweat seeping into a freshly made cut on his shoulder, he puts his lips to the cut and kisses it. This narcissistic gesture recalls Dorian Gray, who kisses his own portrait.

And just like Dorian, Osamu ultimately surrenders himself to the death drive. The decisive factor in Osamu's mental collapse is his inability to distinguish fantasy from reality. While there is no end to the number of painful cuts he can make in his skin, a *fatal* cut would be unrepeatable; this idea takes devastating hold of Osamu's mind. Over and over he imagines his own death as a sensational one-time-only performance, until he reaches a point where he ceases to differentiate between fantasy and reality: "Sometimes it seemed to him that the death he was imagining contained no pain whatsoever, and at such moments he could hardly tell whether the death he was dreaming of was real or being enacted on stage" (353). Just a few pages later we hear that Osamu is dead. Apparently he has killed himself in a suicide pact with his sadistic lover, the one who had first cut him.

Osamu exhibits all the exclusionist tendencies that Mishima considers requisite for the condition of pure narcissism. Although he fantasizes about success and stardom, Osamu does not wish to be loved by other people. He is not sufficiently interested in other people to care about their feelings. And despite his grandiose ambitions, he makes no effort to change the world in order to actualize those ambitions. He is frozen in self-centered stasis. But it would be wrong to say that he is in love with himself. Osamu is not capable of loving himself because his "self" is something of which he has no definite awareness. Rather than pursue this perpetually elusive self, he invests his energies in a pleasing artificial self-image, into which he discharges his anxiety. Osamu is in love with his *image*, and although he thinks he is acquiring a greater realness through his gym workouts and his skin-cutting sessions, in fact he is denying the possibility of his real self even further. This is the psychological process that coincides with the death drive. Eventually Osamu severs all his connections to external reality and replaces reality with his image, which thus becomes the totality of his world.

When Osamu's friends hear that he has committed suicide, one of them offers this analysis: "You have to understand that when men dream of becoming beautiful it is not the same as women's desire for beauty; in men it is always a 'will to death'" (*shi e no ishi*; 371). This line accords with Mishima's view of pure narcissism and the death drive, though as an assessment of Osamu's case it is an oversimplification. In Osamu, Mishima has demonstrated very persuasively how narcissism is not just an inordinate self-regard but a total denial of feeling. The inability to feel, the awareness of one's incapacity for emotional relations with other people, generates an anxiety that leads to self-torture. Osamu's masochism is atonement for his narcissism.[8] Yet his masochism only increases as he grows more confident about his physique and his physical existence, a paradoxical pattern that we can also observe in Mishima himself.

CHAPTER 5

Intoxicating Illusions

> In the violence of the overcoming, in the disorder of my
> laughter and my sobbing, in the excess of raptures that shatter
> me, I seize on the similarity between a horror and a volup-
> tuousness that goes beyond me, between an ultimate pain and
> an unbearable joy!
>
> Georges Bataille, The Tears of Eros

An old Italian manuscript records the fate of a Roman soldier who captained the bodyguard cohort of Emperor Diocletian in the third century after the Cross. This captain, a devout Christian, was concealing his faith to avoid persecution. Eventually he was exposed and sentenced to death. Shot through with arrows by the emperor's archers, he miraculously survived and recovered. In defiance he returned to the palace and proclaimed the power of Christ. This time the emperor's men beat him to death with clubs.

Nearly two millennia later a Japanese novelist poses for a photograph of himself depicted as the Roman captain, who has long since been canonized by the Christian Church. Wearing only a loincloth, with his hands roped to a tree branch above his head and three fake arrows piercing his body, Mishima is gazing to the heavens with what he presumably intends to be a saintly expression.

Mishima's adulation of the martyred Saint Sebastian demands some explanation. What is this Christian icon doing in the fantasies of a modern Japanese intellectual, one who otherwise presents himself as a pro-Japan purist and ultra-traditionalist? The photograph is not a solitary anomaly. Sebastian makes a notorious appearance in *Confessions of a Mask*, and Mishima revisits Sebastian again and again in later writings as he attempts, ever more audaciously, to transform himself into a Sebastian-type figure.

The earliest paintings of Saint Sebastian depicted him as a typical Christian sage, a bearded man of mature years. Over centuries the iconography changed to show him as a martyr suffering for his faith. In the 1300s, during the time of the Black Death, painters stressed Sebastian's physical incorruptibility. Often he was riddled with arrows like a pincushion, to show his power of resistance to torments. The popularity of Cupid paintings in the 1500s gave new meaning to Sebastian's arrows. Now he inspired dreams of love. He became younger, handsome, and more sensuous. Renaissance artists portrayed him as a Christian Adonis. The blatant eroticism of many of these depictions upset religious conservatives. Some Sebastian paintings had to be removed from church altars because of their tendency to excite "lascivious desire" among the faithful.[1]

Mishima knew all this, as his many remarks on Sebastian make clear. He also knew, from his readings of Wilde, Huysmans, Proust, Mann, and others, that a string of late nineteenth- and early twentieth-century European aesthetes had celebrated Sebastian as a homoerotic icon. By attaching his name to Sebastian in fiction and in essays, and posing as Sebastian in that photograph, Mishima was knowingly and emphatically identifying himself with this convention. It is a convention that has irritated some artistic purists. In 1959 one eminent French art historian was complaining that there was nothing left for Saint Sebastian now except "the compromising and guilty patronage of *sodomites* or homosexuals, seduced by his ephebic Apollonian nudity."[2] Richard A. Kaye, a scholar who has chronicled the history of Sebastian as a homoerotic icon, makes a similar complaint: "Sebastian's fate in modern and contemporary representation is, above all else, the story of the mischievous appropriation of Christian symbolism and Renaissance imagery by homosexually identified men."[3]

If that is true, then the scene featuring Saint Sebastian that opens the second chapter of *Confessions of a Mask* is one of the most mischievous appropriations of all. In the scene in question, the unnamed narrator, who both is and is not Mishima himself, recalls discovering a black-and-white reproduction of one of the famous paintings of Saint Sebastian by the Italian artist Guido Reni (1575–1642) in one of his father's art books. The narrator has already described for us many of his own erotic fantasies and fetishes, what he calls the "odd images" that haunt him: visions of young men going to their deaths on the battlefield or being ritualistically stabbed and executed. He has described these desires to us as existing *a priori*, dependent on nothing in this world extraneous to himself. They are, he tells us, the "determinants" (*gentei*) of his life, fully formed and immutable, "remarkably perfect . . . lacking nothing" (1:185–186). When he sees Reni's Sebastian he is entranced by its sensual beauty:

Sebastian's white and incomparable naked body was gleaming against a background of dusk. His strong arms, those of an imperial guard accustomed to bending a bow and wielding a sword, were raised at a fairly gentle angle, and his tied wrists were crossed directly above his head. His face was turned slightly upward, and his eyes, filled with profound tranquility, gazed up to the glory of heaven. It was not pain that hovered about his straining chest, his tense abdomen, and his slightly twisted hips, but a flicker of languid pleasure that was almost like music. . . . The arrows had eaten into his tense, fragrant, youthful flesh, and were about to burn his body from the inside with flames of the most extreme agony and ecstasy. (1:203–204)

The painting triggers in the narrator an instant and overwhelming sexual response:

My blood surged, and my organ swelled as if enraged. A part of me that was now gigantic and ready to burst was waiting for me to use it with an unprecedented ferocity, panting impatiently and chiding me for my ignorance. My hands unknowingly began a motion that they had never been taught. From inside myself I felt something dark and bright rise swiftly to the attack. Suddenly it burst forth, accompanied by a blinding intoxication. . . . This was my first *ejaculatio*, and the first time I indulged in my clumsy and entirely unexpected "bad habit." (204)

In accordance with the conventions of his day, Mishima tries to avoid explicitness through fastidious use of euphemisms, foreign words, and scholarly jargon. "The instant I looked upon the picture," recalls the narrator, "my entire being trembled with some sort of pagan joy" (203). The word "pagan" (*ikyō*) is incongruous here, since paganism is not a concept normally present in the minds of Japanese schoolboys. The author's research has intruded into the narrative. Obviously it is *sexual* joy that makes the narrator tremble. Though there are perfectly good Japanese words for "ejaculation" and "masturbation," the narrator retreats into Latin and speaks only of his "bad habit" (*akushū*). And at no point does he address the question of why this image excites him sexually, rather than emotionally, aesthetically, or spiritually. Instead, and in lieu of real introspection, he offers only this dry parenthesis:

The fact that Hirschfeld places "pictures of Saint Sebastian" in the first rank of those kinds of paintings and sculptures in which inverts take special delight is, in my case, an interesting coincidence. Hirschfeld's observation easily leads us to assume that, in the vast majority of cases of inversion, most especially of congenital inversion, the inverted impulses and the sadistic impulses are inextricably entwined. (204).

An interesting coincidence! It was his reading of psychological literature, particularly the pioneering work on sexuality by Magnus Hirschfeld (1868–1935) and Havelock Ellis (1859–1939), that had given Mishima the confidence he needed to write *Confessions of a Mask*. Ellis' scholarly study *Sexual Inversion*, first published in 1906, includes many anonymous sexual confessions by Ellis' patients, most of which focus on childhood experiences. It contains, for example, the long sexual history of an Englishman, identified only as Case "XXVII," who recalls that as a young boy he was "deeply impressed" by the handsome faces of soldiers and "the male figures of Italian martyrs."[4] Influenced by Ellis, it seems that Mishima had initially conceived of writing *Confessions of a Mask* as an experiment in self-analysis. He even sent a copy of the book to a Tokyo psychiatrist.[5]

Following on from the passage quoted above, without further comment the narrator quotes from a prose poem, which, he tells us, he wrote when he was a boy: "Was not the beauty of Sebastian, young captain in the Imperial Guard, a beauty to be killed [*korosareru bi*]?" The English translation by Meredith Weatherby gives this phrase as follows: "Was not such beauty as his a thing destined for death?"[6] This implies two concepts, beauty and death, which are conjoined by a third, destiny. But Mishima presents the idea as a unity: Sebastian's is a beauty-to-be-killed. Since the Japanese language has no specific future tense, *korosareru bi* could also be translated as "a beauty that will be killed," or conceivably even as "the beauty of being killed"; that is, the term equally implies all these meanings. Hence Sebastian's beauty is not one that, by some unidentified external process or power, has been fated to die. It is that particular kind of beauty that Mishima most cherishes, a beauty on the verge of death. And, as always in Mishima's visions, not only a promise of death but also an implicit *violence* is suggested here. This is not a beauty that will wane from frailty. It is a beauty that demands the violence of being killed and which through its violent destruction will become consecrated, or will consecrate the one who possesses it.

Phallic Destiny

The sex act as fatal violence is an ancient cliché. Its symbolism is accurate enough. Sexual climax is like an eruption or explosion, and the enervation that follows it is indeed like a miniature death. Reni's Sebastian both asserts and confounds this cliché. Shot through with arrows, Sebastian should be weakened and crumpling. Instead he is upright and straight-backed, with all his concentration directed skyward. The tree that is his only background accentuates the erectness of his posture. The prose poem in *Confessions of a Mask* likewise depicts Sebastian as an embodiment of rigid manhood, so filled with anticipation and vitality that he is about to burst: "Beneath his white flesh, his blood was pumping even more fiercely than usual, searching for an opening through which to spurt out as soon as that flesh was torn apart" (1:207–208). These lines give Sebastian a phallic destiny, so that his beauty must be killed just as a sexual desire must be sated.

This formula is everywhere in Mishima's work. Consider the structure of *Sun and Steel* (*Taiyō to tetsu*, 1969), the purportedly self-analytical (though equally self-constructive) essay in which Mishima charts what he calls his "spiritual development." Essentially, this is a process of transforming himself into a Sebastian type. To accomplish this transformation, in *Sun and Steel* Mishima follows an obvious phallic trajectory. The opening line of the essay introduces an image of frustration and pent-up energy, as Mishima complains of an "accumulation of all sorts of things" that he feels unable to express via any kind of "objective art form such as the novel" (33:506). Since words are inadequate for relieving himself of this accumulation, Mishima must seek a "language of the body." Mishima therefore devotes himself to bodybuilding. He builds firmly defined muscles, grows taut and hard, makes his body into a thing of beauty, while recounting ever more extreme experiences of physical stress: kendo practice and military training, the "white-hot frenzy of muscles in action," the thrill of sweat and strength and perfected form. At last, rising to a state of intoxication, he cries out, "I exist!" Mishima's levitation then begins. Forgoing all subtlety, he describes his experience of shooting into the sky in an F-104 supersonic fighter jet, "like a sharp silver phallus tearing through the sky at the angle of an erection. . . . Now I knew how a spermatozoon feels at the moment of ejaculation!" (577). Mishima's stamina is remarkable. Only a few lines later he is off again, airborne once more, this time poetically transformed into the Greek mythical figure of Icarus, and on the final page we can only lag behind him as he soars upward and out of sight, presumably all the way to the sun.

Julia Kristeva says, "Mishima, mistaking himself for Saint Sebastian . . . [carries] to the limit the slavish moment of male eroticism appended to a deathful veneration of the phallus."[7] In similar manner, the narrator of *Confessions of a Mask* does not just make Sebastian into an object of his own erotic pleasure; he dreams of transforming himself into Sebastian. This process of identification is apparent from the moment of his first encounter with the painting, as the narrator seems to relinquish his own viewpoint outside the painting and relishes the sight of the arrows as if they are penetrating his own flesh. He makes a narcissistic investment in the painting, and his response is therefore one of self-directed erotic arousal.

For that matter, Reni's Sebastian himself displays strong narcissistic tendencies. Barely noticing his wounds, he seems enraptured by his own rapture. Germaine Greer calls him "a lover whose body is racked less with agony for the arrows of his persecutors than with his soul's longing for the beatific vision that will be his at the moment of death."[8] The point is that the painting invites narcissistic identification, and we could isolate the single drive at work in the narrator by saying that he wishes to possess the same qualities as Sebastian. He not only admires Sebastian's beauty, he covets it. This impulse gains emphasis later in the novel, when the narrator develops the habit of striking the "Sebastian pose" by crossing his arms above his head whenever he is naked. This culminates in a second masturbation scene, in which the narrator strikes the Sebastian pose and finds himself aroused by his own armpits. The narrator accomplishes the illusion of eliminating his self-consciousness by merging with Sebastian and then auto-erotically directing his own desire toward this Sebastian-self.

But still we have to account for the masochistic nature of much of the solitary erotic activity described in *Confessions of a Mask*. Auto-eroticism is a notion we can understand, but auto-masochism seems paradoxical. Must there not be someone to wield the knife (or shoot the arrows)?

When reflecting on his creative projects, at all stages of his career, Mishima likes to cite these famous lines of Baudelaire:

I am the wound and the dagger!
I am the blow and the cheek!
I am the members and the wheel,
Victim and executioner![9]

This is a verse from Baudelaire's poem "L'Héautontimorouménos," a neologism that translates as "He Who Tortures Himself." These four lines express a profound psychic instability. Here is the modern artist as self-tormentor, suffering for the sake of the art that will, he hopes, make him immortal. Earlier we examined Mishima's image of the suffering poet as a person who aggressively displays his suffering in his works, as if turning himself inside out. But it would be wrong to say that his auto-masochism lacks an object: it is a one-man show, but it is one in which the performer has split himself in two. As I noted earlier, narcissists are like dual beings: Narcissus and his reflection; Dorian Gray and his portrait; Osamu and his mirror. We could add to that list: Hiraoka and Mishima. This trajectory toward dualism is also apparent in *Confessions of a Mask*, where, after his initial encounter with the painting, the narrator withdraws into narcissistic fantasy, taking Sebastian (both as image and legend) with him, and gradually turns Sebastian into a fantasized alternate self. This enables him to relish all the sadistic and masochistic potentialities of Sebastian from, as it were, exterior and interior, both as objective observer and as Sebastian-self.

Many commentators on *Confessions of a Mask* have built their reading of the Sebastian scene entirely around the narrator's anxious awareness of his physical deficiencies: his fragile health, his lack of athleticism, his anemia (induced, he suspects, by too much masturbation). His encounter with Sebastian convinces the narrator that he himself lacks the beautiful body needed to become a tragic hero. "His longing for a beautiful body is one with his longing for the tragic," writes one literary critic.[10] The key to becoming a hero, according to this view, is simply to solve the problem of deficiency, and this is the transformation chronicled in *Sun and Steel*.

No doubt that is all correct. But I think there are some additional issues here that cannot be resolved so easily, issues Mishima does not want to resolve and that relate to taboos that are implicit in his lifelong project.

Let us state the obvious: Sebastian is not Japanese. He is a Westerner, a white man. His sheer foreignness denotes an impossibility: no Japanese boy can become Sebastian. It is not just that the narrator feels shut out on account of his own deficiencies. Rather, by coveting this impossible image he *intentionally* shuts himself out, masochistically renders himself deficient. There are hints of racial awareness in the text, as when the narrator speaks enviously of Sebastian's "white and incomparable naked body" (*shiroi taguinai ratai*; 203). This expression is slightly odd. After all, Sebastian's body is not incomparably naked. The suggestion, presumably, is that his physique is incomparably athletic, or incomparably handsome, or muscular. Nonetheless, the idea that dominates this phrase is whiteness. White as the symbolic color of Sebastian's purity, of his incorruptibility, and of his saintly ascension to heaven; but also white as the actual color of his skin, of his foreignness, of his incomparably exotic otherness.

Sebastian is just one of many non-Japanese objects of the narrator's fantasies and fetishism, which include characters from the fairy tales of Oscar Wilde and Hans Christian Andersen, an unnamed Hungarian fairy tale, the notoriously decadent Roman boy-emperor Heliogabalus, the pirates of *Treasure Island*, and Joan of Arc, whom the narrator wishfully mistakes for a prince. *Confessions of a Mask* articulates a constant yearning for things that are not Japanese, an implicit disavowal of the narrator's own cultural identity. This theme of otherness dominates the first half of the novel. And, one might argue, it also dominates the second half, in which the narrator recounts his ultimately futile attempt to act out the role deemed appropriate for interacting with another other: woman.

Even when we turn to the local Japanese objects of the narrator's erotic interest, otherness remains a defining part of their allure. Hotel elevator boys. tramway ticket collectors. Street toughs. The "night-soil man" (a worker who empties the toilets). In every case here it is social status that marks the dividing line. The narrator is a pupil at the posh Peers School in Tokyo (as was Mishima); he will never have to punch tramway tickets or carry a bucket of shit. Like Sebastian, such people inhabit a realm of existence that is essentially forbidden to him, and a forbiddance is always simultaneously an enticement. As the narrator explains it, his "longing for tragic things" (*higeki-teki na mono e no akogare*) is directed toward "lives and events unfolding without any relation to me, at places for which my sensuality yearned yet from which I will forever be denied" (1:181). This too seems odd. How precisely are ticket collectors and street toughs "tragic"?

The answer again relates to death. We can think of social status as a measurement of proximity to death. The lower classes are closer to death, more likely to succumb to sickness or a workplace accident, more likely to be killed. (The narrator dreams about the street toughs being stabbed to death.) In other words, these objects of the narrator's lust are not individuals; they are symbols of a close proximity to blood, destitution, and destruction. What generates part of the narrator's erotic excitement is his anticipation of transgression. This time it is a betrayal of class, a breaking of taboo by touching one of these symbols of death, these things that are opposed to the natural, survivalist impulses of life.

Yet another taboo relates to Sebastian's profession. He is, after all, a soldier. The Sebastian episode in *Confessions of a Mask* appears to take place in the late 1930s. The scene is therefore the implicitly unpatriotic one of a feeble Japanese boy awed to the point of ecstasy by the sight of a brave and apparently indestructible foreign warrior on the eve of the Pacific War. Japanese magazines of that time offered endless images of brave Japanese youths in military uniform, while newspapers serialized samurai tales featuring beautiful youths laying down their lives or dying in tragic circumstances. But it is the Western military man who holds sway over Mishima's narrator.

What is more, Sebastian is no ordinary soldier. He is bodyguard to the Roman emperor. And why does Sebastian choose martyrdom? Because he cherishes a divine ideal that transcends the person of the emperor. Mishima does not press any of these points in *Confessions of a Mask*. But he does not need to. All the narrator's dreams of slaughter and youthful death gain deeper significance when considered against the background of the war, and it is not impossible to connect his reveries on Sebastian to the cults of self-sacrifice and suicide promoted in Japan during the war years. We may also note the abiding presumption in Japan that the most extreme manifestations of reverence for the emperor, the passionately expressed longings of young men to obliterate themselves and merge ecstatically with the exclusively male institution of the imperial throne, contain strong homosexual undertones.

One scholar writes, "It is hard to think of a novel that demonstrates more effectively than *Confessions of a Mask* the corrosion of identity that results from desire imagined as fully inherent and interior to the self."[11] It is a characteristic of Mishima's attitude that, for all his narcissistic concentration on himself, he disdains introspection. Seldom is he willing even to acknowledge, let alone discuss, the role of external forces in creating and shaping his desires and his fantasies. Yet in *Confessions of a Mask* he offers just enough evidence to show that the narrator's fascination with Sebastian derives not only from the erotic suggestiveness of the image itself (Sebastian's beauty and athleticism, his alluring posture, etc.) but from the implied transgression of various Japanese taboos that the narrator juxtaposes onto the image and the story of Sebastian, and which relate to issues of otherness, military power, the imperial throne, national identity, and race.[12]

To Drown in Life

Mishima leads us into the Sebastian scene via a seemingly unrelated description of a Japanese festival. This festival scene contains Mishima's first exploration of an idea that becomes more prominent in his work as his career progresses: the idea of an eroticism that is not concerned with sexual activity.

In traditional Japanese festivals, a crowd of people carry a portable shrine from the temple where it is stored and parade it through local streets. The ostensible purpose is to revitalize the *kami*, the deity who resides inside the shrine and, by association, to revitalize the people who carry the shrine or come to greet it. Festival time is traditionally considered to be an interruption of ordinary time, and it allows for a temporary suspension of social taboos. This, of course, is a fundamental principle of festivals everywhere, and although Japan's traditional festivals have lost much of their former symbolic importance, many are still effective in generating an atmosphere of transgression. Typically there is plenty of noisy behavior, public drunkenness, and shoving and jostling between strangers. If things get really heated you might also see a few punch-ups and a bit of property damage. The people carrying the shrine must endure a great deal of physical stress, and this is perhaps the distinguishing feature of the Japanese festival experience. The portable shrines, which rest on a series of long wooden poles, are often extremely heavy, and carrying one on your shoulder for half a day can be arduous and painful work.

The festival scene in *Confessions of a Mask* is presented as a traumatic boyhood memory of the narrator. There is nothing unusual about this. One of the taboos traditionally suspended during the Japanese festival is the taboo on frightening small children. Parents purposefully push their children to the front of the crowd and make them greet the rowdy procession, causing the children to scream and wail in fright. Festivals apparently used to be a lot more raucous than they are today, and memoirs by Japanese writers of Mishima's generation commonly feature recollections of these childhood "festival scares." In *Confessions of a Mask*, however, the little boy remains at a distance from the procession. Not only that, as the shrine approaches his house he runs indoors to his mother and watches the procession with her from the safety of a second-floor window. This, as most Japanese readers will know, is bad etiquette. People are expected to go out to greet the deity of the shrine, and it is considered disrespectful to look down on the shrine from a higher position. This means that in formal terms, the boy's encounter with the festival as described in *Confessions of a Mask* already has a transgressive quality.

Mishima's depiction of the shrine procession is an extravaganza of decadence and evil. Gazing from a safe distance at the sweaty, writhing, seminaked bodies of the young men carrying the shrine, the boy perceives a forbidden and deadly erotic realm that simultaneously tempts him and terrifies him:

> Even from this distance, the sight of the golden phoenix on top of the shrine, glittering and swaying above the commotion like a bird bobbing on waves, gave us a feeling of resplendent anxiety. The shrine was engulfed in a poisonous calm, like the air of the tropics, and seemed to tremble with a malevolent indolence on the naked shoulders of the young men who were carrying it. Inside the shrine, behind those crimson and white ropes, behind the black-lacquered golden rails and the tightly closed gilded doors, was a four-foot cube of darkness, a perfect block of empty night, bouncing and swaying on a clear summer's day. (1:197)

There is a tripart structure here that establishes the coordinates of a certain existential order: the menacing darkness of the shrine, the intoxicated congregation of men who bear it on their shoulders, and the boy who watches spellbound from an external position. This structure forms a central plot line of the life story that Mishima is writing for himself. It is a story of the transformation of one who *perceives* into one who *acts*. This transformation is inherently antinovelistic. The novelist, detached and ironical observer of the world, is alienated by his own excess of consciousness from the joyful intoxication of the masses, whom he envies for what he regards as their plain incapacity for self-reflection. (Mishima's envy of the lower classes, as we have already seen, is mixed with contempt.) Mishima determines to overcome this sense of isolation, to experience intoxication "from the inside," as he later says. This becomes a transition from thinking to nonthinking, as Mishima's quest for relatedness drives him away from literature, off the printed page, and into the realm of extreme physical experiences.

Ten years after writing *Confessions of a Mask*, Mishima participated as a festival shrine bearer for the first time. On a hot summer day in 1956 he joined a group of men from his local neighborhood in downtown Tokyo and carried the shrine through the streets. Mishima was by then thirty-one years old, and his interest in boxing and other "anti-literary" activities had already begun to show itself. His festival experience affected him deeply, and he analyzed it at length in an essay titled "On Intoxication" (Tōsui ni tsuite). Mishima was familiar with the comments on festivals in *The Birth of Tragedy*, where Nietzsche's word for festive frenzy, and also for the frenzy of artistic creation, is *Rausch*, which is usually rendered into English as "rapture" and into Japanese as *kōkotsu*. Mishima's preferred term *tōsui*, which contains the kanji for "drunkenness," is correctly translated as "intoxication." The difference in nuance is that *tōsui* implies an external trigger, something that has intoxicated the subject. Japanese readers will also be aware that *tōsui* is often used reflexively to denote a kind of narcissism: *jiko-tōsui*, literally "self-intoxication," another nuance that is perhaps not irrelevant to Mishima's choice of this term.

In his analysis Mishima pays no attention to the religious or symbolic functions of the festival. Instead he concentrates on the physical and sensate experiences of the people carrying the shrine and on the relationship between those experiences and the state of festive intoxication.

During the festival procession, Mishima observes, it is only the spectators who are able to see the shrine in all its glory. To the people carrying it, the shrine is simply a wooden pole striking their shoulders:

A person who acts never sees the totality. The power of the totality flows ceaselessly to its constituent parts, and the power that each individual is able to receive, not via thought but via action, amounts to one small part of the totality that is appropriate to the physical strength of that individual. That is why the shrine did not need to show itself completely to me. And yet in the depths of my mind I was feeling the shrine much more vividly than when I had watched as a spectator, because the shrine was now not only something being seen, it was a weight bearing down on me. This weight, this force pressing down on our shoulders, is the essence of the shrine; there is no other reason for the shrine to be so heavy. By taking this weight on my shoulder, I was able to forget the material structure of the shrine and thus become an additional part of that structure. I was a part of the shrine that was starting to dance on the shoulders of the people carrying it. This is how intoxication begins. (29:306)

That these banal observations hold such importance for Mishima indicates the extent to which the hypersensitivity of his self-consciousness was obstructing his tangible, physical experience of the world. This is the frightening existential condition he explores in the character of Osamu, who lacks a strong sense of his own existence. It seems that Mishima's self-consciousness was so intense as to be *anti-corporeal*, which is why, in the above passage, even the material reality of his own body appears to strike him as a new discovery.

Mishima then considers the relationship between the sounds of the festival and the physical movements of the participants. Here his remarks are more interesting:

I discovered that the intoxication of the shrine bearers comes from a mysterious coupling between the weight on their shoulders and the persistent rhythm of their shouts and foot movements. . . . It has long been understood that manual labor can be performed more efficiently in time to a rhythm . . . but the experience of carrying the portable shrine is rather different. The force we exert as we resist the weight of the shrine does not have the specific purpose that manual labor has, nor does it operate uniformly; for instance, you think you are about to need all of your strength, but then suddenly your body floats upwards and it turns out that just one-fifth of your strength is sufficient. The force that we exert does not obey us . . . but acts with a frightening wantonness of its own, swelling many times in size and then dropping to a tiny fraction of that size. This was the source of the freedom enjoyed by each of the shrine bearers, who were struck not just by the freedom of the force itself, but by a sense that various internal freedoms were also moving vibrantly with it. Incredible though it may seem, *I am making the shrine move.* (308–309)

Mishima makes much of the asynchrony between the shrine bearers' shouts and their steps; that is, between their repetitive chants, which are uttered both by the shrine bearers and by supervisors who are directing the procession, and the often chaotic and stumbling movements of the shrine bearers' legs and feet. Mishima observes that the chants, despite their rhythmic insistency, do not have any effect of imposing order on the movements of the shrine bearers, as might be expected. On the contrary, the chanting seems to generate, or at least intensify, a feeling of freedom and uninhibited release among the shrine bearers. In this odd fact, Mishima thinks that he is close to uncovering the essence of festive intoxication:

> The rhythmical chants are like the shrine's pulse. The chanting does not signify the rule of reason, and does not have any effect of imposing order on our movements. [. . .] Surprisingly, the exertion of physical force by the shrine bearers is closer to consciousness than their rhythmical chanting. The part of us that is chanting is less conscious, more blind, than the part of us that is exerting strength. Herein lies the paradox of the shrine: of the voices and movements and various physical expressions of the shrine bearers, those that are closest to orderliness are the ones farthest from consciousness. (310)

Mishima thinks that every person carrying the shrine feels this incompatibility between the constantly fluctuating exertion of strength and the constantly rhythmical chanting. Intoxication can only be reached, he says, when the shrine bearers overcome this feeling of incompatibility and accomplish a paradoxical fusion between order and disorder. "That fusion does come," writes Mishima. "We drown in life" (310).

The accuracy of Mishima's analysis is clear if we apply his observations to the event that today fulfills a social function similar to that of the traditional festivals: the rock concert (or rock festival). At a rock concert there is the same feeling of liberation from restrictions, with rough physical contact between strangers, a mass of sweaty bodies being crushed together, insistent rhythms and loud chants, and, at the most euphoric moments, all the people in the crowd seeming to merge into a vast organic unity. The paradox of prescribed wantonness, which Mishima sees in the Japanese festival, is observable here too. People going wild at a rock concert think they are escaping from social rules and restrictions. In a precise sense, however, they are never more conformist and obedient than at this moment: all moving as one, all making identical gestures, singing in unison, and, as is often also the case, enduring a fair amount of physical stress. What they have escaped is conformity to their individual selves. The point that Mishima wants to emphasize is that this intoxicating sense of freedom always requires a countervailing force that represses and subjugates self-consciousness. In order for us to experience the totality of life, our individuality must be destroyed.

The Blue of the Sky

There is one image from his experience of the festival that Mishima invests with special importance, returning to it again and again in his writings, so that it almost ceases to be an image and becomes a concept in its own right. In *Confessions of a Mask* the narrator recalls being horrified by the expression on the faces of the shrine bearers, "an expression of the most obscene and flagrant intoxication in the world" (1:199). In his later analysis of the festival Mishima refines his description: "The innocent eyes of the shrine bearers were directed toward a place I did not know. Those eyes, mixing sharpness with rapture, seemed to be looking at something that was beyond the imagination" (29:307). Another ten years later Mishima recalls the experience again in *Sun and Steel*, where he presents it as a conundrum: "I was puzzled by what the shrine bearers were looking at. I simply could not imagine what kind of intoxicating illusion they were witnessing at a moment of such intense physical stress" (33:511).

It is not easy to share Mishima's puzzlement here. Why does he assume that the shrine bearers are looking *at* something? After all, he has already described for us in careful detail the various psychological and physiological changes that accompany the festival experience: a loss of inhibition, a shared physical stress, a sense of communality, a paradoxical coexistence of freedom and constraint. Is it not more credible that festive intoxication derives from these things, rather than from visual stimuli? Is it not, in fact, a characteristic of festive euphoria that at the peak of the revelers' intoxication their eyes are looking at nothing?

Mishima claims that his own experience of carrying the shrine has finally taught him the true nature of the "intoxicating illusion" (*tōsui no maboroshi*) that the shrine bearers are supposedly looking at:

> They were looking at the blue sky. When the festival procession came out onto a wide road, the shrine bearers' entire field of view was consumed by a sky with autumn-like clouds of late summer, and this blue sky was vividly swaying, as if falling down then being lifted up high. I had never seen such a sky. As everyone knows, I am no poet. Shrine bearers know a blue sky that poets do not know. (29:307)

Mishima repeats this claim in *Sun and Steel*:

> They were simply looking at the sky. It was not an illusion that they were seeing, only the absolute blue sky of early autumn. But this was a very unusual blue sky, one I thought I would never see again, a sky that was ceaselessly swaying, at one moment strung up high, then at the next moment plunging down deep, as if lucidity and madness had come together. (33:511)

The internal contradictions of these statements threaten to undermine the answer that Mishima is proposing. There is "no illusion" in the eyes of the shrine bearers, he tells us; they are "simply" looking at the blue sky. But, as Mishima then describes it, there is nothing simple about this sky at all. It is an "astonishing" and "ceaselessly swaying" sky, an impossible union of "lucidity and madness" (*tōmei to kyōki*). The oscillation in the final sentence of the second passage seems intentionally sexual, the sky being first "strung up high" and then "plunging down deep." Mishima's language typically becomes eroticized like this when he writes about experiences that have affected him on a profound psychical level. What he goes on to describe in *Sun and Steel* is an illuminated awareness of the totality of life, an experience that, as he has argued in his essay on the festival, can only be obtained from a momentary disengagement of consciousness. Mishima now revels in his conviction that he has had nothing less than an insight into the tragic nature of reality:

> I had reached a point where there were no grounds for doubting that the blue sky I had seen through my own poetic intuition was identical with the blue sky reflected in the eyes of those ordinary young men of the neighborhood.... What I had seen was no personal hallucination; it had to be one piece of a clear communal vision.... It was only when I too managed to see this strange, sacred blue sky, which normally only that type of person can see, that I was finally able to believe in the universality of my own sensibility, that my thirst was quenched, and that my sickly blind faith in words was dispelled. At that moment I was participating in tragedy, in the totality of existence [*zen-teki na sonzai*]. (511–513)

Mishima's claim is not literally true. Shrine bearers are not looking at the sky. But it seems that only aerial imagery can adequately convey the plethora and abandon of the festival experience. Nietzsche says that festive revelers feel as if they are "about to fly dancing into the heavens."[13] Georges Bataille, Mishima's thoughts on whom we will examine in the next section, speaks of a "vertiginous loss of consciousness" at the festival and of a "flight into the regions where all individuality is shed."[14] Mishima, however, never fully relinquishes his clinical detachment from the scenes he is describing. His eye seems concentrated more on the faces of the men carrying the shrine than on the intoxicating blue sky, as if he is vicariously experiencing *their* intoxication.

Since Mishima stakes so much on his intoxicating illusion, we are entitled to reflect on the meaning of blue sky. On first consideration it seems a trite and shallow image, a staple of children's drawings and bad poetry. Blue sky, clear sky, happy sky. Blankness, vastness, infinity. Is Mishima's blue sky anything more than a cliché?

Gaston Bachelard offers a remark that can guide us: "The unsilvered mirror formed by a blue sky awakens a special narcissism, a narcissism of purity, of sentimental vacuity, and of free will. . . . The aerial Narcissus looks at himself in the blue sky."[15] Mishima's blue sky is like this. It is not really an aerial image at all, and the operation that Mishima accomplishes by deploying it is not an elevation but a reduction. Once again the condescension in his attitude is unmistakable: "Those ordinary young men of the neighborhood . . . only that type of person." It seems that the unliterary, unintellectual young men carrying the shrine have easier access to the tragic "totality of existence" than does the professional writer, who obsessively scrutinizes everything from an external vantage point. Mishima reduces the ecstatic shrine bearers to statues gazing with vacant eyes toward the heavens, and imagines that he sees himself in those eyes. Despite all the talk about community and unity, the dynamic of Narcissus is still operating here.

Though Mishima claims that his intoxicating vision of blue sky first came to him while carrying the festival shrine, we find many intimations of it in his earlier writings, always in a context of tragic affirmation. In a letter he sent to his school tutor and *Literary Culture* coeditor Shimizu Fumio in June 1942, the seventeen-year-old Mishima offered this reaction to news of attacks on Madagascar and Sydney by Japanese submarines, in which some of the Japanese crewmen had scuttled their vessels and killed themselves rather than be captured alive:

> I feel as though something has pierced my heart, something I cannot speak of in ordinary words. All I can do is shed tears of gratitude for the glorious virtues of His Majesty the Emperor. At the same time, I find it difficult to suppress a feeling of serenity, and I think I can hear the laughter of countless gods in a clear blue sky in the south. (38:554–555)

Here, to show that words are failing him, Mishima crumples melodramatically into a string of clichés. This is the artistic maneuver that characterizes the whole final phase of his career. Cliché appeals to Mishima precisely because it signifies a failure of language. He intends his blue sky to symbolize an experience that is beyond literature, beyond language, an experience beyond a limit where words *must* fail.

Twenty-five years later, in the closing pages of *Sun and Steel*, Mishima examines the letters written by pilots of the kamikaze squadron in their final days and hours, letters that are predictably riddled with clichés and ready-made slogans. Mishima is struck by the impersonal tone of the letters. Written by men who knew they were about to die, the letters are uncannily free of strongly individualistic expression. These are words, Mishima says, that "insistently called for superhuman action, which called for each man who wrote them to stake his life on his attempt to rise to their heights" (33:564). The heroism of the kamikaze, Mishima solemnly reminds us, demands a strict elimination of individuality: "To rise to a level at which the divine can be glimpsed, individuality must be dissolved" (568). In that sense the kamikaze pilot can be considered the antithesis of the novelist, whose vocation is founded on a bold assertion of individuality: "Unlike the words of a genius, the words of a hero must be the most magnificent and noble words selected from pre-existing concepts" (564).

As mentioned earlier, *Sun and Steel* ends with a poem in which Mishima is transformed into Icarus, soaring unstoppably upward:

> . . . driven only by an inexplicable, agonizing desire
> to go higher, to go nearer,
> to plunge into the blue of the sky . . .
> (582)

Mishima's blue sky is a sentimental vacuity that both symbolizes and celebrates this drive away from discursive meaning. It is the same sky glimpsed by Saint Sebastian, by the festival shrine bearers, by the kamikaze pilots, and by the suicidal samurai terrorists whose exploits will preoccupy Mishima during the final phase of his career. It is a knowingly clichéd metaphor for the wordless paroxysm of intoxication-orgasm-death.

Eroticism as Continuity

For his more theoretical discussions of eroticism, Mishima borrowed some ideas from the French novelist and philosopher Georges Bataille (1897–1962).

Mishima frequently expressed admiration for Bataille, in whom he clearly discerned elements of himself. Like Mishima, Bataille was an intellectual maverick. As a student he became a devout Catholic and at one point considered joining a monastery. By his late twenties he had lost his faith, but not his religiosity. He devoted himself to private study while pursuing a quiet career as an archivist. Yet he filled his writing (and, it seems, his private life) with scenes of extreme squalor and sexual excess. He was capable of declaring, "The man who admits the value of other people necessarily imposes limits upon himself."[16] Bataille was a founding member of a secret society that planned, and perhaps almost carried out, a ritual human sacrifice. To indicate the nature of his intellectual interests it is necessary only to list the titles of his major works of nonfiction: *On Nietzsche*

(1945), *Inner Experience* (1954), *Eroticism* (1957), *Literature and Evil* (1957), *The Tears of Eros* (1961).

As an erotic focal point, Bataille had a Saint Sebastian of his own. In his mid-twenties Bataille obtained a photograph, taken in Beijing in 1905, of the public execution of a young Chinese man who had been condemned to death for murdering an imperial prince. The gruesome method of execution was *lingchi*, or "chopping into pieces." The photograph captures an extraordinary moment. While his executioners busily carve off slabs of his flesh, the young man is gazing to the sky and smiling with a rapturous expression. Bataille was so stunned by this image that he reached the point of ecstasy. The photograph convinced him of a fundamental connection between religious ecstasy and eroticism, and it is this connection that he pursues in his writings. Bataille's convulsions of agony and ecstasy, his visions of "voluptuousness" in the extremes of pain and suffering, recall the raptures of early Christian mystics.[17]

Bataille is better known today than he was during his lifetime. His work did not gain much recognition outside France until the 1970s. Hence Mishima's interest in Bataille was prescient. Mishima wrote the following lines in 1969:

> In contemporary Western literature, the authors I follow most attentively are Bataille, Klossowski, and Gombrowicz. Their works seem to skip the nineteenth century and join the eighteenth directly to the twentieth, making a raw and violent link between metaphysics and the human flesh. These writers have many characteristics in common, such as their hostility to psychology, their antirealism, erotic abstractionism, straightforward symbolism, and their underlying cosmic vision. (34:710)[18]

The work that attracts Mishima's keenest interest is Bataille's *Eroticism*, a Japanese translation of which appeared in 1959. Mishima published an enthusiastic review (enthusiastic about Bataille, that is, but not about the Japanese translation, which Mishima excoriated), and cited lines from the book in several subsequent essays and interviews.

In his review Mishima hails Bataille as "the Nietzsche of eroticism" (34:111). In other words, Mishima recognizes that Bataille's research into eroticism was related to his loss of faith, to his experience of "the death of God," Nietzsche having proclaimed the death of God in print in 1882. Mishima thinks that what Bataille looked for in eroticism was "the dark reality of the death of God." It is not just that the twentieth-century world is atheistic, says Mishima. The point is that modern people now live in the shadow of God's death, in "the dark day after the death of that cherished existence." The death of God means that the religious-based taboos that cover sex are devalued; all are changed into "empty carcasses." Yet our memory of the dead God is "fresh and raw" (111).

The death of God—the decline of the importance of religious belief in shaping the moral and spiritual dimensions of our lives—is an issue that almost all modern Western thinkers addressed in one way or another. What fascinates and impresses Mishima about Bataille is his stubborn anachronism, his insistent yearning for the sacred in an increasingly profane world. Mishima writes, "Bataille coldly points out that man's rejection of God, man's desperate cry of the denial of God, is not really from the heart. That heart is the core of what Bataille calls eroticism" (34:719).

How then is God to be revived? How is the sacred to be made visible again?

By reading Bataille's *Eroticism* I realized that human life is discontinuity. Human beings are made by cellular division, by solid matter breaking apart, so that each individual body is a separate entity. Life is a state of division, a state of discontinuity. Discontinuity is the essence of life. This is a new way of thinking about life. How is it made continuous? By death, or by eroticism. When we glimpse death at the moment of eroticism, there is continuity. The most extreme manifestations of continuity are in religious festivals and sacrificial rituals. The idea is that human beings have no way of encountering this continuity other than by glimpsing death through eroticism. Bataille's philosophy was a revelation for me, and has given me much food for thought. (39:684)

The basic idea here is not new. Indeed, as the mention of festivals and ritual sacrifice suggests, it is possibly one of the most ancient of human ideas; Bataille had simply rearticulated it using modern jargon. Like animals, our primal urge is to survive. Unlike animals, we live in the foreknowledge that we will die. Human beings are animals that have become aware of themselves as discontinuous beings. This awareness causes us anguish. We long for the continuity we feel we have lost, and this longing is the impetus for all religions. But although we flee from death and everything that implies death, we recognize that death can have a restorative effect on our thinking. The sight of a dead body naturally compels us to take a transcendental perspective, to think beyond the realm of physical objects. By terminating individual life, death seems to assert the underlying continuity of being from which each of us has become disconnected. "When we glimpse death at the moments of eroticism," as Mishima puts it, "there is continuity." In other words, erotic experiences are those that accomplish the blending and fusion of separate individuals by bringing us into proximity to death, and thereby allow us to sense, if only for a moment, the underlying continuity of life.[19]

Sex is obviously an erotic experience. In the disequilibrium of the sex act there is a loss of self, a sensation of overflowing individual boundaries and momentarily dissolving into a unity. Simultaneously we experience an affirmation of life and an intimation of death. What Mishima finds interesting in Bataille, however, is his emphatic affirmation of *nonsexual* forms of eroticism.

Bataille had postulated that ancient religious sacrifices are related to the eroticism of sex, in that they evolved as ritualistic means for communities to "glimpse" death. Sacrifice is a ritual of destruction, but the destruction that this ritual brings about is not an annihilation. What sacrifice destroys in the victim is its "thingly" quality, the victim's condition of existing as a mere object. By the destruction of this condition, something more vital is laid bare. We have already encountered a similar line of thinking in Mizoguchi, who wants to remove the Temple of the Golden Pavilion from the mundane world of objects and turn it into a spectacular psychological event.

Bataille describes the effect of ritual sacrifice in the following terms:

> The victim dies and the spectators share in what his death reveals. . . .
> This sacredness is the revelation of continuity through the death of a discontinuous being to those who watch it as a solemn rite. A violent death disrupts the creature's discontinuity; what remains, what the tense onlookers experience in the succeeding silence, is the continuity of all existence with which the victim is now one. Only a spectacular killing, carried out as the solemn and collective nature of religion dictates, has the power to reveal what normally escapes notice.[20]

This is the passage in *Eroticism* that most intrigues Mishima, who likewise stresses the similarities between sex and sacrifice in regard to the dissolution of boundaries. "Rendering the sacrificial victim naked is the first step toward such a dissolution," Mishima writes, "and killing him is the completion. For in the ritual of sacrificial death we see the proof of the continuity of existence, and this is the foundation of our sense of the sacred" (31:412).

The French Japanologist Annie Cecchi, who examined Mishima's readings of various French writers, notes his affinities with Bataille while downplaying the possibility of influence. "Rather than speaking of the 'influence' of the French philosopher on the Japanese writer," says Cecchi, "it would be more precise to speak of a convergence, with Bataille's influence limited to a philosophical, theoretical, and globalizing formulation of fantasies that were already present in Mishima's imagination from his youngest years."[21] No doubt that is correct. Obviously Mishima did not need anyone to tell him about the congruence of eroticism and death. And as we have seen, the idea of eroticism as a breaking of the principle of individuation, an ecstatic union with the totality of the world, is present in his work right from the beginning. Nonetheless, it does seem to be true that Mishima's reading of Bataille opened his mind to the possibility of seeing eroticism not merely as sexual, decadent, or tragic, but also as a path to the sacred. While Mishima's earlier fictions contain scenes of *physical* eroticism (anguished muscles, tragically dying boys, frenzy of festival shrine bearers, etc.) and *emotional* eroticism (maidens swooning in voluptuous rapture, ecstatic bondings of siblings or lovers, etc.), the idea of attempting to express in his art an intimation of *sacred* eroticism had not, I think, occurred to Mishima prior to his reading of Bataille. A better way to state this, perhaps, would be to say that it had not previously occurred to Mishima that his lifelong yearning for intoxication, and for the tragic, could be categorized as a kind of religious feeling.[22]

It is plausible to read many of Mishima's major works from his final decade as experiments toward achieving effects that resemble manifestations of sacred eroticism: a glimpse of a transcendental collective continuity, an emphatic reinstatement of spirit as opposed to things, a fierce craving for divine intoxication that reason cannot curtail. Whether those experiments are successful is a question open to debate, but the intent is certainly there. "The greatest ambition of any novelist," Mishima tells us in one of his final essays, "is to render into language the silence that is God" (*kami to iu chinmoku no gengoka*; 34:711).[23]

The Rite of Love and Death

The emblem of Bataille's secret religious society was a line drawing of a naked and headless male figure, holding a dagger in one hand and a bleeding heart in the other, with his intestines exposed and a skull for a crotch. Decapitated (by himself?), with his insides exposed to the outside, and with death emanating from his reproductive organs, the figure is a monstrous contradiction, equally likely to generate awe or revulsion.

Mishima has no need to invent such an image. He can take one directly from Japanese tradition. The monstrous contradiction of the samurai warrior who commits suicide by seppuku, driving his sword into his own stomach and cutting open his bowels, serves perfectly as an epitome of Japanese erotic violence, of "assenting to life up to the point of death."[24]

Mishima first turned his attention to seppuku in a short story titled "Patriotism" (Yūkoku), which he began writing soon after reviewing Bataille's book on eroticism. "Patriotism" describes, in rigorous and graphic detail, the double suicide of a young army officer and his wife during the so-called February 26 Incident of 1936. This was a rebellion and attempted coup d'état in central Tokyo by some fourteen hundred troops of the Imperial Army commanded by around two dozen junior officers. The rebel officers were motivated by a passionate, near-religious veneration of the emperor as the living embodiment of Japanese identity and moral goodness. Their noble though vaguely defined aim was to restore the authority of the emperor by somehow rescuing him from the corruption and venality of his advisors, ministers, and bureaucrats. The emperor, however, was furious at the uprising, which he regarded as a mutiny, and ordered it to be suppressed. The rebels soon surrendered and their ringleaders were executed.

The poignancy of the failed rebellion lies in the fact that the rebels were betrayed by the object of their own religious faith. This is precisely the type of situation that fascinates Mishima: the tragic paradox of one who places his faith in an absolute existence or absolute value, only to be rejected and punished by it.[25]

If the word "patriotism" seems incongruous in these circumstances, that is because "patriotism" is not an ideal equivalent of the Japanese word *yūkoku*, which Mishima uses for his title. *Yūkoku* literally signifies "grieving for one's country" and suggests the melancholy or distress of those who believe their country is heading in a wrong direction. In his newspaper articles Mishima expressed a strong dislike for the more conventional word *aikokushin* ("love of one's country"), which was coined in the late nineteenth century as a convenient Japanese equivalent for the Western concept of patriotism. Precisely for that reason, according to Mishima, the word *aikokushin* lacks "etymological pedigree" and "stinks of bureaucrat meddling." Specifically, Mishima objects to the first kanji, *ai* (love), by pointing to its Christian origins. Christian love implies a boundless and unconditional sentiment, he says, as in the phrase "love of mankind," and cannot be legitimately applied in the Japanese context. Since Japan is an "ethnically homogenous nation," he declares, blithely disregarding the presence in Japan of Koreans and other ethnic minorities, Japanese people tend to think of Japan as "intrinsic" and "noumenal" (*sokuji-teki*, a term often used by Japanese philosophers to denote the "thing-in-itself"). Instead of the word *ai* Mishima prefers the word *koi*, which has been used in Japan since ancient times to denote feelings of sensual longing and erotic love. "*Koi*, not *ai*, is the highest emotional expression for a Japanese person," says Mishima. Unlike Christian love, *koi* is not benevolent; *koi* does not give, it wants, and this is the crucial difference: "For the Japanese people, Japan can be an object of *koi* but not of love." Mishima expresses the basic emotion of Japanese people toward Japan with the phrase *wareware wa tonikaku Nihon ni koi shiteiru*, which could be translated as "We have sensual longings for Japan" (34:648–650).

According to Mishima's way of thinking, then, the Japanese title that is conventionally rendered into English as "Patriotism" already contains erotic implications.

Mishima based the two characters in his story on actual people: a lieutenant named Aoshima Kenkichi and his wife Kimiko, who committed suicide together on the evening of February 28, 1936, the third day of the rebellion. Though the lieutenant did not participate in the rebellion, he supported the rebels' cause, and he chose to die rather than obey an order to open fire on them. The Aoshimas killed themselves in the old samurai manner: the lieutenant stabbed himself in his stomach, and his wife cut one of the carotid arteries in her throat.[26]

Mishima pays no attention to the events of the rebellion itself and concentrates entirely on the couple's suicide. Hence from start to finish the story maintains a stifling intensity. Torn between duty and honor, the lieutenant resolves to die. He informs his wife of his decision. She agrees to die with him. They make love for what they know will be the last time, and then they stab themselves to death.

In a note on the story Mishima writes of wanting to investigate the "profound confusions [konton], complexes [fukugō], and complications [sakusō] in the national consciousness of the Japanese people" (34:37). Since the seppuku suicide ritual is a fact of Japanese tradition, that statement is a legitimate one. Nonetheless, it would probably be more truthful to say that Mishima's intention was to rekindle those confusions and complications rather than to elucidate them. Within his oeuvre "Patriotism" has a pivotal significance. For the first time in Mishima's work a Japanese soldier takes center stage. And like Sebastian, this soldier must die because he has committed the supreme transgression of defying an imperial command. For the first time, also, there is the intimation of the sacred, in the form of the divine emperor.

"Patriotism" thus attempts to establish a trinity of eroticism, death, and the sacred, in the manner defined by Bataille, within a modern Japanese setting. As Mishima explains it in a note, "I managed to achieve a scenario where the lieutenant and his wife die a perfect death, in which their supreme physical pleasure and their supreme physical suffering are united under a single principle, and I used the rebellion as a background to make that blissful result possible" (34:310–311). In other words, the formula for eroticism here entails a fusion of extreme pleasure with extreme pain under the gift of death, a gift that is guaranteed to the couple by their ideology of absolute reverence for the emperor.

We can see that there are tensions between these elements. Mishima does his best to smooth over the apparent contradictions between patriotic devotion and sexual indulgence. Even in the "intense madness" of their lovemaking, we are told, the lieutenant and his wife are "frighteningly somber and serious" (20:15). Not for a moment do they lose sight of the "moral basis" of their lives, and each morning they bow solemnly before a photograph of the emperor. They live in the certitude that they are "protected by the solemn authority of the gods," and they experience "a joy that made their bodies tremble' (16). When they agree to die together, the lieutenant is confident that there is nothing "impure" (*fujun*) in the surge of joy that he and his wife feel at the moment of their decision. Their final night of lovemaking will be "legitimate pleasure" guaranteed by a "complete and impeccable morality." Not only will there be no contradiction between the lieutenant's sexual desire and the sincerity of his patriotism, the two converge into one: "Was it death he was now waiting for, or a mad ecstasy of the senses? The two seemed to overlap, as if the object of his sexual desire was death itself" (24).

In an early essay Mishima had insisted that love suicide is a matter of form, not feeling. Emphasis on form, he argues there, is a general characteristic of Japanese literary depictions of suicide scenes: "Even the great Kabuki and Bunraku dramatist Chikamatsu Monzaemon [1653–1725] does not deal with the psychology of love suicide at the instant of death, only with the process that leads the young couple to it" (27:112). For Mishima, the unnaturalness of youthful death is a quality it shares with art. In the same essay, his description of the beautiful "logic" of love suicide recalls the idea of "choosing one's fate" that he identified in his remarks on Wilde's *Salome*:

> The miracle that two people who were meant to die fell in love with each other in life seems to represent a kind of salvation from the unknowable darkness of our world. We idealize those who die in love suicide as if they were gods with an intimate knowledge of fate. Their love was the cause of the deaths, but it is not strange to think that their fated death was the cause of their love. (27:112)

In "Patriotism" Mishima inserts a similar comment about such "knowledge of fate" (*unmei no chie*) in his description of the couple's wedding photograph:

> After the couple had killed themselves, people often took out this photograph and gazed at it, and reflected sadly that a union of two such beautiful people could only have ended in tragedy. Looking at the photograph after the suicide, it almost seemed as if the young couple was fully aware of the deaths that lay ahead of them. (20:14)

Though Mishima borrows his scenario from the events of 1936, the beauty of love suicide is an idea that belongs to ancient Japanese tradition, as does the beautification of seppuku. One of Mishima's early short stories fictionalizes the ill-fated incestuous love affair of fifth-century Crown Prince Karu and his half-sister Princess Sotoori, whose death scene Mishima calls "the oldest love suicide in Japan" (27:113). Japan's medieval war chronicles are full of glorified scenes of double suicide and mass suicide. Samurai embrace each other, weep, write death poems, and tearfully plunge their swords into their bellies; or, after being defeated in battle, they mutually proclaim their loyalty as they fall onto each other's swords. It is probably true to say that over the centuries, double seppuku suicides have been more frequent in Japanese literature than they have in Japanese reality. Nonetheless it is legitimate to speak of a tradition of double seppuku suicide in Japan and to connect this tradition to a particular kind of eroticism. Away from the battlefield, double seppuku suicides by samurai, and sympathy suicides by their friends and servants, often exposed homoerotic attachments or entanglements. After the execution (by compulsory seppuku) of Shogun Regent Toyotomi Hidetsugu in 1595, more than twenty of his young male admirers cut their stomachs to follow him into the afterlife. In the seventeenth century a trend of double seppuku suicides among teenage samurai boys caused problems for authorities. Love suicides of young couples, who stab each other to death because they cannot be together in life, were a popular trope in the plays of Chikamatsu. The abolition of the samurai class in 1871 made seppuku an anachronism. Yet the most infamous double suicide of modern times occurred in 1912, when army general Nogi Maresuke and his wife Shizuko stabbed themselves to death on the day of the funeral of the Meiji emperor.

What needs to be understood from all this is that seppuku was a practice that had long been officially banned and shrouded in taboos; it was a defiant atavism that also possessed a strongly erotic suggestiveness.

This was especially true for Japanese men of Mishima's generation, who had been subjected to the extreme militarist propaganda of the war years. During the 1960s a novelist named Uno Kōichirō (1934–) published a series of samurai action novels featuring highly eroticized suicide scenes. Like Mishima, Uno had been raised in a middle-class family that claimed samurai ancestry, and he shared Mishima's fascination with the seppuku ritual. In an article he published shortly after Mishima's death, Uno recalled the surge of sexual excitement he had experienced as a boy during the war when his mother had sternly informed him that a samurai boy must be ready to cut his own stomach if necessary. "Even now I cannot forget the strange sensation I felt at that moment," wrote Uno. "It was clearly a feeling of sexual arousal. When I imagined myself cutting open my stomach, my penis got stiff. I couldn't understand why my mother was able to talk openly about something so shocking, so sexual." At the same time, Uno speaks of seppuku in reverential terms as a solemn event of "religious" significance. For a

Japanese man to cut open his stomach is "to return to the ancient gods . . . to our forgotten ancestors." Uno also notes the symbolic equivalence between a samurai who stabs himself and the image of Saint Sebastian pierced by arrows: each sensationalizes the implicitly homoerotic notion of a man who does not resist the violent penetration of his own body.[27]

"Patriotism" puts the sexual symbolism of self-disembowelment on flagrant, almost pornographic display. Mishima depicts the lieutenant's seppuku as a mega-ejaculation in the course of which the lieutenant discharges every last drop of fluid in his body: sweat, saliva, tears, vomit, blood, and bile. At the "climax," the lieutenant musters his strength to finish himself off, flinging back his head as, with some assistance from his wife, he drives the blade of his sword through his neck. Then he crumples, dead and emptied.

As Mishima explains in another essay, the violent exposure of the innards traditionally has meaning in Japan, in that "a person's sincerity is said to be symbolized by their internal organs." For that reason Mishima calls seppuku a means of "exhibitionistic persuasion" (34:92). The internal organs, he says, share a distinctive quality of the reproductive organs, namely, that they "have nothing resembling individuality about them." It is this "non-individual quality" (*mukosei*), says Mishima, that strikes us as shocking and obscene. Exposure of the internal organs "upsets the sense of security we feel about the body as a *thing* and aggravates our fear of seeing the body from the inside." When forced to look at internal organs violently exposed in this way, we are confronted with the reality of our "non-individual, universal bodily existence" (94). Mishima argues that Japanese tradition and legends have equated sincerity with this destruction of individuality and this exposure of the body's universality.

Mishima's growing interest in the impact of visual effects was one of the factors that turned him away from novels, from literary fiction, and toward film and public theater. Within the text itself, "Patriotism" relentlessly emphasizes the act of looking. Every action of the couple is regulated by a protocol of spectacle. As the lieutenant shaves his face for the final time, he gazes at his reflection in the mirror and, with the same morbid narcissism we have seen in other Mishima characters, imagines how his face will look after he is dead. Before he and his wife make love for the last time, the two of them scrutinize each other's bodies. The lieutenant tells himself how fortunate he will be "to have every moment of his death observed" by his wife's beautiful eyes. Just before he stabs himself he fixes his eyes on his wife, and watches her watching him. Once her husband is dead, she sits before a mirror to do her makeup. Her last thoughts also relate to looking, as she wonders how their two bodies might appear to the people who will discover them.

Mishima's American biographer John Nathan sneers and cringes through his reading of "Patriotism" as if he is peering into the mind of a singular pervert. Nathan recognizes that the couple's devotion to their transcendent notion of the emperor is "very like if not identical to religious faith," but he is repelled by the graphic violence, which he regards as gratuitous and meaningless.[28]

Along with much of the English-language commentary on Mishima's own death, this strikes me as a case of cultural blindness. For two thousand years the most sacred image of Western civilization has been a blood-drenched martyr, horribly beaten and tortured, nailed to a wooden cross and dying in the most extreme agony. The holy buildings of Europe are filled with depictions of gruesome martyrdoms and executions. What is the meaning of all this graphic and gratuitous violence? That, essentially, was the question posed by Bataille, whose anthropological investigations took him far beyond Christian Europe to African voodoo and the Aztec hecatombs. The seppuku ceremony, and the stylized eroticism that adheres to it, may be peculiar to Japan, but the belief that some profound truth about existence is revealed in the spectacle of sacrifice appears to be universal. In Nietzsche's words:

> Things never proceeded without blood, torture, and victims, when man thought it necessary to forge a memory for himself. The most horrifying sacrifices and offerings, the most repulsive mutilations, the cruelest rituals of all religious cults—all these things originate from that instinct which guessed that the most powerful aid to memory is pain.[29]

At the core of the matter is a tragic view of the world. Mishima shares the conviction of Nietzsche and Bataille, and centuries of mystics and ascetics before them, that authentic knowledge of reality is bound to be painful, and that the pain, moreover, is part of such knowledge. "Purity and cruelty are located in the same dimension," says Mishima, and the only way to know fully the totality of life is to seek "the transcendence that lies beyond the cruelest things in this world" (40:746).

In "Patriotism," by forcing readers and viewers' attention on a graphic depiction of the bloody ritual of seppuku, the effect Mishima aims for, he explains in one of his notes, is that of "a supernatural ritual of exaltation, destruction, and rebirth" as in "a ritual sacrifice of agrarian rites" (34:46). As Mishima sees things, the bloody spectacle of seppuku manifests a form of beauty that "contemporary ethics and modern liberal humanism have outlawed," and yet which appeals to impulses deep in the human psyche:

In Japan's classical literature, crimson leaves and cherry blossoms are metaphors for bloodletting and death. Deeply embedded in the consciousness
of the Japanese people, for centuries these metaphors have trained us to
apply aesthetic formats to our physical fears. Over the changes of history, we have maintained a balance between these two ideas by adjusting
the emphasis of our calculation. During times when there was an excess
of bloodshed and death, such as in war, people's minds inclined toward
crimson leaves and cherry blossoms, and people used traditional aesthetic
forms to consume their very real fears. In peaceful times, such as the one
we are living in now, our calculation naturally inclines in the opposite
direction, and it thus becomes more difficult to apply conceptual and aesthetic formats to bloodshed and dead bodies. This is a problem that cannot
be solved with modern imports like humanism. (32:573)

Regular targets of Mishima's ire in his final decade were humanist thinkers (Mishima often derisively characterizes them as "pale-faced" or "anemic"
thinkers) who reject the irrational side of nature. Prominent among them was
the French existentialist philosopher Jean-Paul Sartre (1905–1980), for whom
Mishima expressed intense loathing, though this was as much for Sartre's physical ugliness as for his existentialism. Mishima borrows the terminology of Bataille
to assert the futility of attempts by humanists like Sartre to resist the irrational
forces inherent in human nature. What Bataille calls an awareness of the discontinuity of life, Mishima equates with the modern idea of nihilism. It is against
this nihilism, he says, that modern intellectuals are resisting. All the different
forms of what Mishima generically calls "intellectualism" (*shuchi-shugi*), in which
he includes rationalism, scientific positivism, humanism, and existentialism, are
merely our most recent attempts to overcome the nihilistic despair that arises
from our awareness of ourselves as discontinuous beings:

> The limitations of the capabilities of intellectualism are the limits of our
> human ability to withstand the discontinuity of life. Time and again,
> intellectualism has attempted to extend those limits, but always without
> success. Existentialism is yet another form of the extremes of this intel-
> lectualist endeavor. But it cannot save us from the ancient bloody darkness
> that unites death, eroticism, and the sacred. (34:413)

"Patriotism" was Mishima's first attempt to manifest this ancient and bloody
darkness in his work. As he explains it, his aim was to recreate an "anti-civilized
ritual" (*han-bunmei-teki na richuaru*) that would excite "the most primal and

animalistic human emotions." By delivering to those who watch it "a shock that makes them want to cover their eyes," he hoped to achieve an effect whereby "the spectators are reborn with the protagonists" (34:47). Mishima has taken the familiar theory that art originated as a condensed abstraction of religious rituals (ritual here being understood not as a form of prayer but as an expression of intense emotions) and applied it in reverse by making his art into a ritualized enactment. Hence the lieutenant and his wife are not characters in the modern fictional sense. They are like masked actors performing the movements of a primal scene. "Patriotism" does not *represent* anything. It is an *enactment* of intense emotions.

There is more than one version of "Patriotism." At one point Mishima apparently planned to write a Kabuki adaption of the story. Instead he made a short film version in which he himself played the role of the lieutenant, dramatically cutting open his stomach and expiring in a vast pool of blood. Mishima took his film to the 1966 Tours Film Festival, where it played under the English title *The Rite of Love and Death* and generated all the controversy he could have hoped for. In 1969 Mishima gave his approval to a ballet staging of "Patriotism" by contributing a program note for the performance.

Much less well-known is an alternative version of the story that features a pair of male lovers. Mishima gave this version the title "Execution of Love" (Ai no shokei) and published it secretly under a pseudonym ("Sakakiyama Tamotsu") in *Adonis*, a magazine for gay men, in October 1960. For many years after Mishima's death his estate denied that he was the author of this work, begrudgingly acknowledging its authenticity only after the discovery of Mishima's handwritten manuscript in 1996.

"Execution of Love" is a graphic description of a bloody double suicide, presented as erotica. A cruel and beautiful teenage boy comes to the home of his schoolteacher, a man in his late twenties, and orders him to commit seppuku. The teacher is horrified, yet excited:

> A beautiful boy has given me the gift of death. Is there a more terrible or more joyful way to die than this? No matter how long I live, I will never have an opportunity for a greater death than this. It is as if my whole life up until now has been constructed just for the purpose of this joyful death. Yes! I'll show him a horrific, heart-rending seppuku! I'll show this boy how a man cuts open his stomach! (43:46)

The boy maintains his cold demeanor, but secretly he is just as excited as the teacher. "At my command a grown man will go quietly to his death," he thinks to himself. "What bliss!" The two then begin their preparations for the seppuku ritual. They admire each other's physiques and briefly embrace, but they do not have sex. The boy forbids the teacher to die quickly: death must be as painful as possible. The teacher stabs himself in his stomach and cuts a line across it. His blood and innards begin to spew out. At that moment, the boy suddenly drops his pose of cruelty and confesses his love for the teacher. The teacher therefore dies both in agonizing pain *and* in delirious joy. The story ends with the boy about to drink poison and collapse over his teacher's lifeless body. The boy's final thoughts: "People will say that ours was a most enigmatic love suicide!" (53).[30]

Self-Deification

There is one more Sebastian in Mishima's literary writings for us to examine. In 1965, with the assistance of a young scholar of French literature named Ikeda Hirotarō, Mishima made a Japanese translation of *Le Martyre de Saint Sébastien*, a five-act play written in French in 1911 by the Italian author Gabriel D'Annunzio (1863–1938). The project seems to have held special importance for Mishima. This was one of very few occasions in his career when he collaborated on a writing project, and he worked on it for twelve months, by his standards an abnormally long time. Knowing no French, Mishima initially searched for a German or English version of the play; since none existed, he taught himself French. Rather than offering the book to his usual publishers, Mishima signed a one-off contract with a publishing house specializing in art catalogues. The book was published in 1966 in a decorative box edition colored in red and gold. In addition to the translation of D'Annunzio's play, the book contained an afterword by Mishima, a long critical analysis by Ikeda, and Mishima's selection of some fifty reproductions of Sebastian paintings by medieval and Renaissance artists. The only criterion for his selection, Mishima admitted, was beauty: "I discarded all the ugly Sebastians, even if they had high artistic merit" (34:240). Mishima never attempted to stage a performance of his translation of the play. He seems to have considered the book complete in itself. It was an art object, an offering in prose, poetry, and pictures to his beloved erotic icon.

D'Annunzio was a popular author in Japan during the war years, and even today his works are probably better known to Japanese readers than to English readers. Poet, playwright, novelist, and proto-fascist, his affinities with Mishima are so striking that it seems odd that they have not yet been studied in detail. The hallmarks of D'Annunzio's work are a morbid sensibility, lush and ornate language, a love of cruelty and sadism, and the exaltation of a decadent beauty that blossoms in death. I have noted Mishima's tendency to think of artistic creation as something inherently malicious and destructive. A similar notion seems to have preoccupied D'Annunzio, who said of himself, "There is always something carnal, something resembling carnal violence, a mixture of cruelty and intoxication, which accompanies the act of generation in my brain."[31]

In his afterword to D'Annunzio's play Mishima is no longer interested in Sebastian as a legendary Christian saint, and instead devotes his attention to the eroticization of Sebastian during later centuries:

> Of so many Christian martyrs, why must Sebastian alone be a young and handsome soldier? Why must he alone be killed by countless arrows shot into his beautiful flesh? And why is his historical actuality like a shadow that is forever beyond our grasp? (34:189)

The real Sebastian, Mishima now argues, is the one given to us by the Renaissance artists. It was as if they were revealing a secret that had been hidden in the legend of Sebastian ever since the third century. As he says this, Mishima makes a dramatic switch to the first-person plural, as if he and his readers are participants in this revelation: "Our recollections and dreams converged like a bundle of light rays on one particular period in history, at which point an entirely new portrait was inserted, one that had been miraculously created by a concentration of group psychology" (188). According to Mishima's reading, the Renaissance Sebastian was not truly Christian; in his symbolic function he was an anti-Christian figure. The new tendency to depict him as "an embodiment of the heroic and lyrical beauty of a young man going to his death" turned Sebastian into "an extreme expression of pagan sensuality" (189). His spectacular execution scene came to symbolize the ritual killing of a pagan god, who is sacrificed as the last sensual expression of a dying culture. Sebastian therefore personifies "the beauty, the youth, the flesh, the sensuality of the ancient world that was made definitive by being executed by Christianity" (190).

D'Annunzio originally conceived his play as a decadent extravaganza, and he takes every opportunity to relish the bloodletting:

> Sebastian: The Lord of Blood—He is the God I have chosen. I have staked my soul on Him, and much more than my soul!
> Emperor: This pale-faced young man desires blood. Blood and suffering and darkness. Very well, then he shall have it! Like an urn filled to the brim with red wine, let his god be drowned in blood up to its crown. Let us teach him the secrets of sacred sacrifice! (25:664)

We can see how such indulgences would please Mishima. But D'Annunzio goes even further, amplifying the melodrama by depicting the emperor as infatuated with Sebastian. Consequently this tale of martyrdom and death also becomes a perverse type of love story. To save Sebastian from the agony of public execution, the emperor tries to kill him mercifully by strangling him with flower garlands, but Sebastian pushes the emperor away. The execution scene reaches an atmosphere of hysteria. Even the archers are besotted by Sebastian's beauty. When they tearfully hesitate to shoot their former captain, Sebastian implores them to prove their love with their arrow tips: "You must complete my fate!" After the archers let loose their first volley of arrows he cries out, "Again! Again! He who wounds me the deepest loves me the most!" (709–710).

In his commentary, Mishima is intrigued by the play's success in synthesizing two contrary worlds, pagan and Christian. Sebastian is supposed to epitomize the Christian spirit, but the play subordinates this notion to the pagan cult of physical beauty, which dominates every scene. By transforming Christian saint into pagan idol in this manner, the play achieves an effect similar to that of Reni's painting. In addition, Mishima argues, the play confounds the opposing roles of the protagonists. The (pagan) emperor confuses the (Christian) Sebastian with the (pagan) figure of Adonis, yet the emperor shows (Christian) tenderness toward Sebastian in attempting to save him.

Mishima defines the tensions generated within this strange love triangle using the Greek terms Agape and Eros, pointing to a conflict between the archers' comradely love for Sebastian (Agape) and their sensual love of his physical beauty (Eros). In an earlier scene Sebastian had incurred the emperor's wrath by destroying some stone pagan idols. But now, says Mishima, Sebastian "destroys himself as an idol" (34:196). To accomplish this, he demands from his men "a cruel form of Agape." This is not something they can easily understand. For Sebastian, however, "only Agape in this cruel form" can comprehend "his aspiration for the glory of martyrdom" and accomplish "his passion for death and resurrection" (196). The archers, "obedient only in accordance with a common feeling of Eros," hesitate and are unwilling to shoot. For this reason Sebastian, their former captain, must *command* them to execute him. Conversely, the emperor, whose erotic love of Sebastian's beauty has already been made clear, well understands that he must order Sebastian's execution "in order to ease him into the pagan world" (196). This results in a highly paradoxical situation where the emperor and Sebastian give the *same* command to the archers. This is how Mishima schematizes what he calls the "ironical tragic structure" of this relationship between the emperor and the martyr:

No matter how much Sebastian denies it, his external beauty belongs to the pagan world. He could almost be a pagan god. The emperor and the whole Roman Empire therefore have no qualms in awarding Sebastian regal power and divine status, even though they cannot understand his self-denial, his fundamental denial of his own *raison d'être*. But since it is also clear that the right to such a denial belongs only to one who possesses absolute pagan youthful beauty, the emperor can do nothing but look on helplessly as Sebastian destroys himself. The emperor must go along with the destruction of the ideal beauty of the ancient world that he cherishes so dearly. Moreover, since the emperor himself belongs to that ancient pagan world, Sebastian's death not only entails the destruction of an idol of beauty of the ancient world as represented by Sebastian's body, it also means that the emperor is assisting in the self-denial and self-destruction of his own world. (34:195–196)

In this reading Mishima outlines a view of sacrifice that is different from Bataille's. Now it is not just a matter of the executioner and the witnesses glimpsing continuity in a violent release of energies as the victim is ritually sacrificed. Here, as Mishima wants us to see it, the executioner and the witnesses also suffer a loss. Sebastian dies by order of the emperor. But the spiritual power that drove Sebastian to transgression, condemnation, and death originated within himself. The sacrificial victim generates a paradoxical situation by openly condemning himself. He is sacrificed *to* the old (pagan) world *at* its expense. The executioner and witnesses are simultaneously bedazzled and perplexed by this spectacle, which once again we might call the spectacle of a monstrous contradiction.

In this essay on D'Annunzio's play it is clear that Mishima is trying to encourage one possible interpretation of his own spectacular death a few years later; namely, not just as a defiant self-execution in a spirit of remonstrance, but as a sacrificial offering that marks the passing of an era. The interpretation cannot be wholly identical, of course, since in the case of Saint Mishima it is the old world that he claims to favor. But even that point may be moot. As Mishima says, for all the views Sebastian expresses to the contrary, he is pagan in spite of himself. A similar contradiction is easily projectable onto Mishima, as he himself must surely have recognized. Just as Mishima encourages us to think of Sebastian as simultaneously embodying both the opposing worlds, old and new, we can view Mishima in similar terms, as a complicated and uneasy entanglement of old and new worlds, sacrificed at a pivotal historical moment when one appears to cede irrevocably to the other. It seems that this is one way (just one of myriad ways, of course) in which Mishima hopes that his story will be told.

"In me," declares Mishima, "beauty, eroticism, and death are all connected in a single line" (40:746). The intuition at the core of his work is, needless to say, the fundamental unity of eroticism and death. And since all erotic longing points to death, Mishima regards sexual classifications as superfluous. As we saw in *Confessions of a Mask*, in his younger years Mishima had studied the scholarly literature on sexuality. But he was always suspicious of scientific attempts to categorize or explain sexual behavior, and he disliked sexual labels. Although in his mature writings Mishima does occasionally use terms such as "sadomasochism," "fetishism," and other pieces of Freudian jargon, he attaches no precise content to them. "While these terms invented by Viennese scientists are convenient to use," he writes, "in no way do they encapsulate specific conditions that actually exist" (35:287). Mishima thinks that sex is too volatile and mercurial to submit to rigid classifications: "A single act such as fellatio could serve as a metaphor for an infinite number of sexual tendencies, as many as we might care to imagine" (284). The sole constant in this quest for pleasure is a dream of unconsciousness, a yearning to lose one's sense of oneself as an object in the world, to achieve an intoxication that leads to oblivion. The final manifestation of the erotic, Mishima writes, is always "a melting and bonding with the totality of the world" and a consequent "ultimate destruction of the self." There are no exceptions. The greatest orgasm imaginable would kill you with its violent ferocity. In the end, says Mishima, all sexual desires, "even the unique perversions . . . meet in the same place" (279).

CHAPTER 6

The Totality of Culture

The Japanese are, to the highest degree, both aggressive and
unaggressive, both militaristic and aesthetic, both insolent
and polite, rigid and adaptable, submissive and resentful of
being pushed around, loyal and treacherous, brave and timid,
conservative and hospitable to new ways.

Ruth Benedict, The Chrysanthemum and the Sword

In May 1960, while on a visit to New York, Mishima appeared in a CBS televi-
sion interview with the American playwright Tennessee Williams. Mishima's
main contention during this interview was that Japanese culture is characterized
by "a mixture of very brutal things and elegance."[1] If we were to condense the
bewildering performative strategies of Mishima's final decade into a single sound
bite, this would probably be it. His contention is not merely that Japanese culture
contains both elegant and barbaric elements, a claim that could probably be made
for every culture on earth, but that the elegant poise that typically distinguishes
Japan's traditional cultural forms is, almost by necessity, counterbalanced and
sustained by a violent, systematic cruelty. From "Patriotism" onward, Mishima
devotes his indefatigable energies to articulating this mixture of brutality and
elegance. He strives to express it in his novels and plays, to enact it in his film
appearances, to theorize it in his lectures and essays, and to exemplify it in his
own persona.[2]

Mishima's preoccupation with identifying Japan's distinctive cultural traits
was fairly typical of his time. By 1960 the success of Japan's postwar resurgence
was evident. But the nation's rapid economic transformation had outpaced the
various psychological transformations that were necessary to support it, and many
Japanese were troubled by a sense of cultural confusion. Japan's new constitution, written by American military lawyers, had renounced forever Japan's rights
to maintain armed forces and wage war. In the land of the samurai it was now
unconstitutional to be a warrior. Meanwhile, the status of Japan's security treaty
with the United States had become a fiercely contentious issue. On top of all this,

the year 1968 was the centenary of the Meiji Restoration: modern Japan was turning one hundred years old. The approach of the centenary year naturally prompted
a great deal of self-reflection, as intellectuals and social pundits debated the state
of the nation. Everyone could agree that Japan had changed dramatically, but
what had been the cost of those changes? To what extent had modernization and
"Americanization" diminished Japan's traditional ways and cultural integrity?
What did it really mean, now, to call oneself Japanese and to speak of "Japanese
values"?

Mishima was an enthusiastic participant in this debate. As is well-known,
he promoted a reactionary agenda of stereotypical Japaneseness, which incorpo-
rated bits and pieces from ancient myth, classical literature, wartime propaganda,
ultra-nationalist zealotry, Buddhist philosophy, the tradition of reverence for the
imperial household, martial arts and swordsmanship, samurai ethics, yakuza
machismo, and a great many other things. One Japanese commentator sardoni-
cally dubbed this Mishima's "encyclopedic Eastern comeback."[3] With his often
outlandish antics, Mishima succeeded in alienating himself from people on both
sides of the political spectrum. Those on the left objected to what they saw as his
crass glorification of wartime militarist dogma and emperor-centered fascism.
Those on the right objected to his eroticization of the sacred imperial institution
and to his ad hominem criticisms of the reigning emperor. Within a short time,
so it seemed, the flippant aesthete had become a dedicated subversive. Hostile
critics began to speak of Mishima as a "dangerous thinker," a label that pleased
him enormously.

Meanwhile, foreign-language translations of Mishima's work had begun to
appear and he was now attracting the attention of academics and journalists overseas. His CBS appearance was just one of many such encounters with foreign
media, and by his early forties Mishima was arguably the most famous Japanese
man in the world. While he clearly relished this fame, it also exerted a heavy stress
upon him. When we come to examine his later writings we must bear in mind that
in these works Mishima was consciously playing to an international audience. He
was possibly the first Japanese writer of modern times to do so.

Mishima's self-reinvention as a modern-day samurai represents an extreme
case of a career shift that was common among Japanese writers, artists, and intellectuals during the twentieth century: the "return to Japan" (*Nihon e no kaiki*).
The career of a Japanese creative artist typically began with a careful study of
Western art forms, an enthusiastic immersion in Western ideas and conventions,
and an attempt to produce convincing Japanese equivalents. But later, usually just
before middle age, many artists suddenly found themselves unable to continue
any further in this mode. It was as if they had come up against an immovable

cultural essence deep within their psyche, an essence they had not even realized was there. At this point they opted to renounce the Western influences that had previously dominated their work. Instead, artists endeavored to assert their cultural autonomy by embracing traditional Japanese ideas and modes of expression. But this too led them into difficulties. The authentic Japanese spirit they searched for proved impossible to grasp or define. Had such a thing ever really existed, or was it just a nostalgic fantasy? And even if it had once existed, how could it be expressed or realized now, after decades of modernization? These anxieties and insecurities soon showed themselves in the work, and consequently the "return to Japan" often assumed ironical, desperate, or even nihilistic forms.

Japanese intellectuals were discussing this problem long before Mishima's frenetic performance. In a famous essay of 1938 the poet Hagiwara Sakutarō had written, "The return to Japan? To us poets, that is the song of a spiritually forlorn drifter who has no place to go."[4]

Mishima too is essentially pessimistic. The premise of all his work during his final decade was that Japan had entered a period of severe cultural and spiritual decline. Mishima was not the only Japanese intellectual saying this, but he was the most vociferous and the most eloquent.

Even Mishima's awkward forays into political debate were propelled by his worry over what he believed was Japan's national identity crisis. It is true that he expressed hostility toward communism, but this did not indicate a newfound interest in politics. Mishima's concern that a communist or procommunist government would assume power in Japan, which during the late 1960s was not an inconceivable possibility, derived from his fears about the consequences for freedom of artistic expression. He was aware of the plight of artists in the Soviet Union and Eastern Europe, and in his articles and interviews he drew attention to the fate of dissident Russian writers who were suffering persecution by the Soviet authorities.

Mishima's anxiety was heightened by the fact that he was beginning to encounter censorship problems of his own. His major novel of 1960, *After the Banquet* (*Utage no ato*), became the subject of Japan's first "infringement of privacy" lawsuit, after the former cabinet minister on whom Mishima had modeled one of the characters sued Mishima and his publisher. After a six-year legal battle, the two parties eventually settled the matter out of court. Mishima got into more dangerous trouble for helping to promote a satirical story by a minor writer named Fukazawa Shichirō. The story, titled "A Dream of Courtly Elegance" (*Furyū mutan*), contained a scene in which a mob of revolutionaries break into the Imperial Palace and decapitate the crown prince and his wife.[5] Mishima and Fukazawa both received death threats from Japanese right-wing groups, and after one angry rightist broke into the home of the story's publisher and murdered a member of the staff, police officers guarded Mishima's house for several months. In 1964 a planned staging of Mishima's play *The Joyful Koto* (*Yorokobi no koto*) at the Bungakuza Theater had to be canceled midway through rehearsals when some of the actors objected to what they considered to be the anticommunist tone of the work.

These and various other difficulties galvanized Mishima to become an active opponent of censorship. In the obscenity trial of movie director Takechi Tetsuji for his soft-core pornographic film *Black Snow* (*Kuroi yuki*, 1965) Mishima testified in Takechi's defense. Meanwhile, French literature specialist Shibusawa Tatsuhiko, one of Mishima's closest friends, was battling against the censors for his work on the Marquis de Sade. For his abridged Japanese translation of Sade's *Juliette*, Shibusawa was prosecuted for distribution of pornography. Shibusawa fought the legal case all the way to Japan's Supreme Court, which ruled against him. Mishima expressed his support for Shibusawa, and his contempt for the censors, in numerous articles and interviews, and wrote the stage play *Madame de Sade* (*Sado kōshaku fujin*, 1965) as a symbolic retaliation.[6]

The specific target of Mishima's dissatisfaction in his cultural criticism is a modern attitude toward culture that he unhelpfully calls *bunka-shugi*, literally "culture-ism." As Mishima describes it, culture-ism is the attempt to sanitize culture by repressing its dangerous and subversive elements:

> Culture-ism tries to sever culture from the life of the bloody mother-womb that gave birth to it, from the act of its cultivation, and to judge it according to its appealing humanistic effects. Culture-ism tries to turn culture into a shared treasure of the human race, something harmless and beautiful, like a plaza fountain. (35:16)

Mishima traces this attitude to the policies of the Meiji period (1868–1912), when the paramount concern of Japan's leaders was to transform Japan into a "civilized and enlightened" nation based on the model of the Western powers, or, as Mishima puts it, "to stop doing all the things that Westerners regarded as ignorant, foolish, grotesque, unbeautiful, or immoral" (35:193). Fundamentally, though, Mishima's fierce objection to culture-ism is not founded on nationalism but on his concern for art and culture. He views such progressive desires to "improve culture" and to become "civilized" as antithetical to the creation of truly great art and culture, though he never explains at length why this should be the case. The following lines are from an article he wrote in angry response to the court ruling against his novel *After the Banquet*:

This verdict is based on an evaluation of art according to its social validity, a disdain for the autonomy of art, a disdain for the totality of art, and
other short-sighted views that have been the norm since the days of the
Meiji government. Instead of judging a work of art as a piece of literature
(or whatever it happens to be), the tendency is to pounce on one part of
it and complain that this part is offensive or pornographic. This has been
standard procedure in Japan since the Lady Chatterley trials of the 1950s
[in which the Japanese translator and publisher of D. H. Lawrence's novel
were convicted of obscenity]. In the trial involving my novel, too, it seems
that the verdict has been similarly evasive, its sole aim being to protect
privacy and property rights. (33:146)

Mishima associates this problematic culture-ism with a bourgeois mentality,
which he denigrates with humor or malice, depending on his mood:

I do not, fortunately, have the bourgeois habit of passively enjoying beauty
as a kind of nourishment for the mind. Bourgeois types like to follow a typically mammalian procedure in everything: ingestion, mastication, diges-
tion, elimination. It is the same whether they are tackling Shakespeare,
Cezanne, or Noh: it is this that is known as "culture" in bourgeois society.
   True beauty is something that attacks, overpowers, robs, and finally
destroys. . . . Culture is no more than a kind of life insurance taken out
against the dangerous blandishments of beauty. (36:600)

Mishima scoffs at what he characterizes as the modern bureaucratic assumption that art can be made to serve political ends. Good art, he insists, is fundamentally apolitical:

The amount of artistic energy that can be put to effective use in politics is
extremely small. The irony is that when politics thinks it has succeeded
in using art 100 percent effectively, art is already dead and useless, as was
seen during the time of the Nazis. (33:633)

On another occasion Mishima writes, "The secret of art is to be found in the
word 'resistance' [teikō]" (29:183). He even seems to acknowledge that his own
reactionary stance is a deliberate strategy for stimulating his creative energies:

Must a writer automatically jump into bed with his era like a whore? Any
novel will inevitably possess a flavor that comes from its own times. But is
it not true that the isolation and asceticism of a reactionary are more likely
to produce work of greater substance? (28:554)

According to Mishima, a transgressive quality in art is vital to a nation's cultural health, and he rails against what he regards as meddlesome and counterproductive interference in cultural activity by media and government. Mishima abhors progressive utopian ideologies. He believes that danger is intrinsic to art, to sex, and to life itself, and that a healthy culture is one that acknowledges its irrational or antirational elements.

Mishima's cultural libertarianism led him to take up some unexpected causes. He heaped scorn upon conservative commentators who were demonizing the rise of hippie culture in Japan:

> Politicians say we should preserve Bunraku and Kabuki, while telling us that we must get rid of psychedelic music. But old does not mean good. There was more decadence in late-Edo *kyōgen* plays than there is in today's hippie culture. (35:192)

And here is Mishima defending the surging popularity of rock music:

> The belief that the electric guitar is dangerous or harmful to young people, whereas Beethoven is wholesome and uplifting and not dangerous at all, is due to the pernicious influence of modern culture-ism. Vulgar minds who are clueless about Beethoven unthinkingly accept this view. And it is clear that the cultural policies of our current government do not deviate from it.
>
> What no one seems to understand any more is that it is music itself that is dangerous and toxic, and the more artful it is the more dangerous it becomes. This is where the real conflict between politics and art is to be found. In that sense, there is not one artist in Japan today who is truly dangerous. (33:634)

Even in his less petulant moods, Mishima insists on a conception of art as combative and disruptive:

> I cannot give up the idea that art is fundamentally about trying to wake people up, about trying to jolt them out of their ordinary and healthy frames of mind. If artists went about their work with the same mentality as ordinary people, there would be no reason for art to exist at all. Art is about things that cannot be brought to life without first destroying things that already exist. . . . Only as a resurgence that has passed once through death can art really take hold of life. In that sense, literature is rather like the secret rituals of ancient times. (29:186)[7]

The Chrysanthemum and the Sword

Mishima's most forceful statement about the problems of "culture-ism" is a long essay titled "The Defense of Culture" (Bunka bōei ron), which he published in the summer of 1968.

If we take this essay at face value, it begins as a state-of-the-nation critique of postwar Japan, focusing on the arts, and then moves to a general discussion of the characteristics of Japanese culture. Mishima takes a stern anticommunist line, repeatedly warning of the dangers to Japanese culture posed by the surge of communist sympathies. His criticisms of communist cultural policies are naturally of less interest to us now than they were to his contemporaries. Today it is really only the final section of the essay, a proposal for a new way of thinking about the emperor, that continues to elicit comment from critics and scholars. But even in this section Mishima's emphasis is firmly on the issue of freedom of artistic expression in Japan, which he fears is under threat.

"The Defense of Culture" opens with an indictment of the contemporary state of Japanese arts and culture. Some pundits in Japan had been hailing the 1960s as a modern-day Genroku, the name commonly used to denote the five decades from 1680 to 1730, a golden age of art and literature in Japan. Mishima is not so impressed:

> Our era is being hailed as the "Genroku" of the Showa period. If so, it is a Genroku of dubious cultural achievements. We have no Chikamatsu. We have no Saikaku, and we have no Basho. Only the lively folk traditions are flourishing. Passions have dried up, brutal realism has fled, and there has been no deepening of poetry. The era we are living in now should be one of wonder for us all. Instead there is a conspicuous lack of wonderment. Something has been lost. . . .
>
> What is Japanese culture, exactly? In the decades since the war this question has been neatly answered for us by culture-minded bureaucrats and foreign office mandarins. In compliance with Occupation policies they have severed the eternal link between "the Chrysanthemum and the Sword." We are now a peace-loving people whose gentle culture of flower arranging and tea making is no threat to anyone. (35:15–16)

Mishima takes the formula of 'the chrysanthemum and the sword' from the American anthropologist Ruth Benedict, whose landmark analysis of Japanese culture was published in 1946. Benedict had placed strong emphasis on what she regarded as Japan's unusual contradictory qualities. It was a nation with "a popular cult of aestheticism which gives high honor to actors and to artists and lavishes art upon the cultivation of chrysanthemums," yet it was also devoted to "the cult of the sword and the top prestige of the warrior."[8] Since Mishima makes no amendments to Benedict's formula we must assume that he agrees with it unreservedly. However, his unwillingness to clarify or amplify the meaning of the two key terms means that in his hands, this formula of "the chrysanthemum and the sword" never rises above the level of a slogan.

Mishima's main argument in the first half of the essay is that culture must be liberated from the stranglehold of "vulgar-minded bureaucrats and equally vulgar-minded culture experts" who are intent, he says, on turning Japan into a "culture state" (*bunka kokka*; 47). Specifically, Mishima attacks government policy makers for their censoriousness:

> [Bureaucratic policies] have cut the chain between the chrysanthemum and the sword, utilizing only the part that is useful for cultivating public morals, while suppressing the dangerous part. The ban on Kabuki revenge dramas and samurai sword-fighting movies in the early years of the Occupation were the most primitive and direct expressions of this attitude.
>
> In time, the Occupation policies became less primitive. The bans were lifted and culture regained some of its respect. This was probably because this was a period of various successful political and social changes, and it was believed that the tendency of culture to revert to its origin had been eradicated. Culture-ism began from this point. In other words, *nothing is allowed to be dangerous any more.* (16–17)

The censorious nature of culture-ism derives, says Mishima, from a naïve tendency to think of culture in terms of *things*: the things that hang on the walls of art galleries, the things that are displayed inside glass cases in museums. In his popular articles on the arts, Mishima always warns readers against taking what he calls an "archeological" attitude to culture. In his pieces on the Kabuki theater, for instance, he often complains about the growing tendency in Japan to think of Kabuki nostalgically, as if it were a precious remnant of a lost era, a *thing* from the past that requires respectful preservation in the present. Mishima considers such thinking to be detrimental to Kabuki's creative dynamism. In "The Defense of Culture" he argues that this way of thinking about culture originated in the West:

> Japanese culture has traditionally made no distinction between original and copy. In the West the culture of *things* was mainly built from stone, whereas in Japan it was built from wood. In Western civilization the

destruction of the originals is a permanent and irreparable event, and the culture of things expires at that point . . .

In both Japan and the West, however, the culture of *things* was at the mercy of a fearsome wantonness until modern culture-ism began to take active measures to preserve it. Considering all the wars and natural disasters that happened over the centuries, the existence of culture as *things* seems entirely haphazard. We certainly cannot claim that the pieces that survive today are the finest ones, carefully selected for us by the hand of history. Perhaps the greatest sculptures of Praxiteles are still sleeping at the bottom of the Mediterranean. This is all the more true for the plastic arts of Japan, whose fate has depended on a culture of wood and paper. During the Ōnin Wars [of the mid-1400s] it was a rare stroke of luck for Kyoto's shrines and temples to survive without burning, and countless cultural treasures were lost.

This issue of materials is probably one reason why Japan places relatively little importance on culture as *things*, and why a distinctive Japanese trait is the transferral of cultural forms onto modes of action, the essence of which is to vanish. In Japan, the destruction of an original is not considered to be an absolute destruction. Indeed, there is no significant drop in value between an original and a copy.

The best-known example of this is the tradition of the ritual destruction and reconstruction of the Grand Shrine at Ise, which has been performed every twenty years since the reign of Empress Jitō [in the late seventh century]. Each time it is destroyed and rebuilt, the original Ise Shrine passes its life to the copy and vanishes, so that the copy itself, the newly built shrine, becomes the original. . . . This distinctive characteristic corresponds to that of the emperor system, wherein each successive emperor is the true emperor and does not stand in an original/copy relation to the sun goddess Amaterasu Ōmikami. (23–24)

This line of reasoning recalls Mizoguchi, who rages against what he sees as the naïve overconfidence of modern Japan in the "thingly" character of the Golden Temple. While culture naturally produces "things," Mishima argues, in its living aspects culture is obviously not a thing. Culture is made of "forms" (*kata*), which are to be thought of as "transparent crystalline structures through which we can perceive the nation's spirit" (22). This is particularly the case in Japan, he says, which has a tradition of making modes of action into works of art:

Japanese culture includes everything from a single form of Noh to the action of a naval officer who is shot to pieces as he leaps from his suicide torpedo, sword in hand, on the surface of the sea one moonlit night in New Guinea; it includes the many suicide notes of the kamikaze pilots. From *The Tale of Genji* to modern novels, from the *Man'yōshū* to avant garde *tanka* poetry, from the Buddha at the Chūsonji Temple to modern sculpture, from flower arrangements and the tea ceremony to kendo and judo, from Kabuki dramas to yakuza movies, from Zen Buddhism to military etiquette, Japanese culture subsumes all the forms through which the Japaneseness of Japan can be seen, including both the "chrysanthemum and the sword." (22)

It is hard to imagine anyone disputing these simple statements. Of course all these things are cultural. Mishima's more urgent point is about intolerance and censorship. Due to the "artistic chauvinism" of culture-ism, he says, the Japanese are today trying to extract only the "static" aspects of their culture and are ignoring its "dynamic" aspects. Culture is not something that can be improved or corrected in this way, says Mishima. Without making his position entirely clear, he seems to advocate a removal of all restrictions on freedom of expression: "The point is not that we must judge beauty logically and give complete approval to the 'chrysanthemum and the sword'; rather, we must judge logic aesthetically and give complete approval to culture" (25). The political dimension of Mishima's essay arises from the question: What type of political system will best achieve this?

The totality of culture requires both temporal continuity and spatial continuity. The former guarantees tradition, beauty, and taste, while the latter guarantees the multiplicity of life. Freedom of expression certainly guarantees the latter, if not the former.

Of course, freedom of expression is not an absolute value. Sometimes freedom of expression itself eats away at culture, as we see happening in Japan at the moment. Freedom of expression has the drawback that it can make us lose the creative and traditional character of culture, and the hierarchy of culture, supporting only a flat surface of the totality of culture, and make us lose the dimensionality [*rittaisei*] of culture. Nonetheless, comparatively speaking, there is nothing better that can preserve the spiritual superiority of tolerance toward the ideas of others. Freedom of expression is a technical and political expedient that supports the totality of culture. That is why the selection of a political system that guarantees freedom of expression is a practical matter, a matter of selecting the best system available. The first enemy of culture is a political system that does not ultimately guarantee freedom of expression. (38–39)

Foreign-language commentary on Mishima sometimes states that he was opposed to democracy, but that is not entirely the case. Mishima dislikes democracy but does not actually want to get rid of it. He warns repeatedly against the naïveté of believing that democracy, alone among political systems, is the true ally of human nature. Mishima thinks of society as our fragile human defense against the destructive forces of nature, including the destructive forces of our *own* nature. "Violence and cruelty are universal to humankind," he writes in an earlier essay. "Indeed, they dwell immediately beneath the human" (28:358). The defect of liberal humanist views of society, argues Mishima, is that they lack a proper understanding of evil:

> The unrestrained liberation of human nature would mean self-destruction. It would lead, by logical necessity, to the complete dismantling of political order, and in the end would allow the existence of nothing but anarchy. At the time of the French Revolution, the thinker who conducted the most profound research into human nature was not Voltaire but the Marquis de Sade. [. . .] Sade's insight was that the wanton destructiveness that characterizes revolutionary uprisings, the period of intoxication during which things are destroyed with no regard for their value, is merely a natural consequence of human nature. Herein lies the contradiction between freedom of speech and all forms of political order. (35:260)

Mishima believes that the essence of democracy is to seek a compromise between the anarchy inherent in human nature and the stability required by government. Democracy merely expresses "the minimum amount of political evil that is needed to deal with human nature" (261). In a democracy, the majority controls the minority; Mishima would prefer things the other way around. He fears that the flattening effect of democracy is contrary to the tragic worldview, which demands lofty heights, and that democracy will create an environment inhospitable to the cultivation of noble types, such as himself. Nonetheless, faced with the looming threat of Soviet-style communism, Mishima grudgingly supports multiparty democracy in Japan as the political system that can best guarantee freedom of expression.

Mishima's idea of "the totality of culture" is opposed, he explains in "The Defense of Culture," to all forms of political totalitarianism, both of the left and of the right:

> There is an ancient conflict between poetry and politics. To ask whether it is possible to achieve a political structure that could tolerate culture comes

very close to asking whether it is possible to achieve a political structure that could *entirely* tolerate eroticism. (35:38)

Though totalitarian systems promote their cultural policies as nationalist or "culture-friendly" in the manner of culture-ism, their true aim, Mishima says, is to destroy the totality of culture: "At the psychological root of the repression of free speech is totalitarianism's envy of all totalities, for the essence of totalitarianism is to monopolize 'totality.'"

Since even multiparty democracy is susceptible to contamination by totalitarian ideology, Mishima argues, Japan needs a fundamental "cultural-collective principle" (*bunka kyōdōtai rinen*) that would be able to resist such contamination. This principle must simultaneously possess an "absolute logical value" and an "undiscriminating cultural inclusivity." As a solution, Mishima proposes what he calls "a cultural conception of the emperor" (*bunka gainen to shite no tennō*; 40). Mishima says he wants to establish a greater cultural significance for the emperor, who, rather than ruling as a constitutional monarch, will symbolize a guarantee of free expression in Japan. Basically, Mishima is suggesting a new way of thinking about Japan's imperial institution, though he offers no explanation of what this would require in terms of specific, practical reforms.

During the years of militarism and war, the Japanese people had been urged to revere the emperor with fear and trembling as a sacred figure, a living god. Japan's postwar constitution then designated a more limited symbolic role for the emperor and prompted intense public debate about exactly what this role ought to be. It became a commonplace to observe that Japan's emperors had historically been little more than expedient symbols. For centuries courtiers, shoguns, and politicians had manipulated the imperial throne in order to legitimize their own authority. In the aftermath of Japan's defeat in 1945, this image of a powerless (and therefore blameless) emperor being controlled by his scheming advisors had held special appeal. In a 1946 essay the novelist Sakaguchi Ango (1906–1955) had written, "It was out of the question for politicians or military leaders to call themselves divine and demand absolute reverence from the Japanese people. Instead, however, they could prostrate themselves before the emperor and call *him* a god, and then foist this notion upon the people."[9] Mishima quotes at length from an article written around the same time by the philosopher Watsuji Tetsurō (1889–1960), who had argued, in a more positive tone, that the emperors of Japan had historically symbolized the unity of the Japanese people. Since the imperial institution had continued to exist even during times when the Japanese state was fractured and divided, Watsuji had written, it must therefore be regarded as being of a different order from the state. It follows from this, Watsuji argued, that the emperor is fundamentally not a political concept, but a cultural one. The emperor is a symbol of the Japanese people as a united cultural community. Moreover, the tradition of reverence toward the emperor, which has endured throughout the history of Japan, is none other than an awareness of this unity.[10]

Mishima discusses these ideas for several pages, quoting from writings by various historians and legal experts. This section of his essay is uncharacteristically sober, though it has attracted a fair amount of attention from scholars who are interested in the historical role of the imperial throne. Suddenly Mishima seems to tire of this discussion and breaks out on his own:

> The emperor system as a cultural concept satisfies two conditions of the totality of culture, in that, while its temporal continuity connects to religious rites, there are also times when its spatial continuity will even tolerate political disorder. This corresponds to the way that the most profound eroticism clings both to ancient theocracy on the one hand and to anarchism on the other. (46)

Mishima is now moving toward the idea that most excites him. His "cultural emperor" will be a modern heir to Japan's ancient rulers, who devoted their lives to sacred rites and poetry. To encapsulate the chrysanthemum-sword duality within a single concept associable with the emperor, Mishima offers an unusual interpretation of *miyabi*, or "courtly refinement." This ancient aesthetic term idealized the artistic proficiencies (in poetry, music, calligraphy, etc.) cultivated by members of the imperial court. According to Mishima, the ideal of *miyabi* signified not only "the cultural essence of the imperial court" but also "a longing for that cultural essence" (46). This statement recalls Mishima's claim that Japanese patriotism is like a "sensual longing" for Japan. In his final writings Mishima will characterize the entire history of Japanese literature as a continually renewed expression of longing for the refinement of the emperor's court. Here, though, he is more eager to argue that this centuries-old ideal of "courtly refinement" is flexible enough to accommodate disruptive or even violent actions. Mishima's contention is that, as a cultural concept, the emperor is not always on the side of state authority and order, but can also "reach across to the side of disorder" (35:46). This, basically, was the point made by Watsuji. But Mishima, in line with his earlier remarks about the transfer of cultural forms into modes of action, wants to think of this "disorder" as constituting legitimate cultural expressions included within the ideal of *miyabi*, which is a quality of the emperor system that Mishima believes has been lost in modern times. "Under the Meiji Constitution of 1889," he writes, "the emperor system fulfilled its temporal continuity by advocating the unity of religion and government, but it did not provide the spatial continuity that might tolerate political disorder" (47). The emperor as a cultural concept is freer and more inclusive than the emperor as a political concept. But in modern times, Mishima argues, the first of these concepts has been sacrificed to the second. Hence the failure of the rebellion of February 1936: "The Showa emperor had lost the power to comprehend the *miyabi* of that rebellion" (47). And in the postwar era things have only gotten worse. All that Japan has today, scoffs Mishima, is "an emperor system for the weekly tabloids" (47).

It seems, then, that Mishima wants the emperor to be a symbol of free expression in Japan, including the freedom to make violent expressions of dissent. But at the same time he says this, Mishima insists that those acts of dissent must be confined to specific types or modes of expression in order to prevent "cultural disorder," a reference to the violent student protests that were erupting around Japan at the time he was writing. "Uprisings for the emperor should be permitted," Mishima says, "as long as they do not contradict cultural forms" (*Tennō no tame no kekki wa, bunka yōshiki ni sehan senu kagiri, yōnin sareru beki*; 47). At this stage in the essay, this is a problematic statement. Having been at pains to stress that culture can include modes of action, Mishima now wants to place a restriction on his definition of those modes. Apparently there are some expressions of dissent that "contradict" cultural forms. Though Mishima does not inform us who will be assigned the responsibility of determining which forms of dissent are the acceptably cultural ones, his implication is that militant emperor-revering samurai are cultural, and therefore acceptable, whereas militant student radicals erecting barricades on their campuses are not. Mishima's use of the word *sehan* (contradict) seems to lead him into a contradiction of his own, since *sehan* can also have the meaning of "uprising." Mishima's emperor will therefore symbolize and guarantee the totality of Japanese culture, including even violent uprisings, as long as the rebels do not rise up against the totality of Japanese culture.

We are now only a few paragraphs from the end of the essay. Mishima suddenly unleashes a barrage of seemingly paradoxical declarations about the dual symbolic nature of the emperor system:

Susanoo, the god who [according to Japanese myth] was banished from Heaven for his violent rampages, subsequently became a hero [on Earth]. Culture teaches us that the final logical origin of revolts and revolutions in Japan is the sun gods who are the targets of those revolts and revolutions. This is the secret ritual of the Yata Mirror [one of the Three Sacred Treasures of Japan]. Revolts and vulgarities of culture are already included in the concept of *miyabi*, which manifests the totality of culture and establishes the emperor as a cultural concept. This is the fundamental principle of the history of Japanese culture. While absorbing and blurring vulgarities, the emperor is the eternal homeland of nobility, elegance, and the commonplace. (35:49)

Mishima has still not dealt decisively with the possibility of the democratic formation in Japan of a communist-controlled government, which, he claims, would be incompatible with the emperor system and would "break the totality" of Japanese culture. He addresses the matter in his closing lines:

> To prevent this state of affairs, the emperor and the military must be joined with ties of glory. There is no other reliable preventive measure. The restoration of this glorious sovereign content must be the restoration not of the emperor as a political concept, but of the emperor as a cultural concept. Only an emperor that represents the totality of our culture is the thing-in-itself. If such an emperor is rejected, or appropriated as a political concept of totalitarianism, Japan and Japanese culture will face a real crisis. (50–51)

This unexpected mention of Japan's military seems to go against much of what Mishima has said about the emperor as a purely cultural symbol. It is perhaps intended to echo the demands of the rebellious army officers of February 1936, who hoped that the emperor would assume direct control over the military and lead Japan into a new age of imperial glory. But Mishima abruptly ends here without explaining himself.

The mixture of cultural criticism, politics, aesthetics, and religion in "The Defense of Culture" perplexed many readers. In a long and forceful critique published one month later, Hashikawa Bunzō scrupulously worked his way through the essay, exposing counterfactual claims and logical inconsistencies and debunking Mishima's sweeping generalizations about Japan as a single cultural collective. Characterizing Mishima's emperor as a "supreme controller of beauty" (*bi no sōransha*), Hashikawa argued that such an emperor had never existed and that the concept of the modern nation-state was in any case incompatible with such a figure. Hashikawa identified a number of factual errors in the section of the essay relating to the political power of the imperial institution over the centuries, and he exposed biases in Mishima's accounts of certain historical events. Finally, Hashikawa pointed out that an emperor system that was "joined with ties of glory" to the military would logically forfeit its "sovereign content."[11]

Hashikawa's critique was regarded by many as a decisive rebuttal, and subsequent critics and scholars have done little but reiterate his objections.[12] And yet, in an "open letter" to Hashikawa, Mishima retorted that critics who challenged him on the grounds of historical inaccuracy were barking up the wrong tree. His method in "The Defense of Culture" was, he claimed, deliberately anachronistic. That is, he was using imperial tradition to argue for the spatial continuity of culture as one element of its (culture's) totality, while at the same time insisting on the modern notion of freedom of expression as its content. I translate the following crucial passage as literally as possible:

> From this most ultramodern phenomenon of a democratic Japan that permits freedom of expression, a phenomenon that has never once existed in the past two thousand years, I want to conversely prove [*gyaku-shōmei*] an emperor who is managing to remain in existence. Not only that, but also I want to conversely define the disorder incited by this freedom of expression as the very essence of the emperor. (35:207–208)

Thus Mishima is not trying to write history, or even to rewrite it; he is trying to *create* it. Mishima knows that his beautiful, freedom-loving emperor has never existed. "The Defense of Culture" is his attempt to bring such an emperor into being. As for the contradictory notion of an emperor as "supreme controller of beauty" existing in a modern nation-state and the legitimacy of a "cultural emperor" who is also tied to the military, Mishima nimbly replies that these are contradictions inherent in the emperor system itself. Hashikawa has merely identified "the two problems that will determine the basic issue of the emperor system in the future" (206).

Putting aside the issue of the emperor for a moment, I see strong affinities between "The Defense of Culture" and Nietzsche's *The Birth of Tragedy*. Nietzsche had attacked the modern age for its overconfidence in scientific method, reason, and utilitarianism. Dreams of improving the world, Nietzsche wrote, are delusions. Life is a ceaseless flux, an endless cycle of creation and destruction. Nietzsche saw the world as composed of two contrary forces or metaphysical categories, which he named after Greek deities: an *Apollonian* impulse to create forms, boundaries, and structures, and a *Dionysian* impulse toward sensuality, cruelty, dissolution, and destruction. The Greeks had enacted the Dionysian in art on the tragic stage, which Nietzsche held to be the high point of Western artistic achievement, but Greek tragedy was subsequently ruined by the antitragic forces of logic and reason. This introduction of rational thinking led to "the excision of the primitive and powerful Dionysian element from tragedy, and the rebuilding of tragedy on non-Dionysian art, morality and philosophy." Nietzsche looked to the works of Wagner for a modern rebirth of tragedy.[13]

Even from that simple outline it should be apparent that the argument of "The Defense of Culture" resembles that of *The Birth of Tragedy*, at least in its broad structure. Mishima employs the chrysanthemum-sword duality to argue, in Nietzschean manner, that the influx of Western modes of thought has had the effect of sanitizing Japanese culture, repressing its dark and aggressive elements. Some of Mishima's remarks indicate that he does not intend this argument to apply solely to Japan. His thesis is that every human community needs to devise and maintain effective "cultural forms" for artistically or symbolically expressing its aggressive side, and that it is both dishonest and unhealthy to suppress cultural forms that serve this purpose.

For all his passionate concern for the freedom of cultural and artistic activity from politics, however, Mishima is ultimately reticent about how the autonomy of individual creative artists is to be ensured. His vision appears to be one of quasi-religious communitarianism centered on the emperor. But how exactly could the emperor guarantee total artistic freedom, or "aesthetic anarchism" as Mishima is now calling it? In regard to this important question, Mishima makes no comment.[14]

Tragic Cultural Will

Among Mishima's later statements, the following passage from an article he published in January 1970 contains the fullest and most lucid summary of his thoughts regarding the relationship between the emperor and the state:

> As I see things, Japan today is a theocracy that has split into two parts. There is the governing nation-state, which constitutes the administrative power base, and there is the nation of religious rites, which constitutes the spirit of the people; the second of these is currently flickering like a shadow behind the first. Modern political science is concerned only with the first. But in the Free World of the future, nation-states will cede their governing functions to independent organizations, civil groups, business corporations, and so on, while the state itself concentrates only on managerial issues, while tolerating freedom of speech and sexual freedoms to their maximum limits. In other words, in the future, a thin and lean nation-state will be deemed the most desirable. Temporal continuity will not be regarded as important, and the emphasis will be entirely on spatial expansion achieved by the globalization of communication systems, information, and trade. The idea of a worldwide state is already being anticipated in many spheres of human activity, such as in sports and the arts. This

sort of managerial nation-state is actually an embryo for a future World Federation. The principles that control this managerial nation-state are humanism, reason, love of humanity, etc. The nation-state thus becomes a logos from which things that are irrational or antirational are strictly excluded.

In contrast, the nation-state of religious rites is usually invisible. Religious rites are symbolic acts that guarantee the eternal temporal continuity of the nation-state, its inherited history, traditions, culture, and such like. Religious rites also preserve the sources of irrational feelings and emotions. Only here does culture find its roots, and only here can true eroticism exist. In Japan, the head of this nation-state of ethos and pathos is the emperor. Here, a richly dense nation-state is the best.

If the governing nation-state can be thought of as a centrifugal force, one that urges things away from the center, then the nation-state of religious rites is a centripetal force that encourages cohesion and unity. The first is spatial, the second is temporal. My ideal nation-state is one that has achieved a balance of harmony and tension between those two dimensions. (36:33–34)

At other times, however, Mishima deviates from this conservative position and argues that the emperor, being a symbol of free speech, has the potential to become "an agitating force . . . a force that urges change and can even achieve revolution" (35:487).

Mishima was pursuing this idea in one of the works he left unfinished at his death, *A Short History of Japanese Literature* (*Nihon bungaku shōshi*). Mishima began writing this book-length work in the summer of 1969. The introduction includes a list of provisional titles for some twenty chapters, but Mishima had completed only four of these by the time of his death.

A Short History of Japanese Literature continues the Nietzschean argument of "The Defense of Culture." Nietzsche had argued for the importance of myth for cultural health. Modernity's ruthlessly critical spirit (basically, our urge to analyze everything we contemplate) has rendered us incapable of appreciating or understanding myth. The charisma of mythic heroes no longer inspires us. Yet a culture without a mythical heritage loses its creative powers. Nietzsche had written, "The state itself has no unwritten laws more powerful than the mythical foundation that guarantees its connection with religion and its growth out of mythical representations."[15] Mishima proceeds on the same assumption, and in his introduction he promises us a history of Japanese literature "that will deviate infinitely from rationalism" (35:537):

My history of literature will demand from readers a most sophisticated, most subtle, and most tolerant sensibility to the Japanese language, and it will demand from the authors I discuss, no matter how ancient the times they lived in, a clearly articulated cultural will. This is because I believe this cultural will to be the essential quality of literary works, and I shall carefully avoid the danger of falling into any murky depths that might precede it. (531)

The "murky depths" are the ones that modern interpretive methods endeavor to illuminate. Mishima is primarily attacking Marxism and psychoanalysis, though he also takes a swipe at the theories of Japanese folklore scholars and ethnographers. As in "The Defense of Culture," what Mishima fears is the universalization of cultural values and the forfeiture of national identity he assumes will be the result. If one peers into the "deep consciousness of a people," he writes, one will eventually come up against a "giant rocky layer common to all humanity" (532). This is the realm of "comparative cultural anthropology," a kind of "low-level internationalism." Like psychoanalysis, Japanese folklore scholars merely show us the "hidden and sickly part" of a primordial human conscious:

> The bland investigative methods of ethnologists are just like the bland analytical methods of psychoanalysts. Ethnologists thrust their hands to the bottom of the garbage dump of each unsavory ethnic phenomenon, and then try to find some deep original experience of their own people or race. Similarly, psychoanalysts thrust their hands into the garbage dumps of individual minds and search for a symbolic code that will provide a universal explanation of human nature. Such methods are the fads of our time. Marx and Freud are the demonic progeny of Western rationalism. Both taught magic and exorcism in ways that appeared to be rational: Marx in regard to the future, Freud in regard to the past. Along with ethnology, that makes three schools of cultural theory that refuse to acknowledge cultural willing. (35:533)

Mishima refuses to "reduce culture to its lowest common denominator" in this way. The Japaneseness of Japan is manifest, he says, in the various forms of its literary culture, and not in any primal phenomena that existed before its literary culture. What Mishima wants to stress is the intentionality of cultural creation. As seen in the above extracts, his term for this is *bunka ishi*, "cultural will" or "cultural willing." Mishima uses this term to denote the process whereby groups of people cooperate in creating (or, in the case of the classical poetry anthologies, collecting) artistic works that initiate cultural styles, which over time come to dominate the public imagination. He makes it clear that "cultural will" does not signify anything like a mystical Hegelian spirit operating independently of the authors' intentions:

> Culture is realized by creative cultural willing, and, allowing at least for a certain amount of, shall we say, unconscious artistic luck, it is founded on conscious decisions and choices. But the workings of culture do not relate only to actions of individuals, as they do in modern works of art. Things that were first determined and selected by a single outstanding individual can, with the passage of time, come to dominate vast numbers of people and become the standard that regulates people even in their unconscious. (533–534)

Almost certainly, Mishima has adapted his concept of "cultural willing" from the concept of *Kunstwollen* developed by the Austrian art historian Alois Riegl (1858–1905). *Kunstwollen* has been translated into English variously as "artistic intention," "aesthetic willing," and even "the will of art." Riegl's theory was that each of the great historical artistic styles springs from a single idea, a collective artistic intention that is neither an impersonal social volition nor something reducible to the ambitions of individual artists.[16] What Mishima chooses to call "cultural willing" signifies a conscious intention in each era to transform culture, not just by bringing into the world a new style or genre of work, but also by effecting an irrevocable change on all the cultural works that have preceded it. And Mishima is unequivocal about what it is that animates such an intention: "The most intense cultural willing of any era is always a growing awareness of crisis" (560).

In his first chapter Mishima looks at Japan's oldest surviving text, the *Kojiki*, translatable as *An Account of Ancient Matters*. Written in the early years of the eighth century, this is a collection of myths and poems that describe the origin of the Japanese islands and the divine ancestry of the imperial family. It features a cast of gods and goddesses, whose volatile mood swings and eccentric antics are not easy for modern readers to fathom. Mishima's ideological agenda is clear from his opening remarks:

> I cannot read the *Kojiki* as a collection of pure and naïve myths. I cannot read it without sensing a terrifying jumble of the dark and the tragic, of extreme vulgarity and the sacred. . . . The brightest lights and the blackest

darkness of Japanese culture are here, and both continue in the institution of the imperial household. (538)

Predictably, Mishima focuses much of his analysis on the episodes that recount the adventures of the ill-fated hero Prince Yamato Takeru.

Prince Yamato Takeru is Japan's archetypal warrior-hero. "Yamato" was the ancient name of Japan, and "Takeru" means "brave," so the prince's name translates almost literally as "Japanese hero." The *Kojiki* identifies him as one of the sons of Emperor Keikō, a ruler of Japan in the second century. Takeru has a troublesome twin brother who repeatedly disobeys the emperor. When the emperor tells Takeru to find and reprimand his brother, Takeru carries out this imperial command with excessive zeal (to put it mildly) by murdering his brother and ripping off his arms and legs. The emperor, alarmed by Takeru's ferocious nature, sends him off on missions around Japan to subdue rebellious tribes and deities, often without any troops at all. Takeru wins a series of brilliant victories, but soon he begins to suspect his father's motive:

> Why is it that Heaven's Sovereign desires my swift death? He sent me off to smite wicked people in the west, but no sooner do I return from there than he sends me out again, without a force, to subdue wicked people in the east. All this makes me think that His Majesty must desire my swift death.[17]

Takeru's adventures contain features that are common to tales of legendary heroes in all cultures. But it is not his indomitable character or his military successes that have endeared him to the Japanese sensibility. What makes Takeru the archetypal Japanese hero is the stoic yet melancholic resolve with which he goes to his death. There is no final victory or triumphant homecoming for the warrior prince. After an exhausting trek across plains, he falls gravely ill. He spends his last moments composing poems about his loneliness, his sword, and his homeland. He dies while carrying out his orders, uncomplainingly, reciting his sad poems of longing for the beauty of Japan.

Mishima is less interested in Takeru's poetry or his exploits on the battlefield than in the symbolic meaning of his banishment. According to Mishima, it is not that the emperor feels threatened by his son's violent nature. The emperor recognizes that Takeru's brutal act of fratricide is a manifestation of his "divine nature," and at one point he even says of him, "In form he is my son, but actually he is a deity" (540). The idea of the cultural emperor looms large over Mishima's reading. Prince Takeru is the "divine emperor" or the "pure emperor," whereas his father is the "human emperor" or the "ruling emperor" (543). Mishima develops his idea of the cultural emperor from this divine emperor, while viewing the imperial system itself as merely a political system governed by the human emperor.

Furthermore, as Mishima wants to see things, Takeru did not overstep his orders. On the contrary, by murdering his own brother he was actualizing the emperor's "divine murderous intent" (541). The "impeccable purity" of this deed apparently consists in the fact that Takeru has been too faithful to the imperial will. The consequence is that the emperor, frightened by Takeru's ferocious zeal, sends him away on his fateful mission. Mishima makes these comments:

> This was probably the first separation, in politics, of divine and demonic things [kami-teki na demōnisshu na mono] from the governing structure. It was the manifestation of the will of government to suppress divine and demonic things and to give them the role of poetry or culture; and, from the viewpoint of the things being restricted, it was the first appearance of a forced cultural willing. (541)

Conventional readings of the Takeru myth have interpreted it as an allegory about the birth of poetry. A typical view is "The existential experience of human alienation in Japanese literature, the ostracism of the self from the collective, is first seen in Takeru; it is this loneliness that creates poetry."[18] According to Mishima, however, the more important idea conveyed by the Takeru myth, and by the *Kojiki* as a whole, is what he calls *shinjin bunri*, "the separation of gods from humans" (539). Mishima characterizes this trope, which is familiar to students of Japanese folklore and mythology, as the opposite of the Renaissance. Rather than culture abandoning the ancient gods in favor of human endeavors, in this case, he says, "culture is on the side of the banished gods, and rather than criticizing them it takes the form of sorrow and lyricism and goes wandering, and only in that form does it represent legitimacy" (542). Takeru, in Mishima's reading, embodies the "tragic nature" of this separation, which marks an epochal moment in the development of human consciousness.[19]

Ivan Morris begins *The Nobility of Failure*, his 1975 study of Japan's tragic heroes, with a chapter on Takeru, and in his acknowledgments Morris credits Mishima with enlightening him about the "psychological significance of failures."[20] But I wonder whether Mishima might not have objected to the judgmental harshness of the word "failure." It is interesting that such harshness is absent from the Japanese translation of the book, which has the title *Kōki-naru haiboku*, or *Nobility in Defeat*. Morris repeatedly stresses the point that since ancient times, the Japanese have "recognized a special nobility in the sincere, unsuccessful sacrifice." But Mishima never speaks about Japan's self-sacrificial heroes in terms of success or failure. The notion of failure does not feature in Mishima's summary of the archetype he says is communicated by the Takeru myth:

> Throughout all subsequent history, divine things would have to be made into legends and myths and heroism; in other words, they would have to be "sacrificed." Takeru does not understand why he is the one who has been selected for that role. Yet, despite his inability to understand, he fulfills his duty with a pure heart and without the slightest feeling of disobedience, even though he does not know why he is being commanded to die. The anguish of one who is forced into a world of absolute agnosticism begins in this episode of the *Kojiki*, and will be repeated many times in the history of Japan, right up to the present day. This archetype of a tragic cultural will [*higeki-teki bunka ishi*] was established with the tale of Prince Yamato Takeru. (545–546)

The use of the word "tragic" seems questionable here, and it might be safer to take *higeki* in its literal meaning of "sorrowful drama." After all, no catastrophic turn of events has landed Takeru in his predicament. He is simply doing as he was told. He makes no effort to resist, but only resigns himself to the inevitable. Strictly speaking, he is too passive to be a tragic hero. What Mishima here calls a "tragic will" is really a fetishism of obedience. The reason for this, obviously enough, is that the model for Mishima's vision is that of a soldier going unflinchingly to his death in battle. Takeru was one of the cultural icons promoted during the war by the writers of the Japan Romantic School, who hailed him as an exquisite antithesis of selfish Western individualism. For the Romantics, Takeru is a poet both in words and in deeds. He epitomizes the "purity" of the Japanese character, and his life is "the poetization of a tragedy that runs deep in the blood of the Japanese people."[21] On impressionable literary-minded Japanese boys this sort of propaganda had an almost diabolical effect. Hashikawa Bunzō, reminiscing years later, speaks of young men "rushing into the jungle to die with copies of the *Kojiki* in their hands."[22]

If we consider *A Short History of Japanese Literature* together with "The Defense of Culture," Mishima's remedy for what he claims is the destitution and fragmentation of modern Japanese culture consists of a communal faith founded on veneration of the emperor as an absolute cultural principle, and a strong communal identity founded on the ancient myths. Setting himself against Marxism and liberal humanism, both of which look to the future and assume the possibility of evolution and progress, Mishima looks to the past. He wants to understand Japan, not historically, but mythically. He wants to repudiate foreign influences by reconnecting the mundane present to the mythical past, and thus he wants to reassert a core Japanese identity.

Or so he says. As with all Mishima's final pronouncements, when reading *A Short History of Japanese Literature* it is impossible to suppress the suspicion that what interests him most is not the tragic story of Takeru but the meta-tragedy of his own life story. *Confessions of a Mask* contains plenty of talk about "longing for the tragic," though as we have seen, this mostly equates to a masochistic impulse toward self-exclusion, with the narrator obsessively focusing his reveries on "lives and events unfolding without any relation to me, at places for which my sensuality yearned, and yet from which I would forever be shut out" (1:181). By the time of his essay on the Japanese festival, Mishima has grown dissatisfied with this self-exclusionary attitude. "Today I cannot just sit silently watching the intoxication of others," he writes there. "I cannot make do with the tragic resignation of being shut out from their intoxication. I feel that I am qualified to experience every kind of intoxication, and that I *must* experience it" (29:305). In the same essay Mishima expresses his determination to accomplish a "tragic effect" in his work, and he describes this effect with a Takeru-like formulation: "I have come to believe that, in literature, quiet intellectual confidence will produce nothing [of worth]. Only a bridge that connects intellectual things to the most irrational intoxication will produce something" (305). Mishima's lifelong ideal of the artist as an "absolute intermediary," a transcendental figure who connects the particular to the universal, at the risk of his own life if necessary (and Mishima, of course, always desires this tragic fate, always *wants* it to be necessary), is merging with his conception of beauty as a turbulent fusion of contrary forces. In the above statements there is also, one senses, a resignation that literature alone no longer has the power to accomplish this "bridging" effect. And Mishima is surely dreaming of his own destiny when he writes of Takeru:

> The cultural burden that he bears means adversity, it means turning his living flesh into a poem, it means isolation, ostracism, and it even means defeat; but through his sacrifice the gods can behold one last flash of their splendor. (35:543)

These thoughts oblige us to consider yet another possible reading of Mishima's final actions: a re-enactment of the myth of Takeru. The tragedy of Mishima Yukio will signify nothing less than the expulsion of divine and demonic violence from modern Japan, in an act of beautiful terrorism that will simultaneously serve as an exorcism.

CHAPTER 7

The Purest Essence of Japan

From today I will not turn back toward home
for I am going away
to serve as a humble shield for our Great Lord.

Poem by a Japanese frontier guard, from the Man'yōshū

The final years of the 1960s were turbulent ones for Japan, as they were for many other countries around the world. Japan saw disruptive protests by university students and massive demonstrations against the American war in Vietnam. The students complained of the blandness of modern urban life, the lack of opportunity for individual expression, the dehumanizing effects of the university examination process, and the authoritarianism of professors and administrators. Student protesters nationwide occupied their campuses and shut down the universities for months on end. Some of the protests turned violent. In January 1969 there were extraordinary scenes at Tokyo University, Mishima's alma mater, where militant students clashed with thousands of riot police in a two-day battle of wooden sticks, projectiles, tear gas, and water cannons. The escalation in violence and lawlessness at the universities caused consternation among the Japanese public. If this was the result when activists gained control of their campuses, what would happen if they gained significant influence in national politics, as had happened in France and Czechoslovakia? Some Japanese commentators raised the possibility of sending in the Self-Defense Forces, the postwar name for Japan's military, to quell the protests if they grew any larger.

Yet the violence in Japan was to some degree rhetorical in nature, as evidenced by the low numbers of fatalities and serious injuries. The French writer Roland Barthes, who visited Japan during the protests, noted this intransitive quality of the violence, the way it seemed to express no content but was like a self-justifying gesture, a "great scenario of signs" that signified nothing.[1] More than a few students conceded the emptiness of their agenda in their own published statements, which reveal just how closely Mishima's existential angst coincided with that of the postwar generation. "I have never felt that I am really alive," wrote one student.

"I don't even know *why* I am alive, and that's why I don't care when I die. I have no hope for the future, no reason to live. So I put on a helmet, pick up a stick, and go to confront death. Perhaps at that moment I will have some kind of sense of being alive."[2] We can imagine these self-consciously despairing words, which seek a solution to nihilism in a theater of violence, being uttered by any number of Mishima's characters.

In October 1968, toward the height of the unrest, Mishima founded a civilian defense group he called the Tate-no-kai, the "Shield Society." The group's main purpose, as he explained it, was to serve as a standby militia that would assist government security forces in the event of a national revolution by procommunist activists. Small groups of reactionary students opposed to the campus revolutionaries had sprung up at universities around Japan, and Mishima was able to recruit members from these groups; within a year the Shield Society had one hundred members. Mishima also received generous support from government ministers and from SDF officers, who permitted him and his recruits to take part in training exercises at military bases.

The Shield Society was thus a product of the nervous, volatile situation in Japan at the end of the 1960s. But like all of Mishima's final enterprises, this one was also an imitation, an ostensible attempt to rejuvenate fading myths and modes of action by re-enacting them in the present. As always, literature played a part in shaping Mishima's vision. "Shield Society" has an unliterary sound to it. But the shields that Mishima has in mind are those of the *sakimori*, frontier guards of ancient Japan whose poems feature in the twentieth book of the *Man'yōshū*. Stationed at forlorn outposts along the Japanese coasts to defend against attacks from China and Korea, the frontier guards filled their poems with expressions of two conflicting types of sentiments. On the one hand the guards sang of their loneliness, and of their longing for their families and loved ones. But together with this sorrowful longing they also proclaimed their martial pride and their willingness to fight to the death for Japan and the imperial throne. The poems, each no longer than a single sentence, are direct and heartfelt, but arguably they are also predictable and melodramatic. Hence scholars have often considered them inferior to the more artful *Man'yōshū* poems composed by courtiers. "No matter what these poems by the frontier guards say," wrote Orikuchi Shinobu in 1938, "the fact is that they were written as pledges of loyalty and obedience to the imperial court. There is not a single poem among them that deserves to be regarded as truly lyrical."[3]

Mishima sees things differently. In his *Short History of Japanese Literature* he argues that it is precisely the fact that the poems originate in the guards' imperial duty that enables them to manifest a kind of lyricism that no courtier could ever emulate, a pained and piercing lyricism that is possible only when forced by the hand of fate. And in this piercing lyricism Mishima hears a reutterance of the tragic spirit of Prince Yamato Takeru, who had gone to his death for the emperor while composing poems of sorrowful longing. "Inevitably," writes Mishima, "in the guards' poems the Takeru element is more subservient, more honest, more human. But their fundamental cry is unmistakable: 'Imperial Majesty, we are ready to become your humble shields and die'" (35:557).

In these blunt declarations of devotion to life and resignation to death, written by Japanese soldiers more than twelve centuries ago, Mishima wants to find the double lyricism, the elegance and the brutality, which he sees as a continuous feature of Japanese culture from ancient times and which he says is now threatened with extinction. The real purpose of the Shield Society, then, is not to fight and to defend, but to manifest and display.

Aesthetic Terrorism

Mishima began using the term *bi-teki terorizumu* shortly after forming his militia. While "aesthetic terrorism" is probably the best English translation, the Japanese term contains a strong suggestion of "beautiful terrorism." Mishima's first use of this term was in the open letter he wrote in response to Hashikawa Bunzō's negative review of his new theory of the cultural emperor. There Mishima defended his position as follows:

> My view is that the general will of Japanese culture has always transcendentally contained the concept of a cultural emperor, and I am attempting to discover signs of it in the genealogy of aesthetic terrorism. In other words, I want to see the emperor as a point of connection between the cultural disorder generated by freedom of expression and the anarchism contained within aesthetic terrorism. By linking culture and politics at this unusual point, if only momentarily, I hope to demonstrate the emperor's unique nature. (35:207–208)

Mishima intends his term "aesthetic terrorism" to cover various well-known instances of political (or sometimes semireligious) violence in Japan since the middle of the nineteenth century: the rebellions, assassinations, and murderous attacks, and the defiant suicides (of the rebels and the assassins) that invariably followed them. There are some obvious problems, however, with the Japanese formulation *bi-teki terorizumu*. For one thing, it is difficult to ignore the irony that Mishima has been obliged to appropriate an English word to denote a concept that he claims is quintessentially Japanese. The fact is that there is no native Japanese word for "terrorism." That is understandable, since awareness of terrorism as a distinct category of violence is a modern tendency and "terrorism" is a word of relatively recent Western coinage. Nonetheless, the irony remains. For that matter, even the word *bi-teki* (literally "beauty-oriented" or "beauty-like") lacks etymological pedigree. It was coined only in the second half of the nineteenth century by Japanese scholars who felt the need for equivalents of Western notions of the beautiful. Thus each element of Mishima's Japanese catchphrase owes its origin to the West, an awkward fact of which he could hardly have been unaware.

Another objection might be that Mishima uses the word *terorizumu*, usually abbreviated to *tero*, in an extremely soft sense. The rebellion of February 1936 was a failed coup, not an act of terrorism. Likewise, many of the political assassinations and acts of insurrection that Mishima praises were not obviously intended to terrorize anyone. It could be argued, however, that this soft usage of the word *tero* is standard in Japan. We might also note that while acts of murderous violence were sometimes perpetrated by radical leftists, Mishima is interested only in those perpetrated by right-wing traditionalists and ultranationalists. Basically, the only acts of Japanese "terrorism" Mishima praises as beautiful are those that were committed by people claiming to be loyal to the emperor. Mishima has little to say about postwar bombing campaigns by Japanese communists, and he has nothing whatsoever to say about the foiled 1910 plot by Japanese anarchists to assassinate the Meiji emperor.

Mishima's claim that Japanese terrorism has contained an aesthetic element is certainly not fanciful. Though Japanese ultranationalists of the early twentieth century did not lack real-world grievances and political objectives, in their writings they often purveyed a pseudo-mystical idealism that was closer to poetry than to politics. The most fanatical among them, those who carried out terror attacks and assassinations, proclaimed in their manifestos their wish to achieve an "aesthetic death" (*bi-teki shi*). To them, death was never a macabre, banal, ugly reality; it was something incandescent and primordial, a return to the spirit of ancient Japan, to the myths and the gods. The true-hearted Japanese hero was too pure for the ugly modern world, and his act of suicidal violence was like a sacred ritual, the purpose of which was to ensure his passage to the realm of the *eirei*, the spirits of dead heroes. The following line is from the suicide note of a swordsman who assassinated a prominent financier in September 1921 and then immediately slit his own throat: "It is not a safe and easy life that I desire, but a death like the shattering of crystal."[4] It was typical for assassins to observe in their notes that the Japanese word for "death" (*shi*) is homonymous with the word for "poem" (*shi*). Nishida Mitsugi, a former soldier who was executed for his role in instigating the rebellion of February 1936, had stated, "I feel that the true purpose of life is to make one's death beautiful . . . and a beautiful thing is called a poem."[5]

Along with the 1936 rebellion, the act of Japanese "aesthetic terrorism" that Mishima regards as the most beautiful, and therefore the most exemplary, occurred in the southern city of Kumamoto in October 1876, five years after the abolition of the samurai class. Some two hundred former samurai who were hostile to Westernization organized themselves into a group they called the Shinpūren, a name that uses an alternative reading of the word *kamikaze* and translates as the "The League of the Divine Wind." On the evening of October 24 the samurai launched simultaneous attacks on military and government buildings around Kumamoto. Scornful of Western ways, the samurai did not use any firearms and attacked only with swords and spears, though a few of them used homemade explosives. Government forces easily crushed the uprising. More than half of the samurai rebels died fighting, and most of those who survived the battle later committed suicide by cutting their stomachs. For this extraordinary display of suicidal heroics, the uprising by the League of the Divine Wind served as a model of Japanese militant extremism for many decades thereafter. The writers of the Japan Romantic School idolized the Divine Wind samurai as quasi-artistic figures whose proud indifference to death expressed a "god-like poetry" (*kaminagara no shi*).[6]

Mishima summarizes the incident in more sober language:

When the new government enacted a law abolishing swords, collecting up these very symbols of samurai spirit, one hundred rebels attacked a Westernized Japanese army barracks with nothing but their swords and spears. Many were shot down by rifles—imported from the West; and all the survivors committed *hara-kiri*. . . . Their reckless action and inevitable defeat was necessary to show the existence of a certain essential spirit. Their ideology was a difficult one; it was the first radical prophecy of the danger inherent in Japanese modernization, which must damage the totality of culture. The painful condition of Japanese culture, which we feel today, is the fruit of what could only be vaguely apprehended by Japanese at the time of the League of the Divine Wind incident.[7]

Mishima's various other comments on the rebellion are speculative and rhapsodic, making them difficult to engage with scientifically. As in the above passage, he reduces the number of rebels from nearly two hundred to a more heroic one hundred, and he endlessly praises the "quintessential Japanese spirit" of their "fanatical and pure experiment" (39:634). On many occasions in his later reviews and essays Mishima uses the rebellion of the Divine Wind samurai as a template for his ideal work of art, which, he now insists, must be an event of historical importance. Always Mishima is preoccupied with the obsessive pursuit of a single idea to its extreme limit, an obsessiveness he has previously called logical consistency:

> If you are consumed with an idea, you cannot be victorious as an artist unless you pursue that idea completely. Unless the artist constructs a complete system, something rather like the League of the Divine Wind, within his work, it will not stand on its own as a work of art. (633)

In broad terms, the coupling of art and terrorism is not perverse. Acts of terrorism are calculated displays of violence that speak to us through their impact on our senses. Visually spectacular and highly dramatic, often they seem to blur or reject conventional distinctions between performance and reality. This, of course, is a feature they share with modern art. Modern artists challenged the boundary between art and reality because they realized that they were addressing an audience whose sensitivity to art had atrophied. The shock tactics of modern art have been an attempt to stall this process of atrophy, to resuscitate art's magical communicative power. What drives modern artists to utilize "terroristic" tactics is the ambition to overcome what Mishima calls "the hell of relativity": the loss of absolute values, the transfer of art into the realm of aesthetics, the disconnectedness of artists from their material, from tradition, and from modern audiences who seemed to have grown immune to art.[8]

From shock to terror is no great step, and the dream of making a work of art that will dangerously overwhelm both the audience who experiences it and the artist who makes it has great appeal to a certain kind of visionary mind. Mishima, acutely aware of a history of sickly, wilting Japanese writers imploding under the pressure of art, determines to break this stereotype by shockingly and triumphantly exploding *into* his art. To that end, the modern tradition of Japanese terrorism offers him an ideal template for his project. As he observes, "The ideology of Japanese terrorism is characterized by its intimate bond to the ideology of suicide" (34:370).

For readers today, this linking of terrorism and suicide in a single idea is bound to seem ominous. Mishima intended his praise of fearless martyrdom as a critique of postwar modernity, which, in his view, was encouraging a weak-willed survivalism. Countless Japanese had given their lives for the emperor, but "the Japanese are not going to give their lives for the sake of democracy" (40:707). Mishima himself lived long enough to witness the emergence of a new form of

Japanese terrorism that was born of the postwar era. In 1970 a group of radical leftists calling themselves "The Japan Red Army" began a campaign of terror that was to continue for almost two decades. The group operated internationally, using methods that had no precedent in Japan and which typify terrorism as we know it today: hijackings and indiscriminate bombings and mass shootings of civilians. As Mishima scornfully observed, the young radicals who joined the Japan Red Army lacked the self-sacrificial heroism—the "kamikaze spirit"—of his generation. After carrying out their attacks, Japan Red Army members fled and went into hiding or sought asylum overseas. In Mishima's view they were a disgrace to the beautiful tradition of *bi-teki tero* and represented yet another example of how Japan had become Westernized, ignoble, cowardly, and ugly.

Why Has the Emperor Become Human?

Mishima's most determined attempt to achieve a terroristic effect in his writing is a short story entitled "Voices of the Heroic Dead" (Eirei no koe). This was published in May 1966, while Mishima was still relishing the controversy he had caused with his film version of "Patriotism." Like that work, "Voices of the Heroic Dead" is more a ritual enactment than a story. It opens with these lines:

> One evening in early spring I attended a Shinto séance conducted by Sensei Kimura, and I was so overwhelmed by the experience that I shall never forget it. While I hesitate to describe in print many of the things that occurred that night, I feel duty-bound to record them as faithfully as I can. (20:465)

The narrator, an unnamed man of unspecified age, describes for us the strange occurrences at the séance. The sensei plays a stone flute to summon the spirits, which then speak through the mouth of a medium, a young blind man named Kawasaki. Two groups of spirits speak, at first separately, then later in unison. Other than the introductory pages and the closing lines, virtually the entire text of the story is presented as a direct transcription of words that are spoken, sung, chanted, and wailed by this multitude of spirits.

Kawasaki, the young medium, is like a youthful self-portrait of Mishima: "He was a beautiful young man, pale-faced, with narrow eyebrows, an anxious and shapely nose, and the gentle lips of a girl." Kawasaki lost his sight in an accident at the age of eighteen: "From then on he saw only the spiritual world" (467). As the sound of the flute begins, Kawasaki's face turns even paler and his shoulders start to tremble beneath his kimono.

Voices begin to speak through the medium. When the sensei asks them to identify themselves, the voices initially give the enigmatic reply: "We are the spirits of those who were betrayed" (475). Hundreds of thousands of spirits are gathering over the Sea of Japan, they explain, to lament the corruption and degeneracy of present-day society. It soon becomes clear that these voices are the spirits of the young army officers who were executed after the failed rebellion of February 1936: "We are the ones who thirty years ago raised a righteous army, only to be branded as mutineers and killed" (478).

The officers claim they had conceived of their uprising as an act of sacred communion with the emperor:

> At that time, Japan, the great land of abundant rice, had turned into a barren wasteland. The people were crying from starvation, women and children were being sold for money, and the imperial domain was everywhere filled with death. And so the gods devised a divine plan. They anointed us with the purest water from the well of history and secretly prepared us, as representatives of the weeping and starving people, to enter into a dialogue with our living god. (484)

The officers describe the events of the uprising, the emperor's ruling against them, and their own executions:

> Our enemies in the military quickly organized a sham trial, and death sentences were handed down before anyone had heard our explanations.
> We were tied to wooden crosses, and the bullets that came hurtling through our foreheads and hearts were stained with the disgrace of mutiny.
> That was the moment when His Majesty's great army perished. That was the moment when Japan's great moral law collapsed. On the day that these true-hearted samurai were shot as mutineers, Nazi-inspired villains among our military leaders began an unstoppable march to war. (490–491)

As seen in the above extracts, Mishima makes the spirits of the heroic dead speak in an unappealingly arch and jingoistic language. Some readers have said it is reminiscent of Japan's wartime propaganda fiction. Yet Mishima also puts heavy emphasis on the homoerotic potential of the young officers' passionate devotion to the emperor. The officers speak openly of their "love" (koi) for the emperor, and they recall their anger and disbelief upon finding that their feelings were unreciprocated. Mishima makes the officers sound like jilted lovers in a cheap song lyric:

> In our dreams we believed it was impossible that Your Majesty would not return our love. . . . We thought that this was all we needed to do: to serve

you, and love you, and love you, and love you, until we went crazy from love [*koishite, koishite, koishite, koi-gurui ni koishi tatematsureba yoi no da*]. (481)

This passage is not entirely gratuitous. At the time Mishima was writing, prison journals penned by some of the young officers who led the rebellion had recently been published, and they contained impassioned accusations against the emperor in language that was often blatantly homoerotic. Mishima had no doubt taken some inspiration from these journals, in which the officers also threatened to return as ghostly spirits to haunt the living. But Mishima exaggerates the fanaticism of their emperor obsession to ludicrous extremes. At one point the young officers jubilantly imagine all the seas and shorelines around the Japanese archipelago turning red with their own "pure-hearted blood" (478). There follows a fantasy death scene in which the emperor gallops up on a white stallion and commands his loyal servants to kill themselves on the spot. The officers cry in unison, "Long live His Imperial Majesty!" (488). Delirious with joy, they plunge their swords into their bellies and drop dead at His Majesty's feet. Love doesn't get any crazier than this.

Next, a second group of "true-hearted samurai" (*sekisei no samurai*), speaking through the medium, identify themselves. They are the spirits of kamikaze pilots who were killed in action during the Pacific War:

Our hope was to be the last kamikaze. *Kamikaze*—who chose this name? When the last plans of the human world have ended in disaster and all hope is lost, when portents of total annihilation are openly flitting back and forth between people's faces like swallows in the roof-eaves, and above us there is nothing but the eyes of a clear blue sky for watching the imminent battle-to-the-death . . . suddenly there blows a wind of salvation, as irrational as anything that can be imagined, blithely disdainful of human thinking and psyche, and of all things that are human. Do you see? *That is kamikaze.* (498–499)

The pilots recount their training and preparation for their mission: "For half a year we trained for death, and we learned how to die skillfully, effectively, and precisely." They recall how people regarded them awkwardly and with mixed feelings: "Even our own officers looked at us with a smile of shame on their haughty lips; it was the unbearable shame of those who know that they are going to keep on living" (499). Like the spirits of the army officers, the spirits of the kamikaze pilots claim they had believed they were entering into a "secret pact with a god" (*kami to mokkei*), toward whom they would "accelerate" at the moment of their death: "The distance between us and him would shrink to zero, and then we, that god, and death would unite as one body . . . we would become one with His Majesty the Emperor" (500–501).

Only the emperor's divine nature, the pilots claim, gives meaning to their heroic sacrifice: "For us to become living gods, His Majesty must be a god." The pilots do not explain why this should be so. They merely assert, over and over, that their faith in the divinity of the emperor is the only thing that guarantees their immortality:

His Imperial Majesty must not allow himself to be swayed by human emotions, or by tears, and try to stop us from dying. For only a god can make authentic tragedy of such irrational deaths, of such magnificent slaughter of young men. If otherwise, our deaths would be nothing more than a foolish sacrifice. . . . Instead of dying as gods, we would die as slaves. (501)

The pilots describe their final moments and then berate the emperor for repudiating his divine status after the war. In an imperial rescript written at the behest of the US Occupation authorities and printed in the Japanese press on New Year's Day 1946, Hirohito, the Showa emperor, had asserted the falsehood of any conception of him as divine. It was an extraordinary moment in modern history. In the middle of the twentieth century, the ruling monarch of a developed nation was being obliged to inform his subjects that he was not, as had previously been reported, a living god. Some Japanese commentators later stated that the emperor's declaration of his human status was more shocking than if he had been killed at the end of the war.

In Mishima's narrative, the spirits of the kamikaze pilots accuse the emperor of tarnishing the glory of their deaths.

When His Majesty declared that he was merely a human being
The spirits of those who died for a god were stripped of their titles,
And there was nowhere for them to be enshrined.
Blood still pours from the hollow frames of their chests,
And though they reside in the world of the gods, they find no peace.
. . .
No matter how pressured or coerced,
Even if threatened with death,
His Majesty should not have said that he is a human being.
He should have stood fast against the censure and scorn of the world

> And preserved his divine status,
> Without conceding its illusory nature, its falseness,
> (Even if he thought this in his heart).
> . . .
> Why did the emperor become a human being? [*nadote sumerogi wa hito
>   to naritamaishi*].
> (512–513)

At the time they were written, these were bold and dangerous statements. Japanese readers had not seen anything like this in print before. But Mishima is not yet finished. At the end of the story, as both groups of spirits are screaming and wailing together, the blood drains completely from the young medium's face and he collapses. The spectators gather round and find that he is dead. These are the final lines:

> It was not only the fact that he was dead that shocked us. The face of the dead boy was not Kawasaki's. To our astonishment, it had changed beyond recognition. It had changed ambiguously into the face of someone else. (514)

Has Mishima symbolically killed the emperor? Some Japanese readers thought so, and on its publication "Voices of the Heroic Dead" provoked outrage and bewilderment. Okuno Takeo, a literary critic who had previously admired Mishima's work, later recalled, "When I first read this piece I felt a horror and a revulsion that made my skin crawl. I could have no more sympathy for Mishima if he was going to write like this. I even wondered if he had been possessed by something and had lost his sanity."[9] Mishima himself encouraged this idea, claiming in interviews that he had written the work in a single sitting as if possessed by forces beyond his control. An alternate draft of the manuscript, discovered after his death, shows that this claim was false, another instance of self-mythification. Other readers complained about the ugliness of the prose, its heavy-handedness and repetitiveness, the triteness of its metaphors and similes. The harshest criticism was directed at the passages of neoclassical verse. The poet Mitsuhana Takao expresses the consensus when he writes, "You would need heroism to call this 'poetry'; it is truly awful."[10]

"Voices of the Heroic Dead" is a tour de force of hyperbole, cliché, bombast, and crude homosexual innuendo. And yet the man responsible for this "awful" piece was simultaneously at work on the novel *Spring Snow*, which contains some of the finest modern Japanese prose that has yet been written. Had Mishima, in the excitement of his mischief making, temporarily lost his objective distance from his material? Or was the vulgarity of the prose itself a kind of aesthetic terrorism, a scornful parody of the language of the wartime propagandists?[11]

As if the storm of critical outrage that greeted the story was not enough for him, Mishima also released a recording of himself reciting one of the long poetic passages, which in the story is spoken by the spirits of the kamikaze pilots. In this recording Mishima speaks in an eerie monotone, with a Noh-style musical accompaniment and various weather effects sounding in the background. The performance is a single unbroken crescendo, by the end of which, over a furious din of flutes and drums and swirling gales and claps of thunder, Mishima is almost shouting his words: "Why has the emperor become human! Why has the emperor become human!" The performance is outlandish, kitsch, preposterous. Yet at the same time, somehow, it is genuinely menacing.

An objection could be made that Mishima has overstated the importance of the emperor's claim to divinity. After all, the conception of the Japanese emperor as a living god was no more than a short-lived modern myth. While Japan's most ancient written documents assert that the imperial dynasty has a divine origin, being descended from the sun goddess Amaterasu Ōmikami, they make no claim for the divinity of the individual emperors. Each was a human being whose ancestors were gods. The emperor was a mediator between the Japanese people and their numerous deities, a sacred figure but not a god.

Nationalists of modern Japan did not initially deviate from this view. "For the Japanese people, the emperor is an object of religious devotion," wrote Ōkawa Shūmei, a prominent nationalist thinker of the 1920s. "You cannot speak of the emperor without acknowledging this religious element. It is through the emperor that the Japanese people connect to the foundational origin of our own lives. For us, the emperor expresses the highest life that unites all our lives."[12] Thinkers like Ōkawa advocated religious devotion to a sacred figure, but stopped short of claiming that the emperor was divine.

It was ultranationalist military officers of the 1930s who hailed the emperor as a living god. Religious reverence of the emperor became a vital element of Japan's wartime propaganda policies. Yet even the pilots of the kamikaze squadrons did not believe that the emperor was divine, as their final letters and diary entries attest. The pilots regarded the emperor with awe as the supreme symbol of Japanese history and culture, a crystallization of the splendor of Japan and its people, but not as a living god.[13]

But here it is important to make a distinction between belief and faith. We do not actually have to believe in society's symbolic order in order to put our faith and trust in it. People can feel bound by a sense of commitment to something that they know is a shared fiction.[14] The divinity of the Japanese emperor is best understood as a shared fiction in this sense. Even Mishima's spirits seem to concede this point, as when they say that the emperor should not have conceded the "illusory nature" (*kakū*) and the "falseness" (*itsuwari*) of his divine status, "even if he thought this in his heart" (513).

For all its excesses, "Voices of the Heroic Dead" succeeds in articulating concerns that were shared, though seldom uttered, by many Japanese of Mishima's generation. Namely, that the war had been worthless, that the emperor had not been properly held to account for his responsibility, that by disavowing his divine status he had nullified the meaning of the countless sacrifices that had been made in his name, and that without a transcendent figurehead postwar Japan was sinking into spiritual barrenness. And while Mishima hyperbolizes the issue of the emperor's divinity, there is no question that the humanization of the emperor after the war was a momentous event in the spiritual history of modern Japan. People ought to have been stricken with panic, yet superficially they carried on as if it were merely a minor readjustment. It is this evasiveness, this willful repression of collective memory, that Mishima wants to attack. His intention is not just to melodramatize the trauma of the loss of the emperor as a value-guaranteeing absolute, but to insist that Japan's experience of this loss has *not been traumatic enough*. This, I believe, is the radical, almost cruel accusation at the heart of this strange and disturbing work.

World of Moonlight and Blossoms

As in "Patriotism," in "Voices of the Heroic Dead" Mishima is addressing issues that are specific to modern Japan. Yet it needs to be recognized that his provocative, reactionary project had parallels overseas. Just as Mishima was re-enacting the violent ideological fanaticism of wartime Japan, writers and filmmakers in Europe were starting to make artistic treatments of fascism and Nazism. Among the most successful results were Luchino Visconti's film *The Damned* (1969), which Mishima reviewed with gushing enthusiasm, Hans-Jürgen Syberberg's *Hitler, a Film from Germany* (1977), and Rainer Werner Fassbinder's *Lili Marleen* (1981). Some commentators saw cause for concern in this new genre, complaining that these works glamorized the material and promoted what was, in effect, a kind of Nazi chic. In a 1975 article titled "Fascinating Fascism," Susan Sontag included Mishima's *Confessions of a Mask* and *Sun and Steel* on a list of recent works that, she argued, glorified ideals that had become associated with fascism: "the ideal of life as art, the cult of beauty, the fetishism of courage, the dissolution of alienation in ecstatic feelings of community; the repudiation of the intellect; the family of man (under the parenthood of leaders)."[15] We can see that this list matches Mishima's interests and attitudes very closely. And just like the Europeans and their Nazi chic, more than the dangerous ideology that he appropriates, Mishima relishes the paraphernalia and euphoria that accompany it: the military uniforms, the blood oaths, the death poems, the martial ethos, the training regimes, the obsession with physical perfection, the intoxication of the "community unto death," the aestheticization of virtually everything that can be aestheticized, and the erotic dream of individual consciousness dissolving into the totality.

The Jewish historian Saul Friedländer said that the bedrock of Nazi aesthetics was a juxtaposition of kitsch and death.[16] Kitsch and death: these are two things that ought to be incompatible. The essence of kitsch is that it is not authentic; it offers nothing but fake emotions and fake effects. This inauthenticity stems from a lack of conviction, an underlying deficiency of faith. The world of kitsch is a vast zone of unfeeling. Kitsch offers the accoutrements of faith without the faith itself. Death is, or should be, the opposite. Death is the one undeniably authentic event, so authentic that it is almost unbearable to contemplate. While kitsch offers a sentimentality that cannot hurt us, death induces terror. The paradoxical bonding of these two opposing elements creates a uniquely unsettling effect.

Material for a Japanese kitsch of death exists in abundance. We find it in the protocols of the seppuku ceremony and the various clichés of samurai machismo, in the aesthetic category of "cruel beauty" (*zankoku-bi*) and the stylized blood-letting of the Kabuki stage, and in the countless glorified death scenes found in historical chronicles and literary works. Consider the suicide scenes in Japan's medieval war tales: a defeated samurai general, his castle in flames, drinks one last cup of sake with his most loyal men; he then takes a brush and tearfully writes a death poem, slits open his stomach, and offers his head for decapitation. Or the final journeys of suicidal lovers in Chikamatsu's tragedies for the puppet theater: the two lovers, their hearts breaking, tearfully walk the road of death, praying to the gods and the Buddha as a wind blows through the pine trees; there is a flash of the dagger with which the lovers stab themselves, and then their two spirits enter the bliss of nirvana . . .

Something very close to kitsch can also be found in the most fanatical excla-mations of the Japan Romantic School. Here is Hasuda Zenmei (1904–1945), one of the mentors of the teenage Mishima, writing at full throttle in June 1939:

Equating poetry with spirit is a distinctive feature of Japanese culture. To my mind it is the most suitable way of speaking about Japan.

Literature does not merely make people decadent. It orders them to die. In its cruel voice the will of greatness survives in us. Do not complain about war or death with cheap modern ideas, for poetry lies in the direction of hearing that voice.

All Japanese people are essentially heroes. It is no "sacrifice" as such when our soldiers rise up, determined to obey the command of the absolute, for one by one they all become heroes. And thus they begin to create poetry. They feel that they have descended from the poetic world, and they are resolved to return to it. Orders are not obeyed as a collective military unit. Orders are already the path that says: "Die!" This command to die is what makes you a "blossom." Just a single blossom. How solemn! How poetic!

Poetry is not life, no matter how lofty the meaning of that life. Poetry is loftier still. It is the world of moonlight and blossoms.

What we crave is a place to die. . . . A bullet strikes you. Your vision becomes blurry. You walk on, you stumble and fall. And beneath your feet you see the spirit of the earth, the grass and the leaves, you see clouds curdling through the sky. This earth, this spirit, this grass, these clouds— all is poetry![17]

An enraptured consciousness dreaming of its own destruction. A promise of transcendent unity. Spirit as poetry, and poetry as portal to immortality. This is the language of the death cult, and although Hasuda exalts what he claims is a "distinctive feature of Japanese culture," Western readers are likely to perceive in his lines an echo of the effusions of the eighteenth-century German Romantics or their unpleasant twentieth-century imitators. At the time Hasuda wrote the above passage, German purveyors of Nazi lyricism were composing poems to the sacred purity of the Reich.

Poetry and purity as synonyms for death. This is the hackneyed, degenerate aesthetic with which Mishima chooses to define his late style. As a conscious recreation of kitsch, it is in constant danger of lapsing into parody, a danger that is abated only by the grim seriousness with which Mishima pursues his project off the page.

For example, it is almost impossible to read *Runaway Horses* (*Honba*, 1969), the novel in which Mishima chronicles the career of a right-wing terrorist in the 1930s, without superimposing our knowledge of the author onto the protagonist. That is just what Mishima intends. Isao, the aspiring young terrorist, is motivated more by narcissism than by any social or political agenda. While he admires the samurai of the League of the Divine Wind, he has not been radicalized by any clearly definable ideology. And although he is ruthless in his determination to carry out an assassination, he does not hate his victim. In fact, he seems to think that the "purity" of his violence would be diminished by such hatred. The one clear objective in his mind is aesthetic: he wants to kill and he wants to die *beautifully*. Terrorism is the means whereby he actualizes this narcissistic vision.

Isao's meditations evoke the most morbid features of Japanese ultranationalist mysticism while juxtaposing kitsch and death in a paradoxical manner similar to that described by Friedländer:

> Purity took the idea of cherry blossoms, the idea of the strong minty taste of mouthwash, the idea of clinging tightly to your mother's gentle bosom, and joined them directly to the idea of blood, the idea of swords striking down injustice, of blood spraying from a neck that has been sliced through with a blade, and to the idea of seppuku. The moment a samurai "fell like the blossom," his blood-smeared corpse was instantly transformed into fragrant cherry blossoms. Purity was this arbitrary transition between contraries. Hence purity was poetry. (13:515)

Arguably, this is no more than another variant of the dichotomies we have tracked in earlier chapters: hypersensitivity and unfeeling, art and crime, creation and destruction, orderliness and intoxication, beauty and terror. The ultimate vision Isao cherishes for himself renders all of these into a cluster of kitsch: "To climb to the top of a cliff at sunrise, pay homage to the rising sun, look down over the sparkling sea, and then, at the foot of a noble pine tree, I want to stab myself to death" (520–521).

Then there is the matter of Isao's attitude toward the emperor. Isao is rabidly devoted to an idealized vision of the emperor, one that seems to take no particular object and which could never be achieved in the real world. This has perplexed readers who want to understand *Runaway Horses* as historical fiction. One Japanese critic, struggling to find words to describe Isao's notion of the emperor, calls it "an abstract conceptual signifier that transcends specificity."[18] We might as well call it "God." Isao himself cannot fathom the source or meaning of his own restless yearning for violence. He longs for an Absolute that is inexpressible, or that can only be expressed in a shocking paradox. Here we may recall how the young Mishima had wondered if paradox might be a shortcut to the divine. Isao, pursuing himself with paradoxes, is almost convinced of the necessity, and even the essential goodness, of doing evil:

It is clear that the supreme moral goodness resides only in the will to kill, and yet the law that criminalizes this will is enforced in the name of the emperor, the immaculate Sun. Thus the supreme morality is punished by the supreme moral being. Who could have devised this terrifying contradiction? Was His Majesty aware of it? (733)

All Isao knows for sure is that he wants to "dirty his hands with a little act of pure evil, a little blasphemy" (734). That last word intimates the religious nature of his attitude. Isao plots an assassination and successfully carries it out, but his fundamental yearning is toward the sacred. Though he lacks the language to articulate it, what he craves for himself is transfiguration. Through an encounter with the sacred he dreams of conferring a kind of holiness upon himself. His act of violence, which comprises assassination followed by suicide, is like a rite of sacrifice in which Isao is both executioner and victim. Here again, one feels, Mishima's vision, which his contemporaries deemed eccentric, comes very close to a phenomenon that is all too familiar to us today.

Evil, insofar as it is a forbidden realm, is related to the realms of the erotic and the sacred. Morality deems it indefensible, but this only increases its allure. One of Mishima's early short stories contains this peculiar aphorism: "Crime is the rage of the gods against those who relish a divine pleasure that human mortals are not supposed to experience" (16:384). That statement makes little sense unless we assume that the first word denotes something like "the guilty feelings of those who commit crime." For Mishima, and for his characters, any act that intentionally breaks the taboo of the law generates a surge of eroticism.

It would therefore be a mistake to read *Runaway Horses* as a straightforward drama of good versus evil. Mishima gives Isao yearnings that are clearly opposed to goodness:

"When will I be able to go to jail?" thought Isao. The fact that there was, as yet, no chance that he would be thrown in jail was displeasing to him in many ways. [. . .] If it were possible, he wanted to die under a pure morning sun, and at that moment he wanted the wind in the pine trees on the cliff and the reflection of the sea to merge with the stench of urine from the rough, damp, concrete walls of a jailhouse. (13:527)

These lines recall Mishima's remark about Oscar Wilde's fatalistic longing for a filthy prison bath. In each case there is a strong suggestion of self-punishment, of evil and blasphemy against the gods as means to turn oneself into a scapegoat. By aligning himself with that which society deems indefensible, Isao seeks a sovereign value that is not subject to external limitations. Only by condemning himself, it seems, can the aesthetic terrorist feel that he is truly free.

In her comments on Syberberg's film about Hitler, Susan Sontag delicately wondered if Syberberg had perhaps been a little too sympathetic to the terrifying world he had recreated so faithfully in art. Mishima makes a similar point, with no delicacy at all, in his review of Visconti's *The Damned*:

> In its Wagnerian manner, its German grotesquerie, its transvestitism, its nervous insanity, its ponderousness, its symphonic sense of psychological danger, its worship of the body, its unceasing dramatic tension, its excesses, its obsession with hurling every single character toward tragedy and death, its ostentation, its sensuality, its love of ritual and ceremony, its intoxication, and its shattering dark lyricism which is like a blue sky suddenly cloaked by clouds, *The Damned* recreates the hate-filled beauty of the Nazis so faithfully that it virtually becomes the thing it depicts. (36:101–102)

I am sure Mishima was burning with envy when he wrote those lines. To become the thing he depicts: this, of course, is the little act of pure evil that the author of *Runaway Horses* will soon commit.

One way of categorizing Mishima's artistic strategy during his final phase would be to say that he attempts to make a progression from writing works *about* crimes and criminality to writing works *with* criminal intentions. His lawsuit and censorship problems were the first direct consequences of this. *The Temple of the Golden Pavilion* is a story about an aesthetic terrorist, whereas "Voices of the Heroic Dead" and *Runaway Horses* are themselves literary acts of aesthetic terrorism. As Japan approached what many were hailing as the completion of its astonishingly rapid process of modernization and democratization after the Western model, Mishima taunted Japan by lauding aspects of its history and traditions that seemed most at odds with that process: aggressive ultranationalism, military glory, samurai ethics, ritual suicide, the way of the sword, religious reverence of the emperor, the ancient myths of violence and insurrection, the kamikaze, and so on.

The writings Mishima published during his final year are mostly very short and minor texts: prefaces and afterwords to books by other writers or to collections of his own works, notes for theater pamphlets, blurbs for book covers, and so on. Yet even in these little texts Mishima never let up his attack. He was unequivocal about his objective: "I am putting a curse on present-day Japan" (*watashi ga genka Nihon no noroite de aru*; 35:207). He provided a glowing afterword for a biography of his former mentor Hasuda Zenmei, who had committed suicide after Japan's surrender. He lavished extravagant praise on yakuza movies for preserving what he said were feudal Japanese concepts of duty and honor. He lamented the decline of Japan's traditional "naked festivals," which had fallen victim to a growing censoriousness that was based, he argued, on a Christian moral outlook imported from the West. Mishima relentlessly attacked those "vulgar-minded bureaucrats" who were intent on turning Japan into a "cultured nation" (35:47). Against this, Mishima urged the Japanese to take pride in their primitivism:

How wonderful it is for civilized people to retain their primitivism! How proud for a modern person to be a noble savage rather than a pale-faced city dweller! And how old-fashioned, how typically nineteenth-century, to be a nation of "civilized people" who refuse to acknowledge the primitive roots that lie deep beneath their nation's culture! (35:126–127)

Mishima scoffed at the pacifism of the postwar constitution, which had obliged Japan to restyle its military as "self-defense forces," a maneuver Mishima denounced as yet another piece of hypocrisy. In defiance he enthused about *Hagakure*, a morbid eighteenth-century treatise on samurai honor and the glory of self-sacrifice, which twentieth-century militarists had plucked from obscurity and promoted as exemplary of the Japanese character. Since 1945 *Hagakure* had become taboo. Mishima scandalously hailed it as "a bible for beautiful murderers" and an indispensable text for "sweeping away the humanistic morals of anemic intellectuals" (35:764).

In this way, each of Mishima's final pieces of writing functioned as a symbolic act of terrorism, a literary grenade lobbed at an increasingly Westernized, secularized, and "civilized" Japan.

The Last Humans

On a superficial level, then, Mishima assumes the role of a radical conservative who is fighting to preserve Japan's cultural identity and fading traditions. But of course this is not the whole story. As I have argued, Mishima's view of the world is founded on artistic models. In his final "terroristic" stage his view has not changed, and the decadent aestheticism that governed the works of his adolescence and his early career still dominates his thinking. Thus it is not enough for Mishima to attach his name to the genealogy of Japanese aesthetic terrorism. It is necessary that this genealogy comes to an end *in him*. Mishima's ambition is not to revive a beautiful tradition but to manifest it for the final time, and his project thus assumes the ironical form of a decadent lyric that flaunts its own futility. These lines are from one of the manifestos he wrote for the Shield Society:

We are the last protectors of the culture, history, and traditions of Japan. . . . We radically oppose all ideologies that aspire toward a "better and brighter society." To act for the future is to deny the ripeness of culture, to deny the dignity of tradition. In taking it upon ourselves to embody history . . . and the beautiful forms of history, we follow the same principles of action as the samurai of the League of the Divine Wind and the [kami-kaze] pilots of the Special Attack Squadron, who in their last testaments stated that they believed no one would come after them. . . . Effectiveness is not an issue for us, because we do not think of our existence or our actions as constituting progress toward the future. . . . We embody the traditions of Japanese beauty [*wareware wa Nihon no bi no dentō o taiken suru mono de aru*]. (35:389–392)

A militia that does not care about its own effectiveness! Nothing matters any longer but the dream of becoming beautiful, of embodying a beautiful dream. To think of the (living) future is already to submit to rational calculation and therefore to negate this dream.

"I refuse to believe in the future," declared Mishima in one of his many media interviews. "I prefer to think that I carry all of tradition on my shoulders, and that literature will end with me" (35:379). Mishima's chief inspiration for this attitude was *Hagakure*, which instructs samurai to deepen their experience of the present by giving no thought for the future. "Only the weak put their hopes in the future," says Mishima, "only people who think of themselves as processes" (35:313). Refusing to believe in the future does not, he insists, mean living only in the present moment: "We must think of ourselves as the result of many generations of culture and tradition, in order to perform our present work fully" (315).

But even as he says this, Mishima repeatedly portrays Japan as a culture in decline. His final statements are full of gloomy prophesies:

I no longer have any great hopes for Japan. Each day deepens my feeling that Japan is ceasing to be Japan. Soon Japan will vanish altogether. In its place, all that will remain is an inorganic, empty, neutral, drab, wealthy, scheming, economic giant in a corner of the Far East. I will not listen any longer to people who are content with that prospect. (36:214–215)

Japan is coming to an end, says Mishima, and he is its final embodiment. During another of his university lectures he told the students:

Right now I have no room in my life for thinking about the future, because I am convinced that I am the last remnant of the cultural traditions and national characteristics of the Japanese people that have continued since antiquity, and that when I am gone it will all be over. I am the purest essence of this thing called Japan, and that is how I will end. (40:281)

And yet, in his final interview, conducted just one week before his death and published posthumously as his "last words," Mishima offered many opinions about the future. Again he linked Japan's national identity crisis to wider trends, to the universalization of capitalist values and the merging of all world cultures into a single common culture:

I suspect that my generation will be the last that truly knows the Japanese language. After us, there will be no one who carries within them the words of the Japanese classics. All that lies ahead is internationalism, a type of abstractionism. . . . In the future the whole world, the capitalist nations at least, will face exactly the same problems. People will still speak different languages, but they will all have the same mentality, the same feelings about life. That day is coming, and inevitably so. For we are the last humans [*saigo no ningen*], and there's nothing any of us can do about it. (40:779–780)

Mishima's pessimism here is surely genuine. He has consistently argued that a culture can only exist if it possesses a unified form of life, and yet Japan, like cultures elsewhere, is rapidly being absorbed by the West. Mishima believes that the universalization of a single dominant culture will mean no culture at all. And his conviction that Japan's cultural identity is defined by its literary traditions has not diminished at all since his youth.

In the passage quoted above, *saigo no ningen* is presumably Mishima's Japanese rendering of *der letzte Mensch*, the phrase used by Nietzsche's Zarathustra to warn of the imminent end of modern culture. The "last humans" who inhabit culture's final phase are timid, insignificant creatures. Chronically cynical and incapable of passion, they do not care strongly enough about anything to stake their lives on it. All they want is comfort and peace of mind. They work, obey, conform, and ask no difficult questions. Contemporary Japanese society, says Mishima, is just like this, a society of sheer relativism where there is nothing but *nichijōsei*, the mundaneness of everyday life. Perhaps Mishima was thinking of Japan's growing population of docile white-collar workers, the "office ladies" and the "salarymen."

For the last humans there is no such thing as transcendence, and without transcendence, Mishima insists, eroticism cannot exist: "Eroticism only releases its true value when it makes contact with something transcendent" (745). In order for people to know life in its fullness there must be a transcendent principle, an Absolute, on which they are willing to stake their lives. In a clear echo of Bataille, Mishima now declares that eroticism means affirming life up to the point of risking death, a paradox he calls "reaching the Absolute from the underside." And Mishima characterizes his own project as an attempt to accomplish just that: "I am going to revive the Absolute, no matter how impossible that may be, and I am going to make eroticism complete [*erotishizumu wo kansei shimasu*]" (750–751).

No matter how impossible. As the ironic inflexion of this remark suggests, Mishima's final position is devoid of anything resembling pragmatic, real-world political goals. Japanese Romanticism is radically apolitical since it strives toward ideals that can only be realized by the imagination. That is why the ever-ambiguous figure of the emperor is so easily appropriated as a Romantic concept. "Romanticism is always one step ahead," Yasuda Yojūrō had written. "Something that has never been heard of before and does not yet exist—that is the only objective it needs."[19] The Absolute that Mishima locates in his beautiful ideal of the emperor is something that can only be grasped negatively, through a nostalgia that has no expectation of fulfillment.

"My novels cannot dissolve into the Absolute that is His Majesty the Emperor," says Mishima in his final interview. "My art can only exist at a point of not being able to reach him." That is really no more than a histrionic restatement of the lesson Mishima had learned from his study of the fin-de-siècle aesthetes two decades earlier; namely, that beauty is a value, and values are not facts. The only thing that can turn values into facts is action. Romantic longing for ideal beauty belongs only to the realm of the imaginary, of the impossible. "The impossible is art, the possible is action," says Mishima. "The possible is death" (770).

The Defeat of Language

Aside from *The Decay of the Angel*, the fourth of his quartet of novels *The Sea of Fertility*, the last installment of which he delivered to his publishers on the day of his death, the final piece of fiction that Mishima published was a little story with the title "Prince Ranryō" (Ranryō-ō). A calm and evocative piece, inevitably it has been overshadowed by the violent drama of Mishima's death scene. Yet in its own way it is a perfect crystallization of his ambition to connect himself to Japanese tradition in such a way as to confer immortality upon himself, while at the same time seeming to bid his farewell to literature and the profession of writing.

"Prince Ranryō" interweaves fact, fiction, autobiography, classical literature, and ancient myth in a manner wholly characteristic of Mishima's late style. The setting is an SDF training camp near Mount Fuji, where Mishima and thirty student members of the Shield Society spent four weeks in the summer of 1969. Mishima took notes while at the camp and completed the manuscript one week later.

Mishima begins by telling us that some of the students had collapsed from heat exhaustion during the grueling training exercises, but not Mishima himself, of course. After dinner and a bath, Mishima returns to his room in the barracks. The room is bare and austere. And Mishima, for once, is happy:

A desk, a steel bed. On the walls, only my raincoat, combat fatigues, helmet, and water flask. Nothing here was superfluous. . . . Outside the open window, beyond the darkness of the barracks yard, I could feel the base of Mount Fuji spreading all around. In that pitch-black darkness, existence itself was softly and densely enclosing the lights of the barracks. The plain and simple way of life for which I had yearned so long was mine at last. (20:565)

A few of the students gather in Mishima's room. One of them is a player of the *yokobue*, a transverse bamboo flute that produces a piercing, high-pitched sound. For many centuries the *yokobue* has been one of the instruments featuring in the music performed at Japan's imperial court. After answering a few questions from Mishima about the history of the flute, the student performs the ancient piece of music known by the title of *Prince Ranryō*.

Ranryō, a Japanese reading of the Chinese name "Lanling," was a semilegendary Chinese warrior-prince who lived in the sixth century. He was famous for his beautiful features, which he is said to have concealed beneath a fierce mask when leading his troops into battle. The piece of music that bears his name was supposedly composed by his soldiers to honor him after one of his great battle victories, and later found its way to Japan. It lasts about five minutes and is usually performed as the accompaniment to a dance by a solo male dancer, who is dressed in princely robes and wears a dragon mask.

In language thick with ornate similes, Mishima describes the music and his responses to it:

The sound grew more joyful, more rhythmical; then it became stern and sorrowful again.
    At one moment it seemed to express a sort of heroic tension, like tears in the corners of strained eyes. Then suddenly it changed to a sound that evoked the merry indolence of a banquet.

Constant throughout these fluctuations was the sound of the boy's breathing, and it was this that formed the core of the lyricism. The boy's forceful and diligent breathing was easily linked to our own stressed breathing during the strenuous marching exercises we had practiced that morning in the scorching heat. At the same time, his sharp breaths seemed to intimate the brevity of adolescence in the cool air of the night.

I realized that the flute was related in equal proportion to two completely opposing things: a lyricism that expressed the overflowing wildness of life, and a lyricism that was gasping on the verge of death. Prince Ranryō had set off from his camp. And as he did so, an absolute form of these two kinds of lyricism was manifest in his extraordinary mask. A lyricism as lucid and absolute as a bow drawn to its tautest point.

The sound of the flute assaulted my ears again and again, like the waves of an evening sea . . .

It was as if I was not listening with my ears, but listening deep inside my head, where there was also a vast dark field, and the sound was reaching me from somewhere far beyond, as if the flute were being played in the extreme depths of my mind. (568–569)

Initially, Mishima avoids using the word *ongaku* (music) and instead writes only of *oto* (sound). This enables him to generate an ambiguity between the "sound" of the flute and the "sound" of the boy's breathing. Mishima manipulates this ambiguity with marvelous delicacy, reducing the clarity of his description little by little as he proceeds, so as to achieve a distorting effect whereby boy and flute seem to merge into a single entity. At one point Mishima tells us, "There was not the slightest warmth in that sound, which was utterly dominated by coldness. It seemed so far away, then suddenly so near" (569). We naturally assume that this refers to the sound of the flute. But in his next sentence Mishima writes, "At that moment I could see a face of some kind rising amid the sound of the flute." This unexpected emphasis makes us wonder if it is perhaps the boy's breath that is dominated by coldness. Mishima then writes:

That sound descended a gentle hill, but then began to climb a very steep slope that seemed as if it would go on forever, and, as the harsh breathing continued with undiminished intensity, somewhere in the distance a death that was frozen as ice seemed to be opening its mouth to welcome the breath of the boy. (569)

Tradition says that a particularly fine *yokobue* performance has the power to conjure up ghosts. Mishima's vision of youthful vitality turning to icy death is obviously intended to recall that tradition. As always, however, Mishima desires more than just a fusion of beauty and death. He wants to capture the special form of beauty that obsesses him, one that contains an intrinsic deathly element yet which is not morbid in any negative sense. An honest expression of the totality of life must, by logical necessity, also contain an acknowledgment of death: this is the idea Mishima was tentatively theorizing in the youthful writings we examined earlier, where he equated the ecstasy of seeing a beautiful thing with a "chilly kind of sadness that deserves to be called tragic" (43:130).

In "Prince Ranryō" Mishima's phantasmagorical description elevates both boy and flute to an ethereal realm of essences, from which all sense of time has been eliminated. Mishima ruminates on the mesmerizing stasis of the flute's long, shrill notes:

> I realized that this music was flowing without developing in any way. Not to develop at all—that is crucial. If music is to be truly faithful to the dynamic continuity of life (just as the flute is faithful to the human breath!), what could be purer than not to develop at all? Again and again the sounds surged forward and then receded, like waves. Yet all this seemed to happen in a single instant. (569)

It is not timelessness that Mishima strives to evoke here, I think, but an intimation of sacred time. He is experiencing the music not so much as a performance but as a kind of sacrament. In this sacrament, the repetitive quality of the music signifies a resistance to all notions of progress. The vital feature, as Mishima says, is "not to develop at all" (*nanra hatten shinai koto*). The solemn, static sounds reactualize a primordial, sacred time that does not belong to the historical present. In this sacred time, Mishima imagines, there is no progress toward the future. There is only an eternal return to a mythical past: a time of legends, heroes, gods, and ancient rites.

With a flute, a mask, a ghostly apparition, and an evocation of beauty hidden in a deathly realm, "Prince Ranryō" obviously aspires to replicate the atmosphere of the Noh theater. Mishima inserts several Noh references into the text. For example, before beginning his performance, the boy has explained that he took up the flute because he wants to die a beautiful death like that of Kiyotsune, a legendary Japanese warrior who was said to have played the flute before committing suicide by drowning. This prompts Mishima to quote some lines from the Noh play in which Kiyotsune appears:

> Without a word to anyone,
> As the moon fades into the dawn

I will stand in my boat, play some clear notes on my flute and sing a
    song,
And I will think of the past and of the future,
And of how every human life comes to an end
Like the foam of a wave vanishing onto a shore.
(568–569)

Legend says that Kiyotsune chose to drown himself rather than accept the ugly
shame of defeat in battle. Leaping into the water for the sake of his own beauty,
he is like a Japanese Narcissus. Having quoted the above lines, Mishima does not
make any comment about the Noh play. But the mere mention of this famous work
conjures up numerous images. Most notably, the play concludes with a vigorous
dance of defiance by Kiyotsune's ghost. People may call him stark raving mad,
he cries, but he has departed from the world with no regrets. Mishima has surely
inserted this reference with an eye on his own posthumous readers.

If the figure of Kiyotsune invites comparison with Mishima, so does that
of Prince Ranryō. "I am sure the prince was not ashamed of his gentle face,"
Mishima writes. "He may even have been secretly proud of it." Mishima thinks
that it pleased the prince to wear a mask in battle, "for his enemies' fear was concentrated on his mask and his courage, while his beautiful and gentle face was
forever protected from harm." Ranryō is said to have vanquished his enemies and
lived a long life. Too long, according to Mishima's ideal. "The secret of Ranryō's
gentle features ought to have been exposed upon his death in battle," Mishima
remarks solemnly, in another scarcely disguised self-reference, "yet the prince
did not die" (567).[20]

Readers who are familiar with the tale of Prince Ranryō will probably notice
that Mishima is obfuscating a little here. According to the legend, the prince did
not wear a mask in order to scare his enemies but to focus the minds of his own
soldiers, who were being distracted by his handsome looks. Mishima omits this
important detail, presumably because he does not want to introduce any sexual
innuendo into a story about himself and the students of the Shield Society. But
the omission is so blatant that the reader cannot help reflecting on what Mishima
apparently does not want to acknowledge in words, namely that the legend of
Prince Ranryō could conceivably be interpreted as asserting that homosexual
desire is incompatible with (or at least impedimentary to) success as a soldier. This
thought would lead us, of course, back to Mishima's own early biography as he
has given it to us in Confessions of a Mask. Yet even if this thought does enter the
reader's mind, after all it is the prince who prevails: by putting on the mask that
is expected of him and performing his role with flair and skill, the warrior-prince

defeats his enemies and then dances his solo victory dance. All the above details are again liable to suggest yet more points of connection to Mishima. As befits a work that seeks to replicate the effects of Noh, even the gaps in this text seem rife with allusions.

After the last note of the flute has faded away, Mishima and the students sit in awed silence. It feels like the longest silence anywhere in Mishima's work. The implication is that words are redundant now because the music has exceeded anything that could be said about it.

The text then ends abruptly with a line that seems to aspire to the mysteriousness of a Zen *kōan*:

After a while, the boy who had played the flute for us suddenly said to me, "If I found out that the enemy you are thinking of and the enemy I am thinking of were different, I would refuse to fight." (571)

This sounds like a declaration of loyalty, albeit an oddly worded one. Perhaps the myth of the warrior-prince, delivered via the notes of the flute, has inspired a bit of comradely bonding. But do the student's words not also seem to imply an antagonism toward the act of *thinking* itself? The purpose of Zen riddles is not to elucidate by rationalization but to cultivate intuition. We have seen how Mishima, in the closing stage of his project, deprecates the importance of reasoning, of calculations toward the future, and urges the acceptance of a tragic worldview. It is appropriate that in his final work he seems to abandon words altogether and turns to the ultimate tragic medium of music. In the scenario that Mishima has constructed here, the flute is announcing the unspeakability of tragic knowledge, summoning Mishima back to his spiritual homeland, to the terrifying mother of culture. Mishima, the seemingly unstoppable torrent of words, is coming to an end here, in the wordlessness of music.

In what is surely a purposeful self-contradiction, however, "Prince Ranryō" comes very close to disproving its own claim about the limitations of language. Mishima suggests that even he does not possess the skills to transcribe the experience of this ethereal music into words. Yet the description he has given us is both technically accurate and superbly evocative, and today all professional *yokobue* players know this text well. The *Prince Ranryō* music is perhaps 1,500 years old. Mishima has come closer than anyone to rendering its effects into language, together with visions of youthfulness and vitality, shared suffering, deathly beauty, and sacred time, all ingeniously intertwined with glimpses of himself.

Death as Art

Mishima brought his project to a conclusion, in the most sensational manner that anyone could have imagined, on November 25, 1970.

On the afternoon of that day, Mishima and four members of the Shield Society staged a violent incident at the SDF headquarters at Ichigaya in central Tokyo. On a pretext of paying a social visit to the commandant, they took him hostage and barricaded themselves inside his office. Mishima used an antique samurai sword to fight off rescue attempts by SDF personnel, inflicting flesh wounds on the hands and heads of no fewer than eight officers and staff members.[21] After issuing a demand that all SDF personnel at the headquarters assemble in front of the main building, for several minutes Mishima attempted to deliver a speech to them from the roof balcony. Above their angry shouts and jeers his voice was barely audible, though journalists' microphones captured snippets of his speech. Mishima was berating the soldiers for their passive acceptance of a constitution that denied their existence, and he was challenging them to join him in a revolt to overturn the constitution.

In a written statement distributed by his students Mishima listed more of his complaints, in a language of strategic vagueness. Japan had lost sight of its fundamental principles. The entire nation had sold its soul for money. Hypocrisy was everywhere. Politics and business were infested with greed and corruption. The people had forsaken their own history and traditions. All that lay ahead was spiritual emptiness. Mishima's final question to the SDF: "Where has the spirit of the samurai gone to?" (36:405).

Mishima returned inside the building and, with the assistance of his students, committed suicide by seppuku. One of the students, Morita Masakatsu, the twenty-five-year-old captain of the Shield Society, then killed himself in the same way.

Foreign commentators are prone to say that Mishima "botched" his seppuku, but that is not correct. Mishima stabbed himself in his stomach, cut a line of nearly six inches across his abdominal wall, and his students removed his head in a few strikes. By the gruesome standards of historical seppuku executions, this one was relatively swift and free of mishap.[22]

Mishima had apparently hoped to capture his seppuku on film, but this proved impossible. The last image we have of him is a press photograph taken within minutes of his death. Mishima's body is lying on the floor, and in front of it is his severed head. Next to this is the severed head of Morita. Mishima's head is illuminated by light; his eyes are closed and his expression is blank. The younger man's death face is remarkably serene, and a trickle of blood is darkening his lips. Mishima would have been pleased with this photograph.

Mishima's death attracted international attention, prompting Japan's leaders to reassure the world that Japan was not veering toward a mood of aggressive nationalism. Mishima was a madman, they said, and his bizarre stunt represented nothing that was true about Japan or the Japanese people. Yet only twenty-five years earlier Japan had astonished the world with the beautiful madness of the kamikaze squadrons, and the wartime slogan of the Japanese people was an insane boast: "One hundred million will die together!" Friends of Mishima, though shocked by what he had done, were more willing to express empathy. In a printed eulogy, Shibusawa Tatsuhiko wrote that postwar Japan had not been mad enough for Mishima, and so Mishima had taken it upon himself to act out Japan's madness for it.[23]

Mishima's death is, in obvious ways, the logical culmination of his life's work and of all the aspects of his thinking that we have investigated in this book. His extreme aestheticism, his narcissism, his eroticism, his desire to transcend modernity and link to the spirit of Japan's classical literature, to turn himself into a sublime object, and his compulsion toward crime, toward evil, and toward the divine terror, all achieve their clearest expression and, we must assume, their personal fulfillment. Mishima's death also affects a permanent change on his literary works, every one of which now appears to point inevitably to this moment, as if every word he had written was posthumous. Through originality in the arrangement of his fate, Mishima has given his work a seemingly indestructible cohesion.

As for Morita's role, on the level of psychodrama it is best to think of him as an alternative Hiraoka. A Hiraoka free of artistic sensibility, with no interest in literature at all. A strong and healthy and happy Hiraoka. A Hiraoka who passed the military inspection and joined the Imperial Army. A heterosexual Hiraoka. This Hiraoka becomes Mishima's executioner. The resultant scenario thus has a classic narcissistic self-sufficiency. Like Dorian Gray, who dies after stabbing the portrait that had for years been absorbing the ugliness of his soul, Hiraoka ultimately confronts his alter ego, killing off the aberrant artificial self into which he has been defensively channeling his vices and his weaknesses; by doing so, he ends his own life.

Morita's presence creates difficulties for Japanese rightists and conservatives hoping to appropriate Mishima's death. No doubt this was Mishima's intention. There is no getting around the fact that a double suicide, and especially a double seppuku by two men, has a powerful erotic suggestiveness. By orchestrating his death scene like this, Mishima lays bare the theme of sexual vendetta we traced as an undertone in his work, discernible in the impotent Mizoguchi's hostility to the Golden Temple and in the depiction of the love-crazed army officers in "Voices of the Heroic Dead." Mishima completes his eroticism in more than one sense: in the ultimate satisfaction of his own sadomasochism, in the psychodrama of the homosexual aesthete who wreaks spectacular revenge on the straight institutions that had once rejected him, and in the defiant assertion of a once-traditional ritual of erotic violence the "anemic" intellectualism of modernity has deemed taboo.

Time has shown that Mishima also succeeded in his ambition of making his death into an event of historical importance. Hirohito, the Showa emperor, out-lived Mishima by nearly two decades, passing away in 1989. But as some Japanese commentators then felt able to admit, there was already a feeling that the essence of the Showa era had faded away with Mishima. The suggestion was that Mishima's death had functioned as a symbolic execution of the wartime emperor and was thus a cathartic event that made it easier for the Japanese to move on from the past. The tragic spirit of Showa—the spirit of the rebel army officers of February 1936 and the spirit of the kamikaze pilots—had not perished in 1945; it lingered, until finally dying with Mishima and his Shield Society. The bafflement and ridicule generated by Mishima's anachronistic display proved that such values no longer existed in Japan. By re-enacting the spirit of Showa, Mishima had effectively brought it to an end.[24]

Today we are familiar with the phenomenon of radical religious or pseudo-religious extremists who hail the greatness of their god as they commit atrocious acts of violence. A serious threat to Western cultural stability now comes from an ultraviolent ideology that promotes "martyrdom operations" of a most spectacular kind. At least one Japanese commentator has compared the famous photograph of Mishima's severed head to images of beheadings recently perpetrated by Islamic jihadists.[25] There is now broad recognition that modernity has produced an environment conducive to terrorism, and the aesthetic dimension of terrorist ideology is acknowledged by experts who study the problem.[26] Set alongside the hideous acts of indiscriminate mass murder that plague our world today, Mishima's artful death scene was carefully self-contained. Even the wounded SDF officers later testified that Mishima had used his sword on them in such a way as to avoid inflicting serious injury. Nonetheless, to those of us who are viewing him from the twenty-first century, Mishima's glorification of the antimodern, anti-Western reactionary as a suicidal warrior, martyred in an extravagant display of destructive violence, surely contains a chilling prescience.

The question that is always asked about Mishima is: Was he sincere or was he acting? This really equates to asking: Is it real or is it art? But in Mishima's case, as I have tried to show, this is a nonquestion. For Mishima, art is not the opposite of reality. Art for him is a different *kind* of reality. Mishima represents an apotheosis of the Nietzschean idea that life can be justified only as an aesthetic phenomenon. His act of aesthetic terrorism was not a failed *coup d'état* but a triumphant *coup de théâtre*, a spectacular piece of performance art that was simultaneously a radical anti-artistic gesture. Mishima believed that he had taken the idea of life as art to its extreme point, beyond which no one could go any further.

Jean Baudrillard says, "The supreme consecration for a work of art: to be realized by the very event that destroys it."[27] Mishima has surely done more than this. The supreme consecration for an artist: to be destroyed by the very event that realizes and completes his entire life's work.

An artist who actualizes all his creative possibilities, good and bad, beautiful and ugly, and succeeds—through the pure realization of a will to power that will not yield to anything in this world—in condensing them into a single momentous event, the effect of which is so beautiful yet so shocking that those who contemplate it are left wondering whether it is a work of art or an act of madness, has surely achieved a masterpiece of some kind. It is, as Mishima intended it to be, a cruel and defiant masterpiece: a terror attack on the modern consciousness, a warning to the "last humans," and a challenge to all those coming after Mishima who would dare to call themselves artists.

NOTES

Introduction

1. Friedrich Nietzsche, *On the Genealogy of Morals*, translated by Douglas Smith (Oxford: Oxford University Press, 1996), 80.

2. See Hashikawa Bunzō's comments on Nathan's book in his *Mishima Yukio ron shūsei* (Shin'ya Sōshosha, 1998), 197.

3. Saeki Shōichi, *Hyōden Mishima Yukio* (Shinchōsha, 1978), 9.

4. Okuno Takeo, *Mishima Yukio densetsu* (Shinchōsha, 1992), 9.

5. Tanaka Miyoko, *Mishima Yukio: kami no kagebōshi* (Shinchōsha, 2006), 300.

6. Hisaaki Yamanouchi, *The Search for Authenticity in Modern Japanese Literature* (Cambridge: Cambridge University Press, 1978), 138.

7. It says something about the state of Mishima scholarship in English that the best book is still John Nathan's biography *Mishima: A Life* (London: Hamish Hamilton, 1974) and the best chapter within a book is still the one by Masao Miyoshi in his *Accomplices of Silence* (Berkeley: University of California Press, 1974) from the same year. There is only one monograph in English written by a Japan specialist and devoted solely to Mishima: Roy Starrs' unsatisfactory *Deadly Dialectics: Sex, Violence and Nihilism in the World of Yukio Mishima* (Honolulu: University of Hawai'i Press, 1994), which barely engages at all with Mishima's writings. In other languages the most valuable study is probably Annie Cecchi's *Mishima Yukio: Esthétique classique, univers tragique. D'Apollon et Dionysos à Sade et Bataille* (Paris: Honoré Champion, 1999), which examines Mishima's relationship with French literature.

8. The girl has been identified as Mitani Kuniko, eldest daughter of Mitani Takanobu, a notable educator and diplomat who at that time was serving as Japan's ambassador to Nazi-controlled Vichy France.

9. If the Hiraoka/Mishima distinction is ignored entirely, things can go badly wrong. An egregious case in point is Naoki Inose's *Persona: A Biography of Yukio Mishima* (Berkeley, CA: Stone Bridge Press, 2012), an expanded English version of a book originally published in Japanese in 1994. Inose offers a journalistic account of the bustling day-to-day concerns of a gregarious Japanese writer: his work schedule, his meetings with his editors and publishers, his theater productions, his public speeches, his trips abroad, his house and its furnishings, his dinner parties, his gym workouts, his mother's thyroid condition, etc. The result is a long but superficial chronicle of the life of Hiraoka, which tells us next to nothing about the art of Mishima.

10. Theodor Adorno, *In Search of Wagner*, trans. Rodney Livingstone (London: Verso, 1981), 120.

Chapter 1: A Zone of Unfeeling

Epigraph: Friedrich Nietzsche, *The Will to Power*, trans. Walter Kaufmann and R. J. Hollingdale (New York: Vintage Books, 1968), 199.

1. "Poetic Theory" remained unpublished and unknown during Mishima's lifetime. It was discovered in the late 1990s during the transferral of his papers to the Mishima Yukio Literary Museum in Yamanashi and was printed for the first time in November 2000 in a special edition of *Shinchō* magazine celebrating the thirtieth anniversary of Mishima's death.

2. Nietzsche, *The Will to Power*, 199. It seems clear that Hiraoka's notion of the "poet of aestheticism" has been influenced by the psychology of the artist offered by Nietzsche in this work.

3. From a 1940 essay titled "Waga kuni ni okeru Rōman-shugi no gaikan" (An outline of Romanticism in Japan), by Yasuda Yōjūrō (1910–1981), the leading figure of the Japan Romantic School, reprinted in *Yasuda Yojūrō zenshū* (Kōdansha, 1986), 11:304.

Chapter 2: Problems of Beauty

Epigraph: Kajii Motojirō, 'Sakura no ki no shita ni wa' (Beneath the cherry trees), *Kajii Motojirō zenshū* (Chikuma Shobō, 1999), 1:143.

1. An observation made by Saeki Shōichi in his *Hyōden Mishima Yukio*, 240.

2. Tasaka Kō, *Mishima Yukio ron* (Fūtōsha, 1970), 270.

3. Kuwajima Hideki, *Sūkō no bigaku* (Kōdansha, 2008), 42.

4. From "Nihon Rōmanha kōkoku" (Advertisement for the Japan Romantic School), a manifesto signed by Yasuda Yojūrō and five other writers, which first appeared in the November 1934 edition of *Kogito* magazine. The advertisement is reprinted in Hirano Ken, Odagiri Hideo, and Yamamoto Kenkichi, eds., *Gendai Nihon bungaku ronsō-shi* (Miraisha, 2006), 2:459–460.

5. Rainer Maria Rilke, "First Diuno Elegy," in *Selected Poems*, trans. J. B. Leishman (London: Penguin, 1991), 60.

6. Fyodor Dostoyevsky, *The Brothers Karamazov*, trans. David McDuff (London: Penguin Classics, 1993), 122.

7. Kajii Motojirō, 'Sakura no ki no shita ni wa,' *Kajii Motojirō zenshū*, 1:143. A complete English translation of this prose poem, along with other works by Kajii, can be found in Stephen Dodd's *The Youth of Things: Life and Death in the Age of Kajii Motojirō* (Honolulu: University of Hawai'i Press, 2014).

8. Yasuda Yojūrō, "Gyokusai no seishin" (The spirit of shattering like crystal), an essay first published in 1943 and reprinted in *Yasuda Yojūrō zenshū*, 19:526.

9. Hashikawa Bunzō, *Mishima Yukio ron shūsei*, 30–31.

10. Noguchi Takehiko, *Mishima Yukio no sekai* (Kōdansha, 1968), 174.

11. Hirano Keiichirō discusses this idea at length in his *Monorōgu* (Kōdansha, 2007), 12–79.

Chapter 3: Originality in the Arrangement of Fate

Epigraph: Quoted by Richard Ellmann in *Oscar Wilde* (London: Penguin Books, 1988), 92. Though Ellmann does not say so, Wilde is paraphrasing a line from Walter Pater's *Appreciations, with an Essay on Style* (London: Macmillan, 1889).

1. Jean-Paul Sartre, *The Imaginary*, trans. Jonathan Webber (London: Routledge, 2010), 193. Inoue Takashi notes the Mishima-esque quality of this line of Sartre's in his *Hōjō-naru kamen: Mishima Yukio* (Shintensha, 2009), 126.

2. This was one of the ideas forwarded by Sartre in *Saint Genet: Comédien et Martyr* (Paris: Librairie Gallimard, 1952), his analysis of his friend, the criminal-turned-novelist Jean Genet. Mishima published a lukewarm review of the Japanese translation of Sartre's book.

3. Mishima is probably alluding to *The Critic as Artist*, in which Wilde had stated, "I would say that the highest Criticism, being the purest form of personal impression, is in its way more creative than creation, as it has least reference to any standard external to itself, and is, in fact, its own reason for existing." Wilde, *Complete Works of Oscar Wilde* (London: Collins, 1990), 1027.

4. Nietzsche, *The Gay Science*, trans. Walter Kaufmann (New York: Vintage Books, 1974), 290. See also Alexander Nehamas, *Nietzsche: Life as Literature* (Cambridge, MA: Harvard University Press, 1987). Nehamas' book is a much-admired study of Nietzsche's philosophy of life as the primary work of art, from which I have taken many hints in this chapter.

5. Yasuda, 'Shintō to bungaku' (Shinto and literature), *Yasuda Yojūrō zenshū*, 11:312.

6. From a short essay by Kobayashi titled "Gyakusetsu to iu mono ni tsuite" (On paradox), first published in 1932 and reprinted in *Kobayashi Hideo zenshū*, 2:249–250.

7. Umberto Eco, *On Literature*, trans. Martin McLaughlin (London: Secker and Warburg, 2005), 72–83.

8. Quoted in Ellmann, *Oscar Wilde*, 92.

9. It should perhaps be emphasized that *Kyoko's House* predates by nearly a decade Susan Sontag's famous *Against Interpretation and Other Essays* (New York: Farrar, Straus & Giroux, 1966), which includes an essay devoted to the idea that "for the modern consciousness, the artist (replacing the saint) is the exemplary sufferer" (*Against Interpretation*, 42).

10. Wilde, *Complete Works*, 922–924.

11. The doggedness with which Mishima pursues his own ideals of formal perfection and "logical consistency" is easily demonstrated by chronicling the course of his relationship with *Salome*. Wilde's play is a tale of lust, rejection, and ritualized death set in a decadent kingdom. Mishima calls it "a catalogue of suicides, beheading, asphyxiation, jealousy, incest, and countless exquisite jewels" (27:289). King Herod lusts for his virgin stepdaughter, Salome. But she has fallen in love with the prophet Iokanaan (John the Baptist), who is Herod's prisoner. When Iokanaan rejects Salome, she turns hostile and implores Herod to execute the prophet: "Give me the head of Iokanaan!" In a climactic scene Salome kisses the lips of the prophet's head as it is presented to her. Horrified, Herod orders his soldiers to kill Salome, and the play ends as she is crushed to death beneath their shields.

In his essay on Wilde, Mishima informs us that as a schoolboy, the first book he selected and purchased for himself was a copy of *Salome*. Scholars have connected this statement to one of the works newly included in the latest edition of Mishima's collected works, a one-act play titled *The Three Wise Men from the East* (*Higashi no hakase-tachi*, 1939). This play, which freely adapts the New Testament story of Herod and the prophesied birth of the Messiah, ending with Herod's command to massacre all the newborn boys, is obviously derivative of *Salome*. After the war nearly half a dozen new Japanese translations of Wilde's play appeared. The work therefore did not remain rooted in Mishima's boyhood memory but was constantly being reborn: Mishima knew many *Salomes*. This is also true for English readers, since Wilde wrote the play

in French and left the business of translating it to others; many have since done so, hence there
are at least as many English versions of *Salome* as there are Japanese versions.
    In 1960 Mishima directed a performance of *Salome* in Tokyo. In a program note he explained
that he had finally realized "my dream for the past twenty years" (31:389). Mishima used the
1938 translation by Hinatsu Kōnosuke, which was the version he had read as a schoolboy, and
he modeled the stage sets on the original illustrations by Aubrey Beardsley. "Rather than *Salome*
by Oscar Wilde," he told the audience, "I would like you to enjoy *Salome* by Hinatsu, Beardsley,
and Mishima." Immediately after completing this production, Mishima began work on his most
famous short story, "Patriotism" (Yūkoku), a tale of love, fate, and ritualized death. Ten years
later, in the autumn of 1970, as he was preparing for his spectacular suicide, Mishima began
preparations for another staging of *Salome*. The last rehearsal he attended was on November
23, 1970, just two days before his death; the production was staged posthumously the following
year. In this way Mishima framed his life with *Salome*, or rather, with his versions and variations of *Salome*.
    12. Nehamas, *Nietzsche: Life as Literature*, 198.
    13. Mishima liked to boast that he was keeping his life and work strictly separate, a claim
biographers have often repeated uncritically. Many people who knew Mishima personally
remarked upon his artistic attitude to life and the impossibility of extricating the man from
his relentless self-dramatizations. The American writer Donald Richie had the impression that
Mishima was "engaged in creating a person called Mishima who would be all of a piece." Richie
says that Mishima rarely took people's character into account when judging them; what was
important was the role one was to play in his life, a role Mishima determined without regard
for the feelings of the person. See Richie's *Japanese Portraits* (Tokyo: Tuttle Publishing, 2006),
31. Mishima's friend Shibusawa Tatsuhiko wrote of him, "He engaged with reality in a realm
of various kinds of narcissistic rapture, beginning with emotional theater. . . . Mishima lived
in a world that was governed not by the principles of truth and falsehood, but by the principles
of pleasure and non-pleasure." Shibusawa, *Mishima Yukio oboegaki* (Chūkō Bunko, 1986), 32.
    Saeki Shōichi, a scholar of English literature who met Mishima many times, was convinced
that Mishima was intentionally styling his aestheticism and dandyism, his aphoristic style, and
even some of his physical mannerisms, such as his famous booming laugh, on Oscar Wilde.
Saeki's vivid description of the Mishima laugh deserves quotation: "No one who met Mishima
could forget his laugh. It was a laugh that seemed to boil up, making his body shake, he would
throw his head back and for a moment entrust his body to this physical attack. It resembled
the hearty laugh of a self-made man; it absolutely was not a laugh of embarrassment, or for
disguising his weakness. And it wasn't the sort of laugh that is contagious. As you watched him
laughing you wondered if he had forgotten about you. He was like a man standing on a high
peak, laughing at the empty sky. . . . His laugh revealed his loneliness. I can remember thinking,
'He's like a Japanese Zarathustra!' " Saeki, *Hyōden Mishima Yukio*, 85.
    14. Shibusawa, *Mishima Yukio oboegaki*, 66.
    15. Wilde, *Complete Works*, 1001.
    16. Nietzsche, *The Birth of Tragedy*, trans. Shaun Whiteside and intr. Michael Tanner
(London: Penguin, 1993), 40.
    17. Edgar Wind, *Art and Anarchy* (New York: Alfred A. Knopf, 1964), 5.
    18. Sontag, *Against Interpretation*, 4-5.
    19. Sontag, *Against Interpretation*, 14.
    20. Wilde, *Complete Works*, 1007.

21. In an interview with the French magazine *Le Figaro* a few weeks before his death, Mishima was asked to name something that was "really important" to him. His reply: "A journalist once asked me what I hate most in the world. I thought for a moment before answering: Solitude. He then asked me what I love the most. With no hesitation whatsoever I replied: Solitude." Interview in *Le Figaro*, December 3, 1970, quoted in Cecchi, *Mishima Yukio: Esthétique classique, univers tragique*, 252.

22. Kiyoshi Mahito, *Mishima Yukio ni okeru Niiche: Sarutoru jitsuzon-teki seishun bunseki o shiten to shite* (Shinchōsha, 2010), 64.

23. Jean-Paul Sartre, *Saint Genet: Actor and Martyr*, trans. by Bernard Frechtman (London: Heinemann, 1988), 372.

24. Quoted by Nicholas White in his introduction to Huysmans' *Against Nature*, trans. Margaret Mauldon (Oxford University Press, 2009), ix.

25. Huysmans, *Against Nature*, 20.

26. Seikai Ken, *Mishima Yukio to Niiche* (Seikyūsha, 1992), 45.

27. George Ross Ridge, *The Hero in French Decadent Literature* (Athens: University of Georgia Press, 1961), 163.

28. Nietzsche, *Twilight of the Idols and The Anti-Christ*, trans. R. J. Hollingdale (London: Penguin Books, 1990), 478.

Chapter 4: The Leap of Narcissus

Epigraph: Wilde, *Complete Works*, 154.

1. I am using the translation by Ted Hughes in his *Tales from Ovid* (London: Faber and Faber, 2002), 74–84.

2. In his psychoanalysis of water images, Gaston Bachelard argues for the inferiority of the mirror, which lacks what he calls the "natural depth" of an image reflected in water. Bachelard, *Water and Dreams* (Dallas: Dallas Institute Publications, 1999), 19.

3. In an unpublished preface for *Confessions of a Mask* the young Mishima had written cryptically, "I am a man who exists only in the mirror" (1:675).

4. Paul Valéry, "Fragments from *Narcissus*," in *Selected Writings of Paul Valéry*, trans. Malcolm Cowley and C. Day Lewis (New York: New Directions Publishing, 1964), 31. Mishima often expressed admiration for the French poet and critic Paul Valéry (1871–1945), hailing him as the "greatest writer of French prose in the essay form" (31:85).

5. Hughes, *Tales from Ovid*, 79.

6. Arthur Schopenhauer, *The World as Will and Representation*, trans. E. J. F. Payne (London: Dover, 2000), vol. 1, 178–179.

7. Hughes, *Tales from Ovid*, 83.

8. Takayama Shūzō makes this observation in his *Narushisu no ai* (Chōeisha, 2011), 286.

Chapter 5: Intoxicating Illusions

Epigraph: Georges Bataille, *The Tears of Eros*, trans. Peter Conner (San Francisco: City Lights Books, 1989), 20.

1. Piero Boccardo and Xavier F. Salomon, *The Agony and the Ecstasy: Guido Reni's Saint Sebastians* (Milan: Silvana Editoriale, 2007), 34.

2. Louis Réau, quoted in Boccardo and Salomon, *The Agony and the Ecstasy*, 29.

3. Richard A. Kaye, "Losing His Religion: Saint Sebastian as Contemporary Gay Martyr," in *Outlooks: Lesbian and Gay Sexualities and Visual Cultures*, ed. Peter Horne and Reine Lewis (New York: Routledge, 1996), 87.

4. Havelock Ellis, *Studies in the Psychology of Sex: Sexual Inversion* (Honolulu: University Press of the Pacific, 2001), 103. Since Magnus Hirschfeld makes no reference to Saint Sebastian in his monumental *Die Homosexualität des Mannes und des Weibes* (Berlin: Louis Marcus Verlagsbuchhandlung, 1920), Mishima must be citing a lesser-known work.

5. In his letter to the psychiatrist, whose name was Shikiba Ryūzaburō, Mishima admitted that he had been unable to resist the temptation to embroider facts with fiction: "Excepting a degree of artistic license, such as the revision of models and the merging of two persons into a single character, what I have written in *Confessions of a Mask* is an entirely faithful and detailed account of facts arising from my own experience. . . . Initially I was more concerned about my physical inability in the normal direction than my essential *Tendenz*. I therefore believed that confession would be the most effective method of psychoanalytical treatment. However, once I started to write, confusions over the mode of expression, by which I mean the contradictions between the act of confession and the autonomous nature of a work of art, rendered this work highly unstable" (38:513–514). Needless to say, these remarks contradict Mishima's boast to his readers that he had written "a completely fictional confession" (1:674).

6. Mishima, *Confessions of a Mask*, trans. Meredith Weatherby (New York: New Directions, 1958), 45.

7. Julia Kristeva, *Tales of Love*, trans. Leon S. Roudiez (New York: Columbia University Press, 1987), 78.

8. Germaine Greer, *The Boy* (London: Thames and Hudson, 2007), 207.

9. Charles Baudelaire, *The Flowers of Evil*, trans. James N. McGowan (Oxford: Oxford World's Classics, 1993), 156.

10. Tasaka, *Mishima Yukio ron*, 53.

11. J. Keith Vincent, *Two-Timing Modernity: Homosocial Narrative in Modern Japanese Fiction* (Cambridge, MA: Harvard Asia Center, 2012), 191.

12. Shibusawa Tatsuhiko thinks that Mishima's "Sebastian complex," as he calls it, is a variant of the Oedipal complex: "What characterizes the rebelliousness of Sebastian, who was loved by Emperor Diocletian, is that he rebels against paternal Rome and the imperial household while craving a force that will work against himself, and this is what eventually leads to his own destruction. This is what Freud would probably call self-punishment. This archetype perfectly applies to all the rebellious and ill-fated young men who feature in Mishima's works" (*Mishima Yukio oboegaki*, 112–113).

13. Nietzsche, *The Birth of Tragedy*, 18.

14. Georges Bataille, *Eroticism*, trans. Mary Dalwood (San Francisco: City Lights Books, 1986), 113–114.

15. Gaston Bachelard, *Air and Dreams, an Essay on the Imagination of Movement*, trans. Edith R. Farrell and C. Frederick Farrell (Dallas, TX: Dallas Institute Publications, 2002), 169.

16. Bataille, *Eroticism*, 171.

17. Bataille, *The Tears of Eros*, 20. Susan Sontag, who mentions Bataille and this Chinese photograph in her book *Regarding the Pain of Others* (London: Penguin Books, 2003), remarks that the expression on the victim's face is "as ecstatic as that of any Italian Renaissance Saint Sebastian" (*Regarding the Pain of Others*, 88).

18. Pierre Klossowski (1905–2001), French artist and writer, noted for his path-breaking study of the Marquis de Sade. Witold Gombrowicz (1904–1969), Polish novelist and playwright, characterized during his lifetime as an absurdist but today a canonical figure.

19. See Bataille, *Eroticism*, 21.

20. Bataille, *Eroticism*, 22.

21. Cecchi, *Mishima Yukio: Esthétique classique, univers tragique*, 245 (my translation).

22. In his late twenties Mishima had written, "If my interest in the demonic had not been so easily linked to beauty, I might perhaps have become a more religious person" (29:180).

23. Mishima's choice of words here was probably influenced by the recent success of Endō Shūsaku's 1966 novel *Silence* (*Chinmoku*, trans. William Johnston (Tokyo: Sophia University Press, 1969)), which addresses the theological problem of the hiddenness of God.

24. Bataille, *Eroticism*, 11.

25. The political theorist Hashikawa Bunzō shared Mishima's fascination with the ill-fated rebellion of 1936, believing that it encapsulated problems of a metaphysical nature. In an essay on Japanese terrorist ideology published in 1961, Hashikawa compared the prison journals of the young officers, in which they vent their fury at the emperor for refusing to support their cause, to the Book of Job and the famous Grand Inquisitor episode of Dostoyevsky's *The Brothers Karamazov*. See Hashikawa, "Terorizumu shinkō no seishin-shi" (A spiritual history of terrorist faith), in *Hashikawa Bunzō chosakushū* (Chikuma Shobō, 2001), 5:216.

26. Specifically, Mishima based his story on the account of the Aoshimas' suicide in Wada Katsunori's book *Seppuku* (Aoba Shobō, 1943), a piece of wartime propaganda that promotes patriotic self-sacrifice. Mishima even borrowed a line from Mrs. Aoshima's suicide note for the story's dialogue.

27. Uno Kōichirō, "Kannōbi no shōri" (A victory for sensual beauty), *Shinchō*, January 1971, 183–189.

28. John Nathan, *Mishima: A Biography*, 179. During a 1976 discussion with Hashikawa Bunzō, Noguchi Takehiko, who had recently translated Nathan's book into Japanese, said, "I don't sense anything grotesque in Mishima. That's how Westerners see him." Hashikawa, *Mishima Yukio ron shūsei*, 210.

29. Nietzsche, *On the Genealogy of Morals*, 42–43. Translation slightly abbreviated.

30. One part of Mishima's oeuvre that has not survived is the collection of miniature theatrical scenarios he wrote for Dōmoto Masaki, a theater producer and Kabuki specialist who worked with him on *The Rite of Love and Death*. Many years after Mishima's death, Dōmoto published a memoir containing a description of some of these scenarios, which he and Mishima had apparently acted out together in Kabuki style, using fake swords and wearing costumes, wigs, and makeup. All are scenarios of ritual suicide: a samurai lord commits suicide with one of his men; a Manchurian prince commits suicide with a Japanese military officer; the captain of a sinking ship commits suicide with a young sailor; a Peers School boy commits suicide with a yakuza gangster; a team of soldiers of the Japanese Imperial Army commit mass suicide together, and so on. Dōmoto, *Kaiten-tobira no Mishima Yukio* (Bunshu Shinsho, 2005), 54–58.

In his memoir, Dōmoto claims that these enactments were nothing more than playful games. In a private interview conducted at his Kamakura home in January 2001, however, Dōmoto told me that these enactments were part of his sexual play with Mishima. Dōmoto said that Mishima had a special fascination with seppuku performed by men in military uniform, and that Mishima was aroused more by the enactment of the suicide scene than by the actual sex. Most remarkably, Dōmoto claimed that Mishima was sometimes able to achieve orgasm at the moment he "cut" his stomach, without any genital stimulation. My interview with Dōmoto was made possible by the kind assistance of Stephen Comee of the Japan Foundation.

31. Quoted in Mario Praz, *The Romantic Agony* (Oxford: Oxford University Press, 1951), 268.

Chapter 6: The Totality of Culture

Epigraph: Ruth Benedict, *The Chrysanthemum and the Sword: Patterns of Japanese Culture* (New York: Mariner Books, 2005), 2.

1. Albert J. Devlin, ed., *Conversations with Tennessee Williams* (Jackson: University Press of Mississippi, 2000), 74. Some additional remarks from Mishima's 1960 CBS appearance are worth quoting: "Today is a very suitable and fitting age to write plays because plays need such a violence of life, such a terror of life. . . . Our civilization seems to be coming to its climax. But I don't think a culture comes to its climax. Sometimes culture seems to descend into hell. But I think a culture has its own way, compared with civilization, and I think culture is a phoenix. Sometimes civilization is destroyed, but culture is a phoenix. Even when it goes down to hell, I'm sure it will come up from hell some time" (*Conversations*, 76–77).

2. Like most of Mishima's later arguments, this one was not new; it was a forceful declaration of a view he had held all his life. In his early thirties he had written, "The Japanese do not lust for bloody displays of cruelty like the ancient Romans did. . . . We conceal our barbarous and cold-hearted tendencies beneath a costume of tears, emotions, and longing" (30:37).

3. Seikai, *Mishima Yukio to Niiche*, 45.

4. Hagiwara Sakutarō, "Nihon e no kaiki" (The return to Japan), *Hagiwara Sakutarō zenshū* (Chikuma Shobō, 1978), 10:489.

5. Muramatsu Takeshi tells us that Mishima originally wanted to publish "Patriotism" side by side with Fukazawa's story in the same magazine, *Shōsetsu Chūō Kōron*, in the hope that the pro-emperor ideology of Mishima's work would "lessen the poison" of Fukazawa's work in the eyes of right-wing extremists. Due to lack of space, apparently, this proved impossible, and the stories were printed one month apart, with Mishima's printed first. See Muramatsu, *Mishima Yukio no sekai* (Shinchōsha, 1990), 305–315.

6. An account of the Shibusawa and Takechi trials is in Kirsten Cather, *The Art of Censorship in Postwar Japan* (Honolulu: University of Hawai'i Press, 2012), 67–115.

7. In his final years Mishima frequently expressed dissatisfaction with his own failure, as he saw it, to produce work that justified his notoriety as a "dangerous" artist. "Yes, I have written many novels, and stories, and plays," he declared in the last year of his life. "But, for a writer, accumulating these works is like accumulating a pile of his own excrement. He never grows any wiser as a result. Yet nor does he ever become foolish enough to be beautiful" (36:213). The following semihumorous remarks, made during one of Mishima's many media interviews, seem to conceal a real frustration: "A foreign journalist asked me, 'What is your mission?' How satisfying it would have been to reply, 'The death and destruction of the human race!' But the truth is that in twenty years of writing I have not even succeeded in making one of my readers catch a common cold" (34:23).

8. Benedict, *The Chrysanthemum and the Sword*, 2.

9. Sakaguchi Ango, "Daraku ron" (Theory of fallenness), in *Sakaguchi Ango zenshū* (Chikuma Shobō, 1998), 4:273.

10. The essay Mishima discusses is Watsuji Tetsurō's "Kokumin tōgō no shōchō" (The symbol of the unity of the people). The essay was first published in 1946 and is reprinted in *Watsuji Tetsurō zenshū* (Iwanami Shoten, 1962), 14:317–396.

11. Hashikawa, *Mishima Yukio ron shūsei*, 116.

12. A useful overview of critical reactions to Mishima's statements about the emperor can be found in Fujino Hiroshi, *Mishima Yukio to shinkaku tennō* (Bensei Shuppan, 2012), 183–195.

13. Nietzsche, *The Birth of Tragedy*, 59.

14. To publicize his arguments among the widest possible readership, Mishima subsequently dictated a simplified version of "The Defense of Culture" for the nationalist magazine *Nihon oyobi Nihonjin*. The message of this version is straightforward: "Even to mention the emperor is to be accused of being right-wing. But I would point to the First Article of the Constitution and retort: Why should we not speak of the emperor? Many times in our history the emperor has been linked to political power, but the emperor has never been a dictator. [. . .] There are many people who take the leftist view that it is antidemocratic to be loyal to His Majesty. But the emperor is a symbol of Japan, a symbol of the history of the Japanese people, and of our culture that has continued since ancient times. The emperor is both a symbol and an embodiment of the historicity, unity, and totality of Japanese culture. To protect Japan always brings us back to protecting the emperor. To protect the totality of our culture, to protect and preserve the unity of 'the chrysanthemum and the sword,' we need a political body that will guarantee freedom of expression. The communist party will not do that for us" (35:194).

15. Nietzsche, *The Birth of Tragedy*, 109.

16. Mishima, who could read German, had probably consulted Riegl's posthumously published *Historische Grammatik der bildenden Künste* (Historical grammar of the visual arts) (Köln: Böhlau, 1966).

17. Ō no Yasumaro, *Kojiki*, trans. Gustav Heldt (New York: Columbia University Press, 2014), 101–102.

18. Kiyoshi Mahito, *Mishima Yukio ni okeru Niiche*, 309.

19. In his early twenties Mishima published a short story based on another episode from the *Kojiki*: the double suicide of Prince Karu and Princess Sotoori. Mishima's handwritten notes for this story contain the phrase "the issue of the separation of gods and humans" (*shinjin bunri no koto*). In his notes Mishima has crossed out the word "issue" (*koto*) and replaced it with the word "tragedy" (*higeki*; 16:630).

20. Ivan Morris, *The Nobility of Failure: Tragic Heroes in the History of Japan* (London: Secker and Warburg, 1975), xiii.

21. Yasuda, "Taikan shijin no go-ichininsha" (The greatest poet of all), in *Yasuda Yojūrō zenshū*, 5:21.

22. Hashikawa believed that this suicidal impulse was the fundamental difference between the ideology of Japanese militarism and that of Nazi Germany: "If the nihilism of the Nazis was expressed in their cursed cry of 'We must kill!' then it seemed to us that the Japanese Romantics were saying: 'We must die!' " Hashikawa, *Nihon rōmanha hihan josetsu* (Kōdansha Bungei Bunko, 1998), 49.

Chapter 7: The Purest Essence of Japan

Epigraph: Satake Akihiro et al., eds., *Man'yōshū* (Iwanami Shoten, 2015), 5:232 (Poem No. 4373).

1. Roland Barthes, *Empire of Signs*, trans. Richard Howard (New York: Hill and Wang, 1982), 106.

2. Quoted in Jōkyō Shuppan Henshūbu, ed., *Zenkyōtō wo yomu* (Jōkyō Shuppan, 1997), 96.

3. Orikuchi Shinobu, *"Man'yōshū* kenkyū" (Research on the *Man'yōshū*), in *Orikuchi Shinobu zenshū* (Chūō Kōronsha, 2002), 1:365.

4. Asahi Heigo, "Shi no sakebigoe" (The scream of death), in Hashikawa Bunzō, ed., *Chōkokka-shugi* (Chikuma Shobō, 1975), 64.

5. Nishida Mitsugi, "Mugan shiron" (A blind personal view), in Hashikawa Bunzō, ed., *Chōkokka-shugi* (Chikuma Shobō, 1975), 67–68.

6. Yasuda Yojūro, "Shintō to bungaku" (Shinto and literature), *Yasuda Yojūrō zenshū*, 11:312.

7. "A Problem of Culture," an article originally published in English and quoted in Henry Scott Stokes, *The Life and Death of Yukio Mishima* (London: Penguin Books, 1985), 225–226.

8. The scholar of aesthetics Arnold Berleant stresses the connections between terrorism and modern art in his essay "Art, Terrorism, and the Negative Sublime," in *Arts and Terror*, ed. Vladimir L. Marchenkov (Newcastle upon Tyne: Cambridge Scholars Project, 2014), 1–16. There Berleant writes, "Is there art in terrorism? It cannot be denied that much of the political effectiveness of terrorist acts comes from their carefully planned aesthetic impact. Indeed, their effect is primarily, often spectacularly theatrical. We can in fact say that such actions are deliberately designed to be high drama. [. . .] Perhaps it now becomes understandable how an artist could consider a terrorist act a work of art" ("Art, Terrorism, and the Negative Sublime," 9).

9. Okuno, *Mishima Yukio densetsu*, 405.

10. Mitsuhana Takao, *Mishima Yukio ron* (Chūsekisha, 2000), 172.

11. Pointing to the erotically charged language of the prison journals written by the young officers before their execution by firing squad, the cultural historian Tanaka Jun comments, "Even if the suicidal aesthetic that Mishima presents in 'Voices of the Heroic Dead' was largely a reflection of his own ideas about beauty, he was foregrounding desires that had indeed been lurking in the political theology of Japanese terrorism." Tanaka, *Seiji no bigaku: kenryoku to hyōshō* (Tōkyō Daigaku Shuppan-kai, 2008), 253.

12. Ōkawa Shūmei, *Nihon oyobi Nihonjin no michi* (Gōchisha Shuppanbu, 1926), 86–87.

13. See the selection of pilots' letters translated by Ivan Morris in *The Nobility of Failure*, 309.

14. Slavoj Žižek makes this argument in *On Belief* (New York: Routledge, 2001), 109–110.

15. Susan Sontag, "Fascinating Fascism," *The New York Review of Books*, February 6, 1975.

16. Saul Friedländer, *Reflections of Nazism: An Essay on Kitsch and Death* (New York: Harper and Row, 1982), 25–27.

17. Hasuda Zenmei, "Shi no tame no zakkan" (Some feelings for poetry), *Bungei bunka* (June 1939): 46–50.

18. Satō Hideaki, *Mishima Yukio no bungaku* (Shironsha, 2009), 353–354.

19. From an essay of 1939 titled "Nihon no roman-shugi" (Japanese Romanticism), reprinted in *Yasuda Yojūrō zenshū*, 11:183. Mishima's contemporary Hashikawa Bunzō recalled that the young men who were seduced by the nationalist mysticism of the Japan Romantic School were determined "not to be polluted by politics of any kind" (*Nihon rōmanha hihan josetsu*, 33). The philosopher Kiyoshi Mahito speaks for most subsequent Japanese commentators when he says, "Mishima's seemingly political, pseudo-fascist actions have nothing to do with the political or economic state of Japanese society; in terms of actual politics they are devoid of content" (*Mishima Yukio ni okeru Niiche*, 274).

20. The philosopher Umehara Takeshi, who was born in the same year as Mishima, said that the enigmatic smile of the Noh mask reminded him of his wartime adolescence: "I knew boys the same age as me who had smiled like that as they went to their deaths, sincerely thanking

the emperor who had ordered them to die." Umehara, *Warai no kōzō* (Kadokawa Shoten, 1972), 77.

21. The names and ranks of the eight soldiers wounded by Mishima, along with details of their various injuries, are given in Andō Takeshi, *Mishima Yukio "nichiroku"* (Michitani, 1996), 419.

22. For detailed descriptions of historical seppuku executions see my *Seppuku: A History of Samurai Suicide* (New York: Kodansha USA, 2011).

23. Shibusawa, *Mishima Yukio oboegaki*, 60–61.

24. Karatani Kōjin makes this observation in his *History and Repetition*, trans. Seiji M. Lippit (New York: Columbia University Press, 2011), 81. The novelist Hirano Keiichirō expresses the same point more sternly when he says that Mishima had "committed double suicide with a failed era" (Hirano, *Monorōgu*, 183).

25. Suzumura Kazunari, *Tero no bungaku-shi: Mishima Yukio ni hajimaru* (Ōta Shuppan, 2016), 41–42.

26. Roger Griffin expounds this view in his essay "Modernity and Terrorism," in *The Routledge History of Terrorism*, ed. Randall D. Law (London: Routledge, 2015), 369–382. In regard to the video letters and other aesthetic practices of present-day suicide bombers, the American scholar of religious terrorism Ariel Glucklich writes, "Suicide terror is art, with its four great acts: the martyr's statement, the noble death, the funeral, and the final—undoubted—denouement: a glorious entry to heaven." Glucklich, *Holy Pleasure and Suicide Bombers* (New York: Harper One, 2009), 251.

27. Jean Baudrillard, *The Intelligence of Evil, or the Lucidity Pact*, trans. Chris Turner (Oxford: Berg, 2005), 119.

BIBLIOGRAPHY

Unless noted otherwise, all Japanese books were published in Tokyo.

Adorno, Theodor. *In Search of Wagner.* Translated from the German by Rodney Livingstone. London: Verso, 1981.

Akasaka Norio. *Shōchō tennō to iu monogatari* (The story of the symbolic emperor). Chikuma Raiburarii, 1990.

Andō Takeshi. *Mishima Yukio "nichiroku"* (Daily chronicle of Mishima's life). Michitani, 1996.

Asahi Heigo. "Shi no sakebigoe" (The scream of death). In *Chōkokka-shugi*, edited by Hashikawa Bunzō, 61–66. Chikuma Shobō, 1975.

Bachelard, Gaston. *Air and Dreams: An Essay on the Imagination of Movement.* Translated from the French by Edith R. Farrell and C. Frederick Farrell. Dallas: Dallas Institute Publications, 2002.

———. *Water and Dreams: An Essay on the Imagination of Matter.* Translated by Edith R. Farrell and C. Frederick Farrell. Dallas: Dallas Institute Publications, 1999.

Baldick, Robert. *The Life of J.-K. Huysmans.* Oxford: Clarendon, 1955.

Barthes, Roland. *Empire of Signs.* Translated from the French by Richard Howard. New York: Hill and Wang, 1982.

Bataille, Georges. *Eroticism.* Translated from the French by Mary Dalwood. San Francisco: City Lights Books, 1986.

———. *Inner Experience.* Translated by Leslie A. Boldt. New York: State University of New York Press, 1988.

———. *Literature and Evil.* Translated by Alastair Hamilton. London: Marion Boyars, 2006.

———. *On Nietzsche.* Translated by Bruce Boone. St. Paul, MN: Paragon House, 1998.

———. *The Tears of Eros.* Translated by Peter Conner. San Francisco: City Lights Books, 1989.

———. *Theory of Religion.* Translated by Robert Hurley. New York: Zone Books, 2012.

Baudelaire, Charles. *The Flowers of Evil.* Translated from the French by James N. McGowan. Oxford: Oxford World's Classics, 1993.

Baudrillard, Jean. *The Intelligence of Evil, or the Lucidity Pact.* Translated from the French by Chris Turner. Oxford: Berg, 2005.

Benedict, Ruth. *The Chrysanthemum and the Sword: Patterns of Japanese Culture.* New York: Mariner Books, 2005.

187

Berleant, Arnold. "Art, Terrorism, and the Negative Sublime." In *Arts and Terror*, edited by Vladimir L. Marchenkov, 1–16. Newcastle upon Tyne: Cambridge Scholars Project, 2014.

Berlin, Isaiah. *The Roots of Romanticism*. London: Pimlico, 1999.

Boccardo, Piero, and Xavier F. Salomon. *The Agony and the Ecstasy: Guido Reni's Saint Sebastians*. Milan: Silvana Editoriale, 2007.

Bungei bunka (Literary culture). 7 vols. Yūshōdō shoten, 1971.

Cather, Kirsten. *The Art of Censorship in Postwar Japan*. Honolulu: University of Hawai'i Press, 2012.

Cecchi, Annie. *Mishima Yukio. Esthétique classique, univers tragique. D'Apollon et Dionysos à Sade et Bataille* (Mishima Yukio. Classical aesthetic, tragic universe. From Apollo and Dionysus to Sade and Bataille). Paris: Honoré Champion, 1999.

D'Annunzio, Gabriel. *Le Martyre de Saint Sébastien*. Paris: Calmann-Lévy, 1911.

Devlin, Albert J., ed. *Conversations with Tennessee Williams*. Jackson: University Press of Mississippi, 2000.

Dodd, Stephen. *The Youth of Things: Life and Death in the Age of Kajii Motojirō*. Honolulu: University of Hawai'i Press, 2014.

Dōmoto Masaki. *Kaisō: Kaiten-tobira no Mishima Yukio* (Mishima Yukio the revolving door). Bunshu Shinsho, 2005.

Dostoyevsky, Fyodor. *The Brothers Karamazov*. Translated from the Russian by David McDuff. London: Penguin Classics, 1993.

Eagleton, Terry. *Sweet Violence: The Idea of the Tragic*. Oxford: Blackwell, 2003.

Eco, Umberto. *On Literature*. Translated from the Italian by Martin McLaughlin. London: Secker and Warburg, 2005.

Ellis, Havelock. *Studies in the Psychology of Sex: Sexual Inversion*. Honolulu: University Press of the Pacific, 2001.

Ellmann, Richard. *Oscar Wilde*. London: Penguin Books, 1988.

Endō, Shūsaku. *Silence*. Translated from the Japanese by William Johnston. Tokyo: Sophia University Press, 1969.

Freud, Sigmund. *Beyond the Pleasure Principle and Other Writings*. Translated from the German by John Reddick. London: Penguin Modern Classics, 2003.

Friedländer, Saul. *Reflections of Nazism: An Essay on Kitsch and Death*. Translated from the French by Thomas Weyr. New York: Harper and Row, 1982.

Fujino Hiroshi. *Mishima Yukio to shinkaku tennō* (Mishima Yukio and the divine emperor). Bensei Shuppan, 2012.

Fukazawa Shichirō. "Fūryū mutan" (A dream of courtly elegance). *Shōsetsu Chūō Kōron*, December 1960.

Glucklich, Ariel. *Holy Pleasure and Suicide Bombers*. New York: Harper One, 2009.

Greer, Germaine. *The Boy*. London: Thames and Hudson, 2007.

Griffin, Roger. "Modernity and Terrorism." In *The Routledge History of Terrorism*, edited by Randall D. Law, 369–382. London: Routledge, 2015.

Hagiwara Sakutarō. *Hagiwara Sakutarō zenshū* (Complete works of Hagiwara Sakutarō). 15 vols. Chikuma Shobō, 1978.

Hashikawa Bunzō. *Chōkokka-shugi* (Japanese ultranationalism). Chikuma Shobō, 1975.

——. *Hashikawa Bunzō chosakushū* (Collected works of Hashikawa Bunzō). 10 vols. Chikuma Shobō, 2001.

——. *Mishima Yukio ron shūsei* (Collected essays on Mishima Yukio). Shin'ya Sōshosha, 1998.

——. *Nihon rōmanha hihan josetsu* (A critical introduction to the Japan Romantic School). Kōdansha Bungei Bunko, 1998.

Hegel, Georg Wilhelm Friedrich. *Introduction to Aesthetics.* Translated from the German by T. M. Knox. Oxford: Clarendon Press, 1979.

Hijiya-Kirschnereit, Irmela, ed. *Mishima! Mishima Yukio no chi-teki rūtsu to kokusai-teki inpakuto* (Mishima Yukio's intellectual roots and worldwide impact). Kyoto: Shōwadō, 2010.

Hirano Keiichirō. *Monorōgu* (Monologues). Kōdansha, 2007.

Hirano Ken, Odagiri Hideo, and Yamamoto Kenkichi, eds. *Gendai Nihon bungaku ronsō-shi* (A history of literary debates in modern Japan). 3 vols. Miraisha, 2006.

Hirschfeld, Magnus. *Homosexualität des Mannes und des Weibes* (Homosexuality of men and women). Berlin: Louis Marcus Verlagsbuchhandlung, 1920.

Hughes, Ted. *Tales from Ovid.* London: Faber and Faber, 2002.

Huysmans, Joris-Karl. *Against Nature.* Translated from the French by Margaret Mauldon. Edited with an introduction and notes by Nicholas White. Oxford: Oxford University Press, 2009.

——. *Là-Bas* (Down there). Translated by Keene Wallace. New York: Dover Publications, 1972.

Inose, Naoki, with Hiroaki Sato. *Persona: A Biography of Yukio Mishima.* Berkeley, CA: Stone Bridge Press, 2012.

Inoue Takashi. *Hōjō-naru kamen: Mishima Yukio* (A fertile mask: Mishima Yukio). Shintensha, 2009.

Jōkyō Shuppan Henshūbu, ed. *Zenkyōtō wo yomu* (Reading the all-Japan struggle). Jōkyō Shuppan, 1997.

Kajii Motojirō. *Kajii Motojirō zenshū* (Complete works of Kajii Motojirō). 4 vols. Chikuma Shobō, 1999.

Karatani Kōjin. *History and Repetition.* Translated from the Japanese by Seiji M. Lippit. New York: Columbia University Press, 2011.

Kaye, Richard A. "Losing His Religion: Saint Sebastian as Contemporary Gay Martyr." In *Outlooks: Lesbian and Gay Sexualities and Visual Cultures,* edited by Peter Horne and Reina Lewis, 86–105. New York: Routledge, 1996.

Keene, Donald. *Dawn to the West: Japanese Literature of the Modern Era; Fiction.* New York: Holt, Rinehart & Wilson, 1984.

Kiyoshi Mahito. *Mishima Yukio ni okeru Niiche: Sarutoru jitsuzon-teki seishun bunseki o shiten to shite* (Nietzsche in Mishima Yukio: A Sartrean existential psychoanalytical perspective). Shinchōsha, 2010.

Kobayashi Hideo. *Kobayashi Hideo zenshū* (Complete works of Kobayashi Hideo). 14 vols. Shinchōsha, 2002.

Kristeva, Julia. *Tales of Love.* Translated from the French by Leon S. Roudiez. New York: Columbia University Press, 1987.

Kuwajima Hideki. *Sūkō no bigaku* (Aesthetics of the sublime). Kōdansha, 2008.

Lowen, Alexander. *Narcissism: Denial of the True Self.* Old Tappen, NJ: Touchstone, 2004.

Marshall, Gail, ed. *The Cambridge Companion to the Fin de Siècle.* Cambridge: Cambridge University Press, 2007.

Matsumoto Ken'ichi. *Mishima Yukio no 2:26 jiken* (Mishima Yukio and the February 26 incident). Bungei Shunju, 2005.

Miller, Henry. *Reflections on the Death of Mishima.* Santa Barbara, CA: Capra Press, 1972.

Mishima, Yukio. "Aesthetics of the Non-Existent: the Poetry of the *Shinkokinshū.*" Translated by Andrew Rankin. *Kyoto Journal,* no. 76 (2012): 106–109.

———. *After the Banquet.* Translated by Donald Keene. London: Secker & Warburg, 1963.

———. "The Circus." Translated by Andrew Rankin. *The East* 35, no. 3 (September 1999): 19–23.

———. *Confessions of a Mask.* Translated by Meredith Weatherby. New York: New Directions, 1958.

———. "A Forest in Full Bloom." Translated by Andrew Rankin. *The East* 36, no. 4 (November 2000): 6–16.

———. *Mishima on Stage: The Black Lizard and Other Plays.* Various translators, with an introduction by Laurence Kominz. Ann Arbor: University of Michigan Center for Japanese Studies, 2007.

———. "On Oscar Wilde." Translated by Andrew Rankin. *The Wildean,* no. 43 (July 2013): 49–56.

———. *The Peacocks.* Translated by Andrew Rankin. London: Travelman Press, 2001.

———. *The Sea of Fertility.* Translated by Michael Gallagher, E. Dale Saunders, Cecilia Segawa Seigle, and Edward G. Seidensticker. London: Penguin Twentieth-Century Classics, 1992.

———. *The Temple of the Golden Pavilion.* Translated by Ivan Morris. London: Vintage, 1994.

Mishima Yukio botsugo sanjūnen (Thirty years after the death of Mishima Yukio). Special edition of *Shinchō* magazine (November 2000).

Mitsuhana Takao. *Mishima Yukio ron* (Theory of Mishima Yukio). Chūsekisha, 2000.

Miyoshi, Masao. *Accomplices of Silence: The Modern Japanese Novel.* Berkeley: University of California Press, 1974.

Morris, Ivan. *The Nobility of Failure: Tragic Heroes in the History of Japan.* London: Secker and Warburg, 1975.

———. *Kōkinaru haiboku: Nihonshi no higeki no eiyū-tachi* (Japanese edition of the above title). Translated from the English by Satō Kazuaki. Chūō Kōronsha, 1981.

Muramatsu Takeshi. *Mishima Yukio no sekai* (The world of Mishima Yukio). Shinchōsha, 1990.

Murasaki Shikibu. *The Tale of Genji.* Translated from the Japanese by Edward G. Seidensticker. 2 vols. New York: Alfred A. Knopf, 1976.

Napier, Susan J. *Escape from the Wasteland: Romanticism and Realism in the Fiction of Mishima Yukio and Oe Kenzaburo.* Cambridge, MA: Harvard University Asia Center, 1996.

Nathan, John. *Mishima: A Biography.* London: Hamish Hamilton, 1974.

Nehamas, Alexander. *Nietzsche: Life as Literature.* Cambridge, MA: Harvard University Press, 1987.

Nietzsche, Friedrich. *The Birth of Tragedy.* Translated from the German by Shaun Whiteside and introduced by Michael Tanner. London: Penguin, 1993.

——. *The Gay Science.* Translated by Walter Kaufmann. New York: Vintage Books, 1974.

——. *On the Genealogy of Morals.* Translated by Douglas Smith. Oxford: Oxford University Press, 1996.

——. *Twilight of the Idols* and *The Anti-Christ: or How to Philosophize with a Hammer.* Translated by R. J. Hollingdale. London: Penguin Books, 1990.

——. *The Will to Power.* Translated by Walter Kaufmann and R. J. Hollingdale. New York: Vintage Books, 1968.

Nishida Mitsugi. "Mugan shiron" (A blind personal view), in *Chōkokka-shugi,* edited by Hashikawa Bunzō, 67–91. Chikuma Shobō, 1975.

Noguchi Takehiko. *Mishima Yukio no sekai* (The world of Mishima Yukio). Kōdansha, 1968.

Odakane Jirō. *Hasuda Zenmei to sono shi* (Hasuda Zenmei and his death). Chikuma Shobō, 1970.

Ōkawa Shūmei. *Nihon oyobi Nihonjin no michi* (The way of Japan and the Japanese people). Gōchisha Shuppanbu, 1926.

Okuno Taeko. *Mishima Yukio densetsu* (The legend of Mishima Yukio). Shinchōsha, 1992.

Ō no Yasumaro. *The Kojiki: An Account of Ancient Matters.* Translated from the Japanese by Gustav Heldt. Columbia University Press, 2014.

Orikuchi Shinobu. *Orikuchi Shinobu zenshū* (Complete works of Orikuchi Shinobu). 40 vols. Chūō Kōronsha, 2002.

Paglia, Camille. *Sexual Personae: Art and Decadence from Nefertiti to Emily Dickinson.* London: Penguin, 1992.

Pater, Walter. *Appreciations, with an Essay on Style.* London: Macmillan, 1889.

Plato. *The Republic.* Translated from the Greek by G. M. A. Grube and revised by C. D. C. Reeve. London: Penguin Classics, 2007.

Praz, Mario. *The Romantic Agony.* Translated from the Italian by Angus Davidson. Oxford: Oxford University Press, 1951.

Rankin, Andrew. *Seppuku: A History of Samurai Suicide.* New York: Kodansha USA, 2011.

Richie, Donald. *Japanese Portraits.* Tokyo: Tuttle Publishing, 2006.

Ridge, George Ross. *The Hero in French Decadent Literature.* Athens: University of Georgia Press, 1961.

Riegl, Alois. *Historische Grammatik der bildenden Künste* (Historical grammar of the visual arts). Köln: Böhlau, 1966.

Rilke, Rainer Maria. *Selected Poems.* Translated from the German by J. B. Leishman. London: Penguin, 1991.

Saeki Shōichi. *Hyōden Mishima Yukio* (Biography of Mishima Yukio). Shinchōsha, 1978.

Saeki Umetomo, ed. *Kokinshū* (A collection of old and new Japanese poems). Iwanami Shoten, 1981.

Sakaguchi Ango. *Sakaguchi Ango zenshū* (Complete works of Sakaguchi Ango). 18 vols. Chikuma Shobō, 1998.

Sakuma Takashi. *Mishima Yukio ron: sono shijinsei to shi wo megutte* (Mishima Yukio: His poetic nature and his death). Doyō Bijutsusha Shuppan, 2009.

Sartre, Jean-Paul. *The Imaginary*. Translated from the French by Jonathan Webber. London: Routledge Classics, 2010.

———. *Saint Genet: Actor and Martyr*. Translated by Bernard Frechtman. London: Heinemann, 1988.

———. *Saint Genet: Comédien et Martyr*. Paris: Librairie Gallimard, 1952.

Satake Akihiro, Yamada Hideo, Kudō Rikio, Ōtani Masao, and Yamazaki Yoshiyuki, eds., *Man'yōshū* (A collection of ten thousand leaves). 5 vols. Iwanami Shoten, 2015.

Satō Hideaki. *Mishima Yukio no bungaku* (The literature of Mishima Yukio). Shironsha, 2009.

Schopenhauer, Arthur. *The World as Will and Representation*. Translated from the German by E. F. J. Payne. London: Dover, 2000.

Seikai Ken. *Mishima Yukio to Niiche* (Mishima Yukio and Nietzsche). Seikyūsha, 1992.

Shibusawa Tatsuhiko. *Mishima Yukio oboegaki* (Notes on Mishima Yukio). Chūkō Bunko, 1986.

Shillony, Ben-Ami, ed. *The Emperors of Modern Japan*. Leiden: Brill, 2008.

Shimada Masahiko. *Katarazu, utae* (Not with a discourse, but with a song). Fukutake Shoten, 1987.

Sontag, Susan. *Against Interpretation and Other Essays*. New York: Farrar, Straus & Giroux, 1966.

———. "Fascinating Fascism." *The New York Review of Books*, February 6, 1975.

———. *Regarding the Pain of Others*. London: Penguin Books, 2003.

Starrs, Roy. *Deadly Dialectics: Sex, Violence and Nihilism in the World of Yukio Mishima*. Honolulu: University of Hawai'i Press, 1994.

Staten, Henry. *Nietzsche's Voice*. Ithaca, NY: Cornell University Press, 1993.

Stokes, Henry Scott. *The Life and Death of Yukio Mishima*. London: Penguin Books, 1985.

Suzumura Kazunari. *Tero no bungaku-shi: Mishima Yukio ni hajimaru* (A literary history of terrorism: Beginning with Mishima Yukio). Ōta Shuppan, 2016.

Takayama Shūzō. *Mann to Mishima: Narushisu no ai* (Thomas Mann and Mishima: The love of Narcissus). Chōeisha, 2011.

Tanaka Jun. *Seiji no bigaku: kenryoku to hyōshō* (The aesthetics of politics: Power and representation). Tōkyō Daigaku Shuppan-kai, 2008.

Tanaka Miyoko. *Mishima Yukio: kami no kagebōshi* (Mishima Yukio: Shadow of the gods). Shinchōsha, 2006.

Tasaka Kō. *Mishima Yukio ron* (Theory of Mishima Yukio). Fūtōsha, 1970.

Umehara Takeshi. *Warai no kōzō* (The structure of laughter). Kadokawa Shoten, 1972.

Uno Kōichirō. "Kannōbi no shōri" (A victory for sensual beauty). *Shinchō* (January 1971): 183–189.

Valéry, Paul. *Selected Writings of Paul Valéry*. Translated from the French by Malcolm Cowley and C. Day Lewis. New York: New Directions Publishing, 1964.

Vincent, J. Keith. *Two-Timing Modernity: Homosocial Narrative in Modern Japanese Fiction*. Cambridge, MA: Harvard Asia Center, 2012.

Wada Katsunori. *Seppuku*. Aoba Shobō, 1943.

Washburn, Dennis. *Translating Mount Fuji: Modern Japanese Fiction and the Ethics of Identity.* New York: Columbia University Press, 2007.

Watsuji Tetsurō. *Watsuji Tetsurō zenshū* (Complete works of Watsuji Tetsurō). 27 vols. Iwanami Shoten, 1962.

Wilde, Oscar. *Complete Works of Oscar Wilde.* Introduced by Merlin Holland. London: Collins, 1990.

———. *Salome.* Translated into Japanese by Hinatsu Kōnosuke. Randai Sanbō, 1938.

Wind, Edgar. *Art and Anarchy.* New York: Alfred A. Knopf, 1964.

Yamamoto Tsunetomo. *Hagakure* (Hidden by leaves). Edited and annotated by Watsuji Tetsurō. 3 vols. Iwanami Shoten, 1941.

Yamanouchi, Hisaaki. *The Search for Authenticity in Modern Japanese Literature.* Cambridge: Cambridge University Press, 1978.

Yanase Yoshiharu. *Mishima Yukio kenkyū: "chi-teki gainen-teki na jidai" no Zain to Zoruren* (Mishima Yukio: Sein and Sollen in an "intellectual and conceptual Age"). Fukuoka: Sōgensha, 2010.

Yasuda Yojūrō. *Yasuda Yojūrō zenshū* (Complete works of Yasuda Yojūrō). 40 vols. Kōdansha, 1986.

Žižek, Slavoj. *On Belief.* New York: Routledge, 2001.

Index

Adorno, Theodor, 10
Absolute, the, 159, 166
aestheticism: and decadence 68–72; and evil, 1, 13–14, 41–43, 61–62; as a lifestyle, 45–46, 55, 80; Mishima's 10–11. *See also* aesthetic terrorism; beauty; decadence
aesthetic terrorism, 9–10, 137, 146–150, 162–163
After the Banquet, 122–123
alienation, 65, 141, 156; of novelists, 95–96
Amaterasu Ōmikami, 19, 128, 155
America, 18, 30–31, 35; "Americanization" of Japan, 121
Antinous, 57
Aoshima Kenkichi, 108
À rebours (Huysmans), 69–72
art: apolitical essence of, 124; and crime, 61–64; and evil, 31; and history, 16–18; Mishima's death as, 173–174; modern decline of, 59–60; as resistance, 124–125; as ritual, 114; as sublimation, 15, 55; and terrorism, 149; visual arts, 55–60. *See also* aestheticism; artists; censorship; life as art
artificiality, 50, 70–71, 80
artists: as "anguish specialists," 52–53; as criminals, 61–63; and history, 16–17; status in modernity, 59
auto-eroticism, 74, 90–91

Bachelard, Gaston, 101
Barthes, Roland, 144

Bataille, Georges, 100, 102–108, 112–113, 165
Baudelaire, Charles, 52, 72, 91
Baudrillard, Jean, 174
Beardsley, Aubrey, 44, 72
beauty: bourgeois misconception of, 124; and death, 22, 89, 116, 119, 159, 165, 168, 170; decadent, 69–72, 115; emperor as "supreme controller" of, 134–135; and evil, 11–12, 41–42, 81; of form over content, 76; Greek cult of, 57–58; of love suicide, 109–110; male and female, 79, 85; of Narcissus, 78; of Saint Sebastian, 89, 115, 117–118; and the sublime, 24–28; in *The Temple of the Golden Pavilion*, 32–39; and terrorism, 146–148, 163; "true beauty," 25, 38, 124; unreal, 21–24, 38, 165; and the war, 28–30. *See also* aestheticism; decadence
Beethoven, Ludwig van, 31, 61, 125
Benedict, Ruth, 126–127
Birth of Tragedy, The (Nietzsche), 96, 135–136
Black Lizard, The, 62
blue sky, 99–102
body: in art, 58–59; mind and, 74; as an object, 83, 90, 92, 97, 111
bodybuilding, 79–80, 83–84, 90. *See also* muscles
Bunraku, 31, 109, 125, 157

censorship, 122–123, 129, 162
Chikamatsu Monzaemon, 109–110, 126, 157

Richie, Donald, 178n13
Riegl, Alois, 139
Rilke, Rainer Maria, 25
Rite of Love and Death, The, 114
ritual, 24, 40, 147, 161, 173; destruction of
  Ise Grand Shrine, 128; as origin of art,
  114, 125; sacrificial, 104–105, 112–114,
  118; seppuku, 108–110; war as, 80
Rococo style, 56–57
Romanticism: 12, 19, 25, 165. *See also*
  Japan Romantic School
Runaway Horses, 62, 158–161

sacrifice: as ritual, 24, 102, 104–105, 112–
  118; in war, 93, 156, 158
Sade, Marquis de, 123, 130
sadomasochism, 16, 24, 88–91, 119, 173.
  See also self-punishment; seppuku
Saeki Shōichi, 4
*Sailor Who Fell from Grace with the Sea,
  The*, 62
Sakaguchi Ango, 131
Salome (Wilde), 44, 54, 177n11
samurai spirit, 148, 152, 163, 171. *See also*
  kamikaze pilots; martyrdom
Sartre, Jean-Paul, 41, 68, 113
Schopenhauer, Arthur, 76–77
Schrader, Paul, 3
Sea of Fertility, The, 165
Sebastian, Saint, 86–94, 102, 111, 115–119
Seikai Ken, 71
self-consciousness, 28, 35, 75–80, 91,
  97–98
self-creation, 45
self-harm, 84. *See also* muscles
self-punishment, 49, 69, 160
self-sacrifice: in Japanese tradition, 141–
  142; of Mishima, 40, 70, 118, 143
seppuku: eroticism of, 106, 110–111; in
  "Execution of Love," 114–115; as
  kitsch, 157; Mishima's, 3, 171–172; in
  "Patriotism," 106–113; in *Runaway
  Horses*, 159. *See also* suicide
sex, 88–89, 105–106, 136; in *Kyoko's
  House*, 82–83; Mishima's sexuality,

3, 44, 172–173, 181n30; sexual labels,
  119; sexual symbolism of seppuku,
  110–111. *See also* homosexuality;
  sadomasochism
Shibusawa Tatsuhiko, 56, 69, 123, 172
Shield Society, The, 145–146, 163, 166, 169,
  171–173
Shimizu Fumio, 101
Short History of Japanese Literature, A,
  137–143, 145–146
Spring Snow, 154
Stokes, Henry Scott, 3
style: of character, 45–46; in literary
  criticism, 43
sublimation, 3, 15–16, 55
sublime, the, 25–29, 35–38, 40, 172
suffering, 14–16, 58, 108; of artists, 51–52,
  91
suicide: of Japanese terrorists, 147–149;
  love suicides, 109–110, 115, 157;
  Mishima's, 2–3, 14, 16, 171–172. *See
  also* martyrdom; seppuku
Sun and Steel, 90, 92, 99–102, 156
Syberberg, Hans-Jürgen, 156, 161

Takechi Tetsuji, 123
Tanaka Miyoko, 4
Tasaka Kō, 25, 92
Temple of the Golden Pavilion, The, 32–40,
  41, 65–66, 105, 161
Terrace of the Leper King, The, 74
terrorism: aesthetic, 9–10, 37, 143, 147–149,
  158–159; Japanese ultranationalist, 46,
  148; Japan Red Army, 150; Mishima's,
  27, 162, 173–174
Tokyo University, 7, 144
tōrima (passing devil), 63–65
totalitarianism, 130–131, 134
Toyotomi Hidetsugu, 110
tragedy, 15–16, 58–59, 135, 142–143
transcendence, 24, 36, 38, 112, 164–165
transgression, 44, 51, 61–62, 64, 71; in art,
  125; in *Confessions of a Mask*, 92–95;
  in *The Temple of the Golden Pavilion*,
  40. *See also* criminality; evil

ABOUT THE AUTHOR

British author Andrew Rankin was educated at the universities of London, Tokyo, and Cambridge. His other books include *Snakelust*, a translation of short fiction by Nakagami Kenji, and *Seppuku: A History of Samurai Suicide*.